Loving Your Husband

How to Transform Your Marriage and Honor Your Covenant

Patsy Loden

Publishing Designs, Inc.
Huntsville, Alabama

Publishing Designs, Inc.
P.O. Box 3241
Huntsville, Alabama 35810

© 2010 Patsy Loden

Second printing, 2014
Third printing, 2018
Fourth printing, 2022

All rights reserved. No part of this book may be reproduced
or transmitted in any form or by any means without written
permission from Publishing Designs, Inc., except for the inclusion
of quotations in a review.

Edited by Peggy Coulter

Design and layout: CrosslinCreative.net
Images: iStock.com, Dreamstime.com, Fotosearch.com

Scripture quotations taken from the New American Standard Bible®,
Copyright © 1960, 1962, 1963, 1968, 1971, 1972, 1973, 1975, 1977, 1995
by The Lockman Foundation. Used by permission. (www.Lockman.org)

All scripture quotations are from New American Standard Version unless
otherwise noted.

Publisher's Cataloging-in-Publication Data

Loden, Patsy, 1933—
Loving Your Husband / Patsy Loden.
256 pp.
Eleven chapters.
1. Christian Women. 2. Marriage Workbook 3. Christian—daily life
I. Title.
ISBN 978-0-929540-74-0
248.8

Printed in the United States of America

Dedication

To my "Forever Valentine," Fernando Woody Loden, III. It was his dream that I put my class "Loving Your Husband" into book form. It was his pushing me that made it a reality. Our love story began when he stuck his face in my car window at our first meeting, and his leaving this world did not end our love's journey. It will last through eternity—though in a different way. To my Loden I owe my love and gratitude for a life full of love and a life well-lived with never a dull moment!

Endorsements

Patsy certainly built her lessons on a framework of pertinent Bible passages—plus she was generous with real-life situations to nail Bible truths into everyday usefulness. Her material has already passed "the rubber meets the road" test, because she has taught it for a number of years and culled many things that just don't work. I had to say "Amen" to Patsy's observation that marriage is always a work in progress! I've always believed that a marriage never stands still. If it's not getting better each day, then it is going backward! In fact, my review of *Loving Your Husband* is peppered with "Amen" throughout.
—*Jane McWhorter,* Author, Lecturer

For a number of years World Video Bible School has offered Patsy Loden's course *Loving Your Husband* on DVD. The course has been well received and we believe that the book, *Loving Your Husband*, will be another excellent tool for study.
—*Rudy Cain,* World Video Bible School

Patsy Loden's book *Loving Your Husband* sensitively unfolds Scripture to reveal how to become a godly, cherished wife. The book is a power-packed marriage manual which demonstrates a depth of understanding about marital love. It reflects a lifetime of experiences based on God's Word with practical insights and helpful suggestions to guide women along the relational journey with their husbands.

Patsy takes a courageous, personal risk in being quite transparent about her own marital relationship. She divulges mistakes, growing edges, and triumphs along the way. This risk pays big dividends for the reader. Her biblically and psychologically sound advice is coupled with helpful introspective, challenging exercises.

As a clinical therapist, Christian marriage counselor, and instructor in counseling, I find many practical uses for this outstanding and much needed tool. I highly recommend this book to any woman who is serious about answering God's call to the spiritual vocation of wifehood. It is a must-read!
—*Ryan N. Fraser,* Clinical Therapist, Freed-Hardeman University

Patsy Loden's intense desire to teach fundamental, practical ways to achieve joy in marriage is presented in *Loving Your Husband*. Her book draws from her observations and experiences. Most important, her book is a testimonial of her desire to live in God's way and encourage all women to do the same.
—*Maggie Colley,* Preacher's wife, Lecturer

I especially like the generous use of scripture from both the Old and New Testaments in *Loving Your Husband*. No home can be what God intends without this foundation. I appreciate the concept of much kindness between husband and wife. Her "surprise ways" of showing and expressing love are beneficial. One of her best admonitions is to tell each other daily "I love you" in words and action.

—*Irene Taylor,* *Preacher's* wife, Lecturer

When I taught the *Loving Your Husband* material, I learned right along with the class. It was easy for us to see that Patsy had fully lived God's teachings. We were amazed at the heavenly instruction, and we understood more about our human side. Patsy was always there for my questions. I felt under-qualified, but her encouragement lifted above my insecurity. She often told me. "Hold their feet to the fire!" Anyone who is given the opportunity to study this material will benefit from it and can become more like the "worthy woman" found in Proverbs 31.

—*Karen Honeycutt,* Elder's wife

I am so thankful that we finally have this beautiful book on loving our husbands written by a fine Christian woman! We all need to learn ways to improve. The wisdom and instruction contained in *Loving Your Husband* is truly priceless to every wife, regardless of age!

—*Tammy Gravelle,* The Gospel of Christ

Notes from Class Members and Husbands

I have really become a better wife because of this class! My marriage is deeper and closer because of the discussions your book brought to the table. Thank you! —Amanda H.

Sister Loden shares her experience, knowledge, and wisdom as a "sweetheart" with Christian women seeking ways to improve their marriages. When Diane, my "sweetheart" of 44 years, participated in a recent class, we became closer to each other and to God. Each week, Diane shared the insights of the class session and we both worked through the exercises each week. Even silver and gold anniversary wives benefit alongside the young-marrieds! —Ron B.

I really liked the format of the class, especially when we exchanged answers. That helped me to realize that everyone has similar issues. I even enjoyed the homework! I had to stop and think about my marriage. It opened up communication between my husband and me. We still need improvement, but your class has set us on the right track. Thank you so much for sharing your life so openly and honestly. —Sandra W.

I had not planned on attending your class at first, only because I thought there would be no way I would be able to manage it with my hectic schedule. My sister changed my mind by promising to cook dinner on class nights. I am so thankful she talked me into attending! I had forgotten how to love my husband and forgive him. My kids had my attention. He told me often how this bothered him, but it took your class to open my eyes. I thought I didn't have time or energy to give attention to my marriage, but now I see what I have been missing! Now both of us are committed never to let our marriage slip. Wow—what a great change! Thank you for enriching my marriage through your willingness to share your life's journey. Jeanette T.

The past few weeks have been great. I enjoyed every class, and I'm sad that it is over. All the scriptures were so appropriate; I realized we must please God according to His word. I learned about real situations and solutions and how we are to fight Satan. It is good to have a notebook to review. We tend to get a little rusty sometimes and need reminders. You explained the lessons so well, even a cavewoman could understand! Thank you for helping me. You are a jewel. —Robbie

I must admit at first I thought the class was more suited for newlyweds—not for people like me, married nearly 40 years. But I quickly found the class to be Bible based, encouraging, informative, fun, and exciting. It was inspiring to study with Christian women whose ages varied so much. Thank you for preventing us for "bashing" our husbands. The class was always positive. When I first heard about the class, I thought it would be the place for me to get some things off my chest. Well guess what? It was the right place to be, but I found I needed to change in order to find contentment. Thank you for teaching us the true meaning of submission. I always thought submission to man was God's curse on women because of Eve's being deceived in the Garden. Shame on me, I taught this to my three daughters. I have already begun to share with them my newfound knowledge, and I look forward to our encouraging each other as we change our mindset. I have a new appreciation for God's commands for His children.—Doris D.

I have a new perspective on my relationship with my husband since the *Loving Your Husband* class. I realize now that he is the "buffalo" that God has made for me! I must be the one to help him help me. I understand now that it is all about the way that a situation is presented. And I must *never* criticize him! What a great service for those of us who thought we had a good marriage! Now it can be a *great* marriage. I am excited about using my new-found knowledge to make my marriage better!—Tommie W.

I am truly grateful to have witnessed first hand the wonderful work you have so thoughtfully done over the years. It has given me a greater appreciation for my relationship with my husband. He has given me support during the class. I have learned that husbands and wives honor God when they love and enjoy each other; a good relationship and wisdom are both gifts from God. We must be willing to sacrifice personal preferences to live peacefully in accordance to God's design. I thank you from the bottom of my heart for reminding me that my worth is "far above rubies." I understand now that the marriage relationship is *always* a work in progress—even at the end of one of our lives. Thank you for your devotion to this wonderful work.—Diane B.

Jason and I have grown much closer from your work. We have had so much fun with our homework, often laughing until we hurt! One thing that hit home with me is the sadness of seeing those I love grow so far apart. It is heartbreaking to see one partner want to work on the relationship and another who sees nothing wrong with never growing. I think that is why this class was so important to me—I am determined that I am not going to end up that way. Thank you so much for the class; I have learned so much and will forever remember the truths we studied.—Selby

I am so glad for the insights you shared with my wonderful wife Cassandra. When the class first began, I couldn't help but wonder if Cassandra was not qualified to teach it. I was not sure that anyone was able to "love your husband" as deeply and richly as she loved me. Nevertheless, I believe we both now see "there's always room for improvement." I've been reminded to shower her with compliments more frequently, to communicate my love to her more regularly, to listen, listen, listen, and to make her the queen of my earthly life each day — not just on special days. Thank you for helping me to remember that each day is special because I am able to live it with her, my suitable helper, and for Christ, our perfect model. I pray that we can continue to grow closer to each other as we grow closer to God. That is the first step in the success of any relationship — put God first, and everything else falls into place. Jesus gave the second step: "love your neighbor as yourself." I think it's interesting that Paul repeats this principle in Ephesians 5:33, "Each one of you also must love his wife as he loves himself." Again, thank you for reminding us to apply these principles in our marriage. — Todd P.

Letters from Ladies

Dear Patsy,

The "Loving Your Husband" class has changed my relationship for the better, as well as my life. This is a class that requires an open mind. I have taken this class more than once, but every time I learn something new about me. You cannot be passive in this class. You are made to look at yourself, and take responsibility for your actions.

As I started in this class I found areas in my relationship that could have caused problems if left alone. I was able to correct those and open up better communication with my mate. This class has given me a better understanding of who I am and what God wants from me. It has enabled me to be a better example to my family.

We all want the best for our families. I believe this class gives us the tools to do this. Now don't think for a minute that my relationship is perfect. I will be the first to say it is not. I have to work daily to be the wife Christ wants me to be and the wife my husband deserves. I am extremely blessed with one of the most loving and understanding men on this planet. He works as hard if not harder for our partnership than I do. This class and his love have allowed me to ask for forgiveness for my shortcomings knowing that I will not be beat down verbally. I am better able to pray for things I need in myself as I now can see them more clearly.

The greatest thing this class has taught me is the amount of power women have in the home. We are the maker of the home. My attitude sets the tone for my home. If you want a warm and comfortable space for your family and friends, then you must set it up for that. I do not want my family to walk on eggshells. I know when I am not my best. I take a few minutes to pray, listen to my favorite song, do something before I infect my family with negative behaviors. You may want to try this yourself. You may really be surprised by how much happier your home will become. I pray this class will continue to help each one of us have the home the Lord wants for us.

In Christ,

A Loyal Student

Dearest Patsy,

I was very happy to learn that you are undertaking the writing of a book about your "Loving" classes. The year 2008 will mark the tenth year since I participated in your "Loving Your Husbands" class in Tupelo, Mississippi. I often think of your lectures and the subjects and ideas we explored over those few weeks so long ago. I remember completing that class and thinking that I had really accomplished a major achievement—but the real achievement, in retrospect, has been the implementation of the principles and Bible lessons that I learned from you. Those lessons have made the journey of the last ten years a happier, more fulfilling one for both my husband and me.

These quotes from lessons three and four, respectively, have influenced my actions and decisions on many occasions:

> "Marriage is a privilege to be shared by two . . . not a convenience to be experienced by one at the expense of the other."

> "Marriage is that relationship between man and woman in which the independence is equal, the dependence is mutual, and the obligation is reciprocal."

Quotes such as these and the many scriptural references incorporated in your lessons actually changed my life and marriage in so many positive ways. When I began your class in September of 1998, my original intention was to find ways to change what I considered to be my husband's undesirable traits. However, what I learned from you and what I daily remind myself of, is this . . . the only person I can ever really change is me. And what a challenge that was and continues to be!

Your patience and concern for educating women through your persistent study of God's Word is remarkable and commendable. I pray that God will bless you in this writing endeavor and also bless those who will someday read and learn from the great wisdom you share.

With love and respect always,

Mary Ann

Contents

Foreword

Many years ago, Patsy Loden started a personal marriage-improvement plan which drew heavily on scripture. The bedrock of the plan was her love and knowledge of God's Word. Through constant determination to be the kind of wife God wanted her to be, Patsy grew in love for her husband Woody, and quite naturally, his love for her multiplied.

I have witnessed firsthand many of the creative touches Patsy employs in loving her husband, from serving daily candlelight breakfasts to carefully keeping herself attractively dressed for him. In return she has been the recipient of his devotion and acts of kindness—including the many years of poster-size valentines made by professional sign painters.

Fortunately, Patsy has chosen to share the honest marriage enrichment plan that worked for her, so we are beneficiaries of her years of study and implementation. She forthrightly admits that it was a learned attitude—not the one with which she began her marriage. She shows us how to improve our own marriages, regardless of age. And yes, there is homework! But it is designed to help us transform theory into practical application. The exercises given with each lesson encourage introspection and self-evaluation.

Through an imagined conversation with Sarah, the wife of Abraham, and other motherly mentors, Patsy learns the Scriptures. Then she teaches us how to be godly wives. Her lessons are refreshingly candid and sometimes surprisingly frank with discussions often avoided in other class books. Patsy has taught this "Loving Your Husband" class many years. Numerous, positive testimonial letters have poured in from her students. Now with this book, you too may enrich your marriage and become one of "Patsy's Girls."

—Laurel Sewell
Henderson, Tennessee

Preface

Dear Reader,

You can make love happen in your life. How do I know that you can be successful in your love journey by following the suggestions in Patsy's book? I know because her book is based on the teachings of the greatest teacher of all—Christ.

I also know from personal experience! I have been married to Patsy for more than fifty years. Our love for each other still grows, and I give her the credit. Patsy continues to make this happen. She has tried everything written in her book on me, and I love her more each day.

I have urged Patsy to write this book for several years, and I feel confident that many husbands will enjoy the benefits of these biblical concepts, just as I have.

Sincerely,

Woody Loden

F. W. Loden III

Acknowledgements

For our Father's gracious mercy, grace, and Word, I owe my praise and honor. What changes He made in me! What honor He has given me to teach the next generation of His way! I am humbled and grateful for work to keep me growing as I walk my last miles on earth with Him.

To my ever helpful Peggy Coulter, I owe much. Her guidance has been invaluable and made the book what it is. To the women who have studied with me through the years, I am indebted for the new concepts they taught me that made this work better. To the loving husbands who so diligently went the second mile by working *all* the lessons to please their wives and make their marriages more loving, I am grateful. Without their co-operation, their "rut houses" would never have enjoyed the transition into "love houses." Thank you, men!

To my precious Loden, who inspired me to write my journey of love. And finally, to you, Dear One, for having the courage to admit that you want to find a better way to love your husband. I owe you my respect, honor, and prayers for your success!

Introduction

Symbols

Our goal in this study is to learn how to build our own house of love by using the teachings of wise women of old whose legacies encourage us to have the same joy and peace with our husbands as they had with theirs. Join Wisdom as she takes you forward to meet Mother Sarah, Queen Mother, and Shulamith. Also join me and share the wisdom I absorbed from living with these women. What a journey it will be! Stay with me and practice, practice, practice until you become like them—daughters of Sarah.

Shulamith refers to her husband as a gazelle or a young stag (Song of Solomon 8:14). Since we don't have the same animals here, we are going to refer to our beloved husbands as "the Buffalo." Why? Because in the early days of our country, the Plains Indians looked upon the buffalo as their lifeline. A simple search on the Internet provided this explanation:

> The buffalo was food and clothing, tools and utensils. The Indians regarded the buffalo as a spirit being, blessing them with everything they needed to survive. They believed the buffalo to be a spiritual lifeline for them. In short, the buffalo was life to the Plains Indians.

Can you see the parallel to the position the Godhead gave to Adam and to every husband thereafter? Your husband is the provider of the essentials of your life. He is the one who helps you live close to God. He leads you in prayer to the Great Father of all. As your head, he is to lead you in God's path. With him as your guide, you will live an abundant life. The buffalo is an apt symbol for your husband. Next to the Godhead, he is your life.

Also, a friend related to me this fact: the under hair of the buffalo stomach is the finest, warmest wool in the world. It ranks above cashmere. Does that speak to you of the great warmth your soul will receive when you cuddle next to your dear buffalo's heart? I want to help you to appreciate him to the fullest.

In our journey together, the symbol for you is the butterfly. Why? Because you are going to allow Jesus to transform you from an ugly caterpillar into a beautiful butterfly, who will lovingly ride on the back of her handsome buffalo (Romans 12:2).

Building a House of Love vs. Keeping House

One woman in my class said: "Miss Patsy, you are so hard on us; I have just got to change." Those are words of advice and wisdom for you as you begin to build your house of love. The reason I will be hard on you is because your marriage is so important to you, your family, the country, the world, and especially the Father.

The two women I wanted to please most were my mother and my mother-in-law, but I found no solace or guidance in either. Both were strong women who did many good works and reared fine children, but their roles as wives showed me what I should not be. They were good at keeping their houses, but not at building houses of love for their husbands. And which do you think a husband would prefer: a tidy house or a loving wife?

Loden and I lost our fathers the same day, Thursday, October 18, 1973. I flew from Memphis to Houston where my father had died in a hospital after a blood clot hit his heart following surgery.

Friday, when we went to the funeral home in Eden, Texas, to view his body, my mother went to the casket, threw herself over him, and sobbed, "Oh, Jim, Jim, you will never know how much I loved you."

My mother, in her deep grief, spoke truth. My daddy had told my sister and me that he knew Mother would not care if he died. He felt she did not love him.

As I stood before the casket, I made a silent vow before God that my Loden would always know I loved him. However, it was five more years before I began changing—changes caused by what I learned when I enrolled in a "loving class."

I was a pouter and I punished Loden by giving him the silent treatment. I've tried to forget that. I've also tried to forget that I was a plotter of revenge. Then one day I looked directly at myself in the mirror and said, *Patsy, you are acting just like your mother, and you are going to change.* I became Sarah's daughter. You can do that too, if you are willing to put forth the effort.

I am still a work in progress, but I can assure you that I would not go back to being the person I was for anything in this world. Love and praise from my Loden were all I needed to keep me growing and loving. I hope you will make that same decision and allow the Holy Spirit's words to mold you into the image of Jesus. Then you will experience true joy with your husband.

Why do I insist that you follow God's Word and diligently work to become all you can as a person and as a wife? Because I have experienced joy as a wife and seen other women bring more happiness into their marriages by obeying God's Word! I know you can!

Lovingly,

Patsy Loden

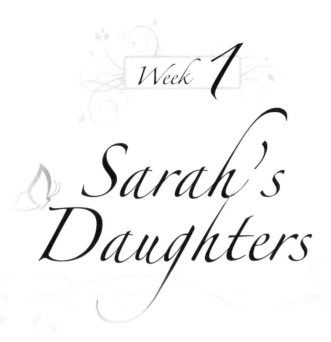

Week 1

Sarah's Daughters

From the Father of the Bride: "Unless the Lord builds the house, they labor in vain who build it" (Psalm 127:1).

Our Golden Rule: "But the goal of our instruction is love from a pure heart and a good conscience and a sincere faith" (1 Timothy 1:5).

Teacher's Commitment: I will give my best effort to help you understand God's will for you. Allow the Holy Spirit to guide you through His Word, so when you reap what you have sown, you can enjoy the harvest.

Student's Commitment: I will give myself the time and the desire to work each day to attain God's will for my life.

Motto: "Act Your Way into Feeling." Memorize that phrase now and sear the words indelibly into your heart. It will help you in every situation. You will learn later the full extent of its meaning.

Day 1

Journey of Love

Address yourself by saying these words aloud: *Dear Sarah's daughter.* Doesn't this phrase have a lovely ring? The Father says women who are obedient to their husbands, do good, and show no fear are daughters of Sarah (1 Peter 3:6). Wasn't that your goal when you made the wise decision to study God's desire for you as a wife?

Did you enter into marriage with a manual? Probably not! Perhaps you didn't even have premarital counseling. Most likely you entered into the most serious human relationship with no idea of which way to go or how to develop a loving relationship. You might have the same idea that most new brides do: a good marriage just happens!

From this study, you can learn how to develop a marriage, avoiding the errors I made before learning God's way. But I did learn, and what a blessing that was for me and Loden! (I call my husband Loden so as not to confuse our son Woody IV with him.)

What preparation did you make for a good marriage?

Did you use the information given you by a counselor or by someone else?

How did you use this advice in the first disagreement you had with your husband?

Do these questions remind you of some of the mistakes you made early in marriage? Of course. You had many decisions to make from the first day, and you did not always make the right ones. I know because I made almost every mistake possible. Now I am a walking encyclopedia of what not to do. Just ask me if you don't believe that!

I was eighteen years into marriage when Dorothea came to Batesville and taught a class on how to love your husband. That was in 1978, and I have been improving my loving skills since then. Because of Dorothea, I began changing my ways. My marriage became what I wanted. It was not Loden who had been so terrible; it was I.

When I changed, Loden began loving me in the ways he had desired from the beginning. My actions had kept him from reaching me with his love! And I knew that what I had learned from the Word was the path our Father wanted me to travel. I began learning to love Loden in God's way, and then using my experiences to teach other women what the Father had taught me. That is the meaning of Titus 2:3–5: older women teaching younger women how to love their husbands and children.

Why do we have to learn how to be loving wives and mothers?

Why does the Father want older women to teach younger women?

I began to develop my "Loving" course soon after being enlightened by Dorothea and have been continually improving it since. What is the reason for this study? It is to enable you to learn to make wise choices according to God's Word.

You have decided that you want to be a daughter of Sarah, so you must devote the time necessary to read the material, to meditate on it, and to complete the exercises in each chapter. If you do not complete them on time, you probably will never go back to finish the work. How tragic if you miss the opportunity to understand God's way and to reap the rewards of being the wife He intended! However, just knowing the material will not bring you the relationship with your husband that you desire. You must allow God's principles to become your nature in order to reap the full measure of happiness with your husband.

You must allow God's principles to become your nature.

Never forget that woman was created to be a help suitable to her husband; that is our most serious role. In fact, the wife you are to your husband is going to be exactly the bride you will be to Christ. After all, He is our spiritual bridegroom and He expects us to be a loving bride to Him. Why? Because He gave His all for His bride and promised to love, cherish, and look after her until He returns to take her home to live with Him forever and ever.

What joy and what contentment you will have here on earth, pleasing both Christ and your beloved in your marriage relationship! What is the greatest honor on earth? It is being given the role of truly meeting the needs your husband cannot meet for himself.

🌿 During your teen years, did you carry your problems to your mother or to your father? How did your parent of choice help?

🌿 How did you celebrate your victories in the family?

The way you answered those questions will probably be the way you deal with life's problems and successes as an adult. We tend to copy the actions of parents in adulthood because that is what we learned in childhood, that is, unless we deliberately choose to learn another way of living, which prompts the motto of our study: *Act your way into feeling!*

Most of us are reactive instead of proactive. We often say, "You made me do it!" It is human to want to shift personal blame. In this study we are going to unlearn that kind of action and replace it with acting, feeling, and living God's way. We can be contented, forgiving, sad, angry, or unforgiving; it's our choice!

21

How are we programmed by our Father? (cf. Genesis 1:26–31).

What does this tell us about God's expectations of our conduct? (Read Ephesians 5:1–2.)

Day 2

Learning God's Way

Here are some comments from husbands.

- "I love you, but I don't know how to show you. Please teach me how."

- "I wrote you a note with that beautiful watch I gave you. My note said, 'I love you—please take time for me.' When our children left home I asked you this question, 'Will you now have time for me?'"

- "I am really tired of my marriage. She has just worn me out with her ways."

- "Isn't she beautiful? Isn't she the most beautiful woman you have ever seen?" (The words of a man very much in love after more than 50 years of marriage.)

- "Thank you for taking care of me and supplying all my needs. I love you very much. I have always loved you." (The words of my precious Loden after more than 51 years of marriage.)

Which of the five comments sound most like your husband? How does it reflect his view of your marriage?

Who really determines whether you are a good wife—you or your husband?

Someone in every class asks, "Why don't husbands have a course on how to love their wives?" I cannot answer. I can only tell you that once you become the wife God meant you to be, you will see wonderful changes in your husband because love begets love. Jesus said, "You love because I first loved you." First

Peter 3:1 assures you that if you are the wife you were meant to be, you will influence your husband without a word—and he may change.

Write the words of 1 Peter 3:1 for your learning.

Go back and read 1 Peter 2—the entire chapter. It discusses Christian submission in a general way, the submission of slaves, and finally, Jesus' submission to His Father. The opening word of chapter 3, *therefore,* means "in like manner." The Holy Spirit is instructing wives, then husbands, to live "in like manner" as Jesus and His Father. Jesus gave Himself over to His Father without reservation (cf. 2:22–23). In the same way, the wife is to commit herself to her husband without fear.

Write 1 Peter 2:22–23. Memorize this passage and learn from it.

Committed is used to describe Christ's will. It means "to deliver or entrust something to a person." Jesus gave Himself over to His Father to direct His life; His fate was in His Father's hands. Jesus totally trusted His Father to do what was best for Him, even when that included the cross.

Are you willing to entrust your whole being to the care of your husband? That is a serious question with many implications. The way you answer this question determines one of two paths: your marriage will grow and develop or your marriage will wither and die.

It is your choice! Just as the salvation of the world rested on Jesus' choice to commit or not commit to His Father's control, so your marriage is in your hands to a great degree. God could not make Jesus the King of kings and Lord of lords until Jesus was willing to drink the cup of suffering given Him by His Father. Your husband cannot love you as God intends until you willingly put yourself into your husband's care without fear.

Teach your husband without a word—and he may change.

Notice in 1 Peter 3:7 how the Father takes care of you by instructing your husband to treat you as a fellow heir in Christ. He should live with you according to knowledge. It is his responsibility to take care of your needs. He is to handle you with the same honor one would give a very precious, delicate dish. That kind of treatment ensures that his and your prayers will not be hindered by bad behavior.

What is Jesus teaching you by His submission to His Father?

Why should we be serious about living together as a loving wife and husband? Why go to the trouble of working so hard to please one another? To find these answers is to find the pot of gold at the end of the rainbow. The answers are simple, but living them daily is complex!

In Genesis 1 we read of the creation of the universe, the world, and finally, those who would inhabit the world. All the fish, the birds, the creeping things, and the beasts of the field were created in pairs—male and female. Adam was a rational creature, the only one of God's creation who could talk and share ideas with Him.

Adam's interaction with the animals was supervisory; he was their master, their guide. He very quickly became lonely and probably despondent. The quickest and best way to break a person's will is to isolate him. The wise God knew Adam needed someone to meet his needs, so He created Eve.

Can't you imagine this first wedding ceremony? The Father of the bride, the groom's Father, and the one to unite them was the dear Father! He instilled in Adam's mind the marriage ceremony so Adam could teach future generations what the Father wanted marriage to be.

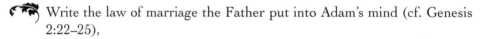 Write the law of marriage the Father put into Adam's mind (cf. Genesis 2:22–25),

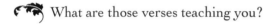 What are those verses teaching you?

Marriage was the first social institution. Is it the foundation of all other relationships? Is a country only as strong as the family unit? Yes! The basic teaching of God's Word was given into the hands of the family unit.

What does Ephesians 6:1–4 teach about the responsibility of children and fathers?

What does it teach about the wife's role?

God commanded the husband and wife to become one. Does the wife have the responsibility of helping the husband to carry out his responsibilities? Of course. She is to be a part of child rearing—the greatest part in many ways. Our nation is suffering from the disintegration of the family. Our nation's morals are at the lowest level ever. Children are continuously being born to unwed mothers who have no idea how to change a diaper, let alone to rear a child in the Lord!

So you are to be commended for realizing your special role as a wife and mother and for desiring to improve how you serve. You will learn how to be the wife God wants you to be, and you will have the joy and pleasure of seeing that your family is happy.

What did the contented husband of Proverbs 31 say about his wife? (cf. v. 28).

What does the Father say about a daughter who is a ruby? (cf. vv. 29–31 KJV).

What do these verses tell you about your importance to your husband and to God?

Day 3

Some Ground Rules

The purpose of this study is to learn to be a better wife, not to learn intimate things about others. The only person you have a right to change is yourself. Other lives are God's business, not yours. To demand that others change to become what you want them to be is to ask them to accept you as their god. That should not be, because there is only one God and Father of mankind. You will, however, have the most influence on your husband, and that is a very scary and challenging thought. In most cases you can have more influence over your husband's choices than God does. We learn this lesson from the women mentioned in the Scriptures.

What do the following women have in common: Eve, Sarah, Jezebel, Jezebel's daughters, and Sapphira? Believe it or not, all of them led their husbands to go against God's will.

Thankfully, we also have examples of women who helped their husbands grow in faith. Sarah heads the list, although she made an error with untold consequences when she arranged for Hagar to birth a child for her and Abraham. That decision is still plaguing Sarah's children today.

The only person you have a right to change is yourself.

Abigail also served David when her husband Nabal was intending to kill him (cf. 1 Samuel 25). Many years later in the city of Ephesus, Priscilla joined with her husband Aquila in teaching Apollos the way of the Lord more perfectly (Acts 18:24–26).

So it is with you. Your influence may be bad or good. You are the one who chooses whether you follow God or go your own way. God's eternal law is that you reap what you sow (Galatians 6:7).

List other women of the Bible who were suitable helpers instead of bad influences.

Criticism of your husband is slander, which is sin.

God is very explicit on the subject of slander. W. E. Vine in his *Expository Dictionary of New Testament Words* defines slanderers as "those who are given to finding fault with the demeanor and conduct of others, and spreading their innuendos and criticisms in the church" (cf. 2 Timothy 3:3). The purpose of this study is to transform ourselves into more loving wives, not to become nosey neighbors. Intimate details shared in this circle are private and personal property. They must remain in our hearts. Only thieves take for their own use property that belongs to another. If one of us has a problem, we are here to offer solutions, to serve as a support group. We must never conduct ourselves in ways to hurt others. So be gentle and kind in your remarks.

Mark this down and remember it: *Criticism of your husband is not allowed in this class.* You are here to discuss yourself and your needs, not to criticize your husband. Life from now on will be geared toward positive attitudes and not negative ones.

Write out God's teaching about talebearers (Proverbs 11:13).

What does He call one who slanders? (Proverbs 10:18). What is God's opinion of slanderers?

What is the lament of Jeremiah 9:4?

✿ What is God's teaching about the wives of deacons? (1 Timothy 3:11).

In Hebrew, *slander* means an evil account or report. If any confidential matter discussed in class is repeated, then an evil report will have been given. *Fool* describes one who is dull or stupid. When our conversation consists of passing along tidbits of gossip, how should we be described? What kind of person has nothing better to do than to spread tales about others? Such behavior is a symptom of poor self-control and low self-esteem. Running others down does not build up the gossiper. It lowers others' esteem of her instead! We really do not fool ourselves. Slandering and gossiping do not fit the commands of Philippians 4:8.

✿ List the things to "think on" from Philippians 4:8.

✿ Are these thoughts positive or negative?

✿ How is our Father trying to train us to think?

Dear One, when you criticize your husband and talk negatively about him, you are slandering him. Slander is a sin. Remember Jesus' comment about the heart in Matthew 12:34–37? He said the good heart would bring forth good fruit and the evil heart would bring forth evil fruit. Every day we all make a choice as to what type of fruit we will deliver to others.

✿ What does Jesus think about our use of thoughtless words? (Matthew 12:36–37).

You are to be the help suitable to your husband and you are to build him up in every way you can. If you treat him with the love and respect due him—given him by our Father, no less!—you will reap the rewards God has promised you.

It is vital to your future that you obey God's commands to you as a wife. God never excuses poor conduct for any reason. Two wrongs do not make a right.

✿ What does Matthew 7:21 teach about obedience to God?

❧ Here are four scriptures that give some wonderful promises from our Father. Write beside each what it teaches you. Reread these often and see how the meaning will grow as you develop into Sarah's daughter.

Psalm 37:3–9

Psalm 84:11

Psalm 119:2

1 John 2:17

❧ For your uplifting, we cannot overlook Jesus' promise to His apostles and to us in John 17:13. Write it for your joy.

Since your present earthly life and your future eternal life depend on your choices, you must learn to make wise decisions, so give this study your all.

Attend every class. Each class builds upon the previous one.

Make a commitment to memorize the verses prescribed. The Holy Spirit directs you through the words of Scripture; listen and learn His guidance for your decisions.

Choose to follow faithfully the "doing" exercises. Often a husband proudly tells me what he is doing to please his wife and how he delights in making her happy.

Use the rules of good living with your family, with the church, and with every person you meet. Let God's commands for living become your nature. That is the goal of your life: to become like Christ.

Keep acting in love's way. If you have been slack in your loving ways, your husband may be shocked by your new conduct. He might also test the genuineness of your changes by responding negatively! Be prepared and keep your actions loving, so he will know you are sincere.

Remember what you are striving to obtain. The Father's goal for you is found in Romans 8:29. Write it out and remember it. Now read 3 John 11. Write it down and meditate on it. What are you striving to attain?

You will fall into one of these three categories in this study:

1. *A hard worker.* You are going to study the scriptures, memorize the assigned verses, and do all the homework, attitude exercises, and hands-on suggestions. Love is going to flourish and mature in your marriage.

2. *A smug student.* You will ignore commands and suggestions that do not suit you. One of my students draped her legs across the chair in front of her and casually filed her nails during class. She proudly announced that all the letters I had written her husband were stacked neatly on his desk—unopened. I later learned that her husband had given up a very prosperous position and moved the family back to the city where his wife wanted to live. How will this marriage grow?

3. *A hard-working student with an uncooperative husband.* Nancy became very close to me during our weeks of study. Her husband bent over backward to oppose God. I told her that one day she would find contentment and joy in Christ and be at peace because she had done what the Father wanted her to do. During later trips to her city, I always visited her. As time went on, I remarked, "Nancy, I can see in your face that you have found your peace with Jesus."

Your salvation does not depend on anyone but you and Christ.

Nancy had indeed found her inward joy and was able to serve her husband until he died, though sadly, it was only her agape love that was allowed to bloom, because he refused to change his emotionally abusive ways. I pray this will not happen to you, but if it does, Christ will give you the strength you need to endure and flourish even in such a marriage. Your salvation does not depend on anyone but you and Christ working to perfect you in His image.

Into which of the previous categories do you plan to fall?

What do you desire to get from this class?

❦ What vow do you make to yourself, before the Father, about being a wife?

❦ How do you see your marriage five years from now?

Day 4

How to Enjoy Success

Here are my suggestions for you to reap the most from this study:

Have a serious attitude. Being a suitable help to your husband is the most serious and joyful position you will ever have.

Keep your Bible at hand. You will need to refer to it often.

Memorize a scripture each week. Jesus used the Scriptures to defend Himself against Satan's temptations. The Word of God is your lifeline as Jesus is your life.

Read the Song of Solomon. This is God's marriage manual. If you have difficulty understanding it, purchase Tommy Nelson's *The Book of Romance*, and study it both privately and with your husband.

Read the book of Proverbs. It was written by a very wise man under the guidance of the Holy Spirit. Keep a notebook at hand to jot down special meaningful verses. Keep reading Proverbs; you will understand more and more of it as you grow in Christ. Each reading will give new insights into your life's choices.

Apply the lesson principles daily. Practice, practice, practice. It takes from one to seven weeks to change a habit. You will have to make conscious and concerted efforts until good actions become second nature. No pianist became great until his hands moved without conscious effort. So must it be with your correct conduct. Christ is love, and your aim is to become love.

Keep a diary of your growth. Jot down your goals and guides for accomplishing them. Note your activities and evaluate your progress daily. As you reach one goal, move to the next.

Jot down, at the end of each day, three good things that happened to you. One woman reviewed her book after a year of notations and realized how much her journal had contributed to her new positive attitude.

If you come to class with a positive attitude, if you have the determination to learn, and if you do all you can to develop a marriage of joy and continued growth that will blossom until death do you part, then you will find some answers to help you walk in the pathway of love. It all depends on the choices you make.

Becoming a "ruby" wife requires daily effort, and one can never say it is finished. Each stage in a marriage has its challenges, its problems, and its own special joys. One has to be willing to change. As Marshall Keeble said, "Be adjustable, be adjustable, be adjustable."

"Be adjustable, be adjustable, be adjustable."
—Marshall Keeble

You will truly reap great rewards and have a peace within your inner soul, knowing that you are cherished just as you cherish your dear mate. Let's take up our building tools and begin to build our houses of love. You will often read Wisdom's advice for building your dream house: "The wise woman builds her house, but the foolish tears it down with her own hands" (Proverbs 14:1). Solomon's father, David, had earlier given him this sage advice in Psalm 127:1. Memorize it.

Be the wise builder and build your house of love upon the foundation of God's laws. You will have much fun while we seriously study God's way for the wife, and you will also grow very close to those who are learning with you. Talk with your husband about your desire to build a house of love with him, and both of you make a commitment to work together to build your marriage to be as wonderful as the love Christ and His bride have for one another.

Make a list of the things you will say to your husband in regard to this promise to one another.

Day 5

Meet Wisdom

We are almost ready to begin studying God's blueprint for your house of love and for your becoming Sarah's daughter. In so doing, you will also become one of "Patsy's girls." We are truly a family of women when we have made this journey together. I cherish you for your willingness to be fashioned into the image of Christ. My prayers are with you and yours.

Now you need to meet Wisdom, the first guide on your journey of love. Her character will unfold as you search the Scriptures and answer the following questions:

🌿 Read Jeremiah 10:12. Where was Wisdom when the earth was created? How did God use Wisdom?

🌿 Now read what Wisdom — her name in Proverbs — has to say in Proverbs 1:20–33. What does she call those who hate knowledge?

🌿 What does Wisdom beg you to do in verse 23?

🌿 What does Wisdom promise you in Proverbs 3:1–26?

🌿 What do these verses promise you?

Verse 2

Verse 4

Verse 6

🌿 What does Wisdom advise you to do in verses 7–8?

What does the Lord do for those He loves? (vv. 11–12).

What do verses 13–18 teach you about Wisdom?

What is wisdom to your soul? (v. 22).

What assurances are yours from Wisdom? (vv. 21–26).

What is the wise choice for internalizing the words of Wisdom? Where do the wise go for instruction?

Read Proverbs 4. What does Solomon say about Wisdom in verses 7–9?

How much is Wisdom worth? (Proverbs 8:10–11).

What does Wisdom say about herself in Proverbs 8:12–36? What does verse 36 teach?

❧ Why should you practice the teachings of Wisdom as you try to become the suitable helper of love for your husband?

❧ Read Wisdom's invitation (Proverbs 9:1–6). How will you answer the summons Wisdom extends to you on how to build your house of love as she has built hers?

Memory Verse

"I can do all things through Him who strengthens me."

Philippians 4:13

My Take-Home

1. Purchase a journal pretty enough to be appreciated. Begin making entries about your past as they come to mind. Dig deep within your heart and look at your core being. Write down your Christlike attributes. Reverse your thinking and ponder ways you have not grown. List fruits of the Spirit you need to add. This is the time to realize how much you need God's Spirit to come into your heart through His Word and begin transforming your mind into that of Christ's.

2. Copy 1 Corinthians 15:49 and 2 Corinthians 13:5 into your journal. The more you think like Christ, the happier your family will be and the more joy you will have in your heart. We act as we think. This study is the beginning of acquiring anew God's knowledge to use the rest of your life.

3. Think about David's request of the Father in Psalm 139:23. What is this scripture saying? What was David's heart like when he penned these words?

4. List some of your mother's positive traits. Circle the ones that you inherited.

5. List some of your mother's negative traits. Circle the ones that you inherited.

6. How will you develop the one trait that you need the most? Begin immediately. Think about it hourly, and work on perfecting it by the minute.

My Homework

1. Make a note of a prayer request to help you become one of Sarah's daughters. Date your prayers so you can go back and notice how the Father has answered each one. Such will increase your faith. Writing events, prayers, attitudes, and goals in your journal is a step toward accomplishing them instead of just thinking about them.

2. Believe your memory verse, pray about it, and meditate on it. Think about the love of Jesus, His example of living, and His sacrifice. Ponder on how these worked to transform John, the Son of Thunder, into the Apostle of Love. Dream of the day you will be addressed by your Father as one of Sarah's daughters and by your husband as "my ruby." Then you can look in the mirror of your love home, and your soul can say, "With the Lord's strength, I did it!" With the strength given you by Jesus, you can be the wife the Father intended. Keep that thought in your mind each day.

Week 2
Choosing Your Standard

Called to Be Perfect: I can be holy like Christ! "But like the Holy One who called you, be holy yourselves also in all your behavior . . . After you have suffered for a little while, the God of all grace, who called you to His eternal glory in Christ, will Himself perfect, confirm, strengthen and establish you" (1 Peter 1:15; 5:10).

From the Father of the Bride: My sound doctrine is the curriculum. Teachers are to be older women (Titus 2:3–5). The students are young wives. The lesson: "And be subject to one another in the fear of Christ. Wives, be subject to your own husbands, as to the Lord" (Ephesians 5:21–22). The result of the teaching: "So teach us to number our days, that we may present to You a heart of wisdom" (Psalm 90:12).

Wisdom Speaks: "The fear of the Lord is the instruction for wisdom, and before honor comes humility" (Proverbs 15:33).

Wear This Habit from Christ: "I can do nothing on My own initiative. As I hear, I judge; and My judgment is just because I do not seek My own will, but the will of Him who sent Me" (John 5:30). Can you wear the habit of obedience to Christ as He did to His Father?

Gear Up for Problems: Satan is after you the same way he was after Eve. God has the only answer. It is explained in Ephesians 6:10–11: "Finally, be strong in the Lord and in the strength of His might. Put on the full armor of God, so that you will be able to stand firm against the schemes of the devil." Read about your full armor and wear it daily (cf. Ephesians 6:14–17).

The Ultimate Gift to Children: Being reared in a loving family, learning the will of God, and seeing firsthand how to be a loving wife/

husband — this is the best inheritance you can give your children. And they don't have to wait until you die to receive it! Think about it.

Day 1

Sound Spiritual Food

The wise Father of the bride wrote these words to Sarah's older daughters:

> Older women likewise are to be reverent in their behavior, not malicious gossips nor enslaved to much wine, teaching what is good, so that they may encourage the young women to love their husbands, to love their children, to be sensible, pure, workers at home, kind, being subject to their own husbands, so that the Word of God will not be dishonored (Titus 2:3–5).

Back up to Titus 2:1 and note that Titus was told to speak the things fitting for sound doctrine — "whole and healthy" doctrine. In other words, these words would lead to the soul's well-being. You eat good food to have a healthy, whole body, and God wants you to have healthy and godly teaching so your soul will be wholesome. Your marriage is very important to the Father, and He wants you to feed it a good diet.

The Best Teachers

The Father of the bride knows that mothers are the best teachers for their daughters. And she does not have to be a biological mother; a surrogate mother will do. So find a godly mother figure with whom you can have instant access. She will bless your life. No matter how much love a man may have for his daughter, he cannot teach her to be a good wife and mother. He does not have the same ideas, hormones, or physical make-up that Eve had when she was created. Therefore, the Father issued a command: older women must pass their knowledge to the next generation. The knowledge of how to be a wife and mother is not innate, so every woman must learn that for herself. We learned in Week One that Wisdom is from before time and has taught women from ancient ages her lessons of life.

From whom did you learn to be a wife? Did she teach you God's way for a wife to live?

Godly Women and Christian Attitudes

The teachers of the younger generation must be mature Christian women whose lives testify that they possess godly wisdom and Christlike attitudes. Additionally, they must be women who can keep what they know about others tucked securely in their minds, refusing to spread tales about one another. They are to be clear-headed, have self-control, and be godly in their conduct if they are to teach what is good to brides.

🌿 Write the name of a woman you know who meets the above criteria. Have you asked her to help you learn how to emulate her life?

I asked a dear friend who had reared a wonderful son for advice. Here is her wisdom:

> Live as a family in work and play. Then when the children become teens, they will not resent the presence of their parents. Always greet your child when he comes home from an evening out, kiss your child goodnight, and engage him regularly with loving and non-threatening conversations. Be alert for traces of alcohol and drugs.

A man cannot teach his daughter to be a good wife and mother.

I followed that advice, and it produced the same results in our children. Many mature "mothers" have helped me become a better person. Therefore, I want to help you learn God's way; it is payback time for me to all those godly mothers who made my path easier to tread.

Learn Love

Love has to be taught. Mankind is the only creature endowed with the same emotions as the Father. His agape love must be learned because it is a love of the will, and the will must be tamed to God's way by learning self-control. Kindness is the opposite of selfishness; kindness is a learned way of thinking and acting.

🌿 Define agape love. If you need help, read John 3:16. Think about who gave what. What was the cost? How can you develop this type of love?

Who Shall Be Praised?

A young wife must be taught that the home is where she is the queen and where she will do her best work for the family, for the Lord, and the community. Worldly wisdom would have a young woman think that being a homemaker is the lowest of the low in job descriptions—a total waste of talents. "Not so," says the Father. As the all-seeing and all-knowing one, the Father created woman to find her greatest joy and work in being a suitable help for her husband and a loving mother to her children. Here are His words to such a queen: "'Many daughters have done nobly, but you excel them all.' Charm is deceitful and beauty is vain, but a woman who fears the Lord, she shall be praised" (Proverbs 31:29–30).

What is your idea about the "wife" role being the most important one for you? Are you willing to give your whole being into developing this goal?

A Good Name

You hold God's honor and His name in your hands. How? By your conduct. The world takes great delight in pointing a finger at those who profess God's name and then live a life of disrepute. You have heard the saying, "If that person is a Christian, I don't want any part of Jesus, because I don't want to be like her." The Holy Spirit guided Solomon to write these words: "A good name is to be more desired than great wealth" (Proverbs 22:1). God holds His name very, very dear, and He does not want us to cause the world to blaspheme His Word. The Bible is God-breathed. It is as if God were speaking the words Himself when we read them (2 Timothy 3:16). If we speak against His Word, we speak against the character of Jesus also. "Keep My name holy" is His command to us. Woe to us if we cause Him to be maligned by our lives and words!

Follow the blueprint; you are responsible for building your home.

Loden and I told Woody and Lisa: "We worked very hard to give you a good name, one you could be proud to wear. Now you give us a good name. Don't disgrace the name you wear, because it is Christ's name as well. Make us proud." I asked our son if that admonition helped him make decisions in his teen years. He told me there were activities he shunned because of our good name. Your Father feels the same way about you, so honor His great name by your actions and words.

Find a verse comparing a good name to riches. Judging by your life and words, what kind of name are you giving your heavenly Father? How are you willing to improve your service to Him?

God's Law and Order

Marriage is important to God. We must never forget that God is the Father of the bride and groom. He united them for life. He created marriage for man's and woman's welfare; it is very important to God.

Law and order prevail in all of God's creation. Marriage is no exception. When Eve was given to Adam by the Father, they both were perfect in every way. There has never been such a beautiful, pure, holy couple since then. This was God's pattern for marriage from the beginning, but man fouled the plan. Still, God's law is immutable and stands until the end of time, according to Jesus in Matthew 19:4–6. What the Father has given you is a book of instructions—a blueprint for building your house of love. You must be wise enough to follow this blueprint, for you are responsible for building your home.

Copy Proverbs 14:1. Memorize it, love it, live it.

Day 2

Your Plan and Compass

If you can realize the importance of marriage in God's plan, you will appreciate your role as a suitable helper and joyfully fulfill His desires for you. The husband-wife relationship is an Old Testament picture of God and Israel and a New Testament picture of Jesus and His bride. This is the closest, most intimate relationship known in all creation, and God wants every Christian marriage to be a good example so the world can see the beauty of the Christ-church union and be drawn into a relationship with Jesus. That is why He wants the older women to train the younger women to be examples to the world. Eve was the crowning act of creation, and as a wife, you are the crown of your husband. It was to wives that the command was given to build a home. Their work is crucial to the foundation of the home. Wives have a greater interest in the home. They spend more time there and are with the children more. The emotions of the home are regulated mostly by the mother, so she needs to be a good thermostat. As the saying goes, "If Momma is not happy, no one is happy."

Read Proverbs 12:4. Write it down and ponder your position with your husband.

We all need help in learning how to live. If we do not grow mentally, our brains begin to die. It is the same with being a Christian; we start out as babes in Christ, but we are to grow into adulthood. From the bottle to meat is the way Hebrews 5:12–14 describes the growth of spiritual life. As a wife, you need help in growing to be a daughter of Sarah. Don't rob yourself of the happiness offered in being a mature wife. Bible perfection does not mean flawlessness; rather, it means maturity in growth toward being Christlike. You need to give abundant blessings to your family and to the church. Then your love will flow to others around you. Its influence for good reverberates just as a stone produces far-reaching concentric ripples when thrown into a pond.

Read Jesus' desire for you in John 10:10. The last word in that verse means "above the ordinary." Jesus wants you to have a relationship with Him that is above what the world offers. Then all your other relationships will be above the ordinary because you follow His example of heavenly living instead of painful worldly living. Write what this verse tells you about your desires to be a help suitable for your husband.

We have numerous examples of how messed up, sad, and unproductive people can be when they have no direction in decision-making or good parenting. That is why we must study God's Word. What a blessing that we have the mental capacity to develop and make rational changes. All other creatures live and react according to their natural instincts, but God equipped you with the ability to change your ways, no matter how bad they are. You can always improve. That is why the Father gave you the Bible. The Holy Scriptures, if obeyed, prevent you from making mistakes in your relationships with Him, with fellow humans, and with your spouse.

You are human; you are going to stumble. But the following psalm holds a promise of God for you to hold with joy!

 Copy and meditate on Psalm 37:23–24. What hope does this give to me?

Training for Queen

The Father instructs you as a trainer instructs an athlete training for the Olympics. Train to become Christlike, because that kind of life does not come naturally. Make a vow before God. Vow that you will give your all to become a wife of noble character.

> But have nothing to do with worldly fables fit only for old women. On the other hand, discipline yourself for the purpose of godliness; for . . . godliness is profitable for all things, since it holds promise for the present life and also for the life to come (1 Timothy 4:7–8).

Remember, you have Christ's royal blood flowing through your heart. You must train to become the queen of your household just as His bride must train to abstain from sin and be holy and blameless for her Bridegroom (Ephesians 5:27). Christ said it was through the washing of water with the word that His bride was made holy, so you must have His washing and His Word to become as He intended you to be—a part of His bride, the church. If you are a faithful bride to Christ, you will be a more loving wife to your earthly husband. Christ through His Word draws the blueprint for your love home with your husband and with Christ.

🌿 How is your marriage to be an example of Christ and His bride?

❧ *Day 3* ❧

Your North Star

The purpose of this class study is found in Colossians 1:9–12, and it is also my prayer for you.

> For this reason also, since the day we heard of it, we have not ceased to pray for you and to ask that you may be filled with the knowledge of His will in all spiritual wisdom and understanding, so that you will walk in a manner worthy of the Lord, to please Him in all respects, bearing fruit in every good work and increasing in the knowledge of God; strengthened with all power, according to His glorious might, for the attaining of all steadfastness and patience; joyously giving thanks to the Father, who has qualified us to share in the inheritance of the saints in Light.

This verse is your north star. Through the knowledge of the Word of God you are going to know how to live, think, and make correct judgments in your daily walk so your feet are always pointed toward Christ, the bright morning star (cf. Revelation 22:16). One must strive to acquire knowledge through study, through observation of others' conduct, and by experience.

God considers a simple act to be a noble act.

God considers a simple act to be a noble act: give a cup of cold water in the name of Christ to a weary traveler! Life is not made of many grand and noble decisions. Life for most of us consists in the daily routine of doing the same things over and over. As one of my grand teachers remarked, "Life is so daily." When we approach these monotonous daily tasks without complaint, our Father is pleased—just as you are pleased when your children act in a pleasant, agreeable, healthy way each day.

Right and wrong are not determined by what we think, but by what God thinks, so it is always in your best interest in your pursuit of contentment and joy to concentrate and practice what you learn from Him. The blueprints must be followed exactly to have your love house turn out as God intended.

To emphasize this truth one more time, please look up the following verses and write what they teach you about God's compass for your life.

🌿 Where do we learn truth? (Titus 1:1–3).

🌿 Where does God expect us to be holy? (1 Peter 1:13–16). Why? Outline how you learn to be holy (2 Peter 1:3–4).

🌿 What choice does Paul say we have? (1 Thessalonians 4:1).

Abundant Marriage

By now I am sure that you have deduced that the knowledge of God's Word is the answer for your daily decisions. Those who live by the Bible will find true wisdom. They will also find an anchor for the soul and will reap all of God's promises. Do you recall Jesus saying He came to give you the abundant life? "Above the ordinary" defines *abundant*. Is that not what you want?—a marriage different from that of your neighbors who fuss and quarrel and talk rudely to one another! No one wants that kind of relationship. A marriage that fosters the growth of each family member and one that is pleasant and kind is best.

Follow the Father's compass to be the best wife. Being perfect, as Matthew 5:48 instructs us to be, is not the sinless perfection of Jesus and the Father; rather, it means to have reached the end; to have become complete, mature. It is the idea of goodness. It is a constant alertness that motivates us to continue learning God's Word, meditating upon it, and allowing its wisdom to mold us into the holiness and perfection of our Father's nature.

"Wives, be subject to your husbands, as is fitting in the Lord." Col. 3:18

We noted from 2 Peter 1:3–4 that God's divine power grants us everything we need to have life and godliness. But what does *everything* include? Your Father wants you to develop your faith to the point that you rely on Him for everything you need in life and godliness. You cannot look to the world's wisdom; it is faulty. Look only to the Word of God for your blueprint for life and for your love house. He will never fail you. Take note of the adjectives and adverbs the Father uses as He talks to you. They are very instructive. The words *all, everything,* and *abundantly* are indicative of God's giving us an ample supply that runs over, if we will only follow His way and walk with Him. As His child grows in faith, she will look more to her Father's grace to supply little needs and big needs in life. Our God is a generous and loving Father to His children.

Day 4

Run and Win

Paul often used the Olympic Games for examples of Christian living. In 1 Corinthians 9:25–27 he refers to an athlete's discipline. The site of the first Olympic Games was on top of a mountain in Greece. The men who competed—no women were in those first games—lived there. Each morning the men walked down the mountain, trained on the plain, and then walked back up the mountain in the evening. This was a 24/7 routine. These super men were very serious about winning. The victor had a wreath of laurel placed on his head to signify he was number one in that event. He was also given the privilege of erecting a statue of himself, at his own expense, on the road to the top of Olympia. The famous statue of the discus thrower is an example of such an honor.

Paul is telling us that living the Christian life should be as serious to all Christians as it was to those first century athletes. You must work diligently to develop self-control for holy living. Unlike the Olympics with only one winner in each category, you can be a winner and receive a gold crown at the end of your race just because you finished. You need only to follow the trainer's advice and run to win.

Write a rule for holy living from Colossians 3:18.

You must learn this command from Colossians 3:18 in order to please God, to please your husband, and to please yourself. We will study this command in detail later; it is not what you may think. It produces great rewards, and you will live in peace and joy once you learn its benefits. Remember what it takes to develop a new habit: practice it from one day to seven weeks. If you want to be an Olympic champ by the end of our study, you must practice, practice, practice to perfect your performance. Don't give up when you slip. Keep applying God's will until you learn how to be your husband's ruby. Submission is for your own good and protection. God made you; He knows you best. He knows how you function as a woman. Your Father will never ask anything of you that will harm you. All His commands are designed for your abundant life, remember?

What is the requirement for an athlete to be a part of the Olympic team?

How committed to winning must the athlete be? How committed are you to finishing the race?

God's Word: Your Compass

How accurate is your compass? Notice God's idea of perfection:

All scripture is inspired by God and profitable for teaching, for reproof, for correction, for training in righteousness; so that the man of God may be adequate [perfect KJV], equipped for every good work (2 Timothy 3:16–17).

Since the Father created marriage, surely it is included in "every good work," and we can rest assured our blueprints for our love house are the best that can be found. *Inspired* in Greek means "to breath." It is as if God is speaking the words to you—and He is! He is truly talking to you as you read His Bible.

Your compass, the Word of God, is used for these purposes:

1. *Instruction.* God will show you exactly what He desires for you to learn. He is the perfect instructor in every phase of life, because He created you and knows best how you should live a holy life.

2. *Reproof.* In the legal field, when one is caught in the act of committing a crime, he is found guilty of the offense. In the spiritual realm, God's laws must be followed or one is found guilty of an offense against God's law. For instance God says, "Be angry and yet do not sin. Do not let the sun go down on your anger." If one becomes agitated at every little thing and lashes out at the offender and holds a grudge against that person, then one is guilty of breaking this law of God, so the verdict from God is "guilty." Sin's literal meaning is "to miss the mark" The guilty one did not solve the problem that day as commanded; he missed the mark. Think of an arrow (one's action) hitting the bull's eye. The action is obedience; it hit the mark. When your arrow (action) misses the bull's eye (God's command), you have sinned.

3. *Correction* means "to restore to an upright position." Ephesians 4:28 is a good example of God's correcting our behavior. The man who has been a thief learns God's Word and becomes His child. He must begin a new life immediately. No longer does he acquire money by robbing but by honest labor. Not only must a thief stop stealing, but he also must reverse his thinking and attitude. Instead of taking from others, he must now give to those in need. He must change his thinking and actions to conform to God's commands. God does not rearrange His plan to conform to subjective human thoughts.

4. *Training* instills self-control and the cultivation of sound judgment and prudence. God's Word will help you develop skills necessary to live a godly life and learn to be holy as He is holy and to be perfect as He is perfect. You will be ably equipped to every good work, including a happy marriage. God's teachings will guide your actions in an acceptable manner before Him and before every person you meet, including your husband.

Read Ephesians 2:10. How is God's compass leading you?

✿ Are you willing to allow the Bible to be your guide for a lifetime? How will you put forth the effort to change in the ways God designed for your living above the average?

Your Standard

All of us like to march under a banner, a standard that represents a leader to whom we are devoted. Think of the American flag that flies continually over the White House. It represents the values of our nation, the foundation upon which she was built, and that for which she stands.

Now move from the political to the spiritual. You have selected Jesus as your standard because He is above reproach—a perfect example for you. No human being can qualify as a standard of perfection. Therefore, you must reach for Jesus who is more than human:

> For a child will be born to us, a son will be given to us; and the government will rest on His shoulders; and His name will be called Wonderful, Counselor, Mighty God, Eternal Father, Prince of Peace (Isaiah 9:6).

God does not rearrange His plan to conform to human thoughts.

Does that scripture cause chills to run down your spine? Do these qualities cover every facet of your life? We will examine each of the ways Isaiah describes Jesus and see if all of them combined meet your total need for a leader.

A Son Will Be Given

Son refers to Jesus who was truly the Son of God and also the Son of man, so you can with confidence believe that Jesus understands both heavenly thinking and earthly thinking. Being both divine and human, Jesus can be the perfect go-between for you and His Father.

✿ What lesson does Jesus give you in John 14:6? Do you truly believe this enough to follow His standard?

Government Will Rest on His Shoulders

Government means ruler-ship. Every society, every country, every family, and every human must have a governing body to make and enforce laws. Otherwise there is chaos. Who could better understand government than the one who made all the authorities of the world? Colossians 1:16–18 informs us that everything — thrones, countries, rulers — was made by Christ, that He has the first place in all and everything, and by Him they are held together.

Again, let's look at the word *everything*. What does that leave out? Jesus is the total government of all creation. He rules according to the laws His Father gave Him. Therefore He is the perfect government, because He is perfect in all His ways. He told Pilate he could have no authority over Him unless it had been given him from above (John 19:11).

 What name is given Jesus in Revelation 17:14? What does that title mean to you and your allegiance to Christ?

Wonderful

A dictionary definition of *wonderful* is "that which causes wonder; marvelous; amazing; very good; excellent; fine; generalized term of approval." God gave His approval to Jesus as the one to whom the earth should listen. Nature obeyed His every command, and the common Jewish populace all thought Him to be at least a prophet, while the apostles looked upon Him with wonder as the Son of God. Could we do less?

Stop and consider how wonderful it is that Christ loves you and gave His life for you. He asks only that you obey His commands to prove your love.

 Name some actions of Jesus that cause you wonder when you think of them.

Counselor

Counselor is a legal term. It refers to a qualified person (lawyer) who gives advice on a point of law. Jesus is such a person. He has both the knowledge and experience regarding God's law. He is the Word, the communication of God to humanity (John 1:1). He can help you to understand what the will of the Father is and then give you advice on how to carry out God's law. Trust Him to guide you daily both in good and bad.

 What does 1 Timothy 2:5 say about your Counselor?

🌿 What does Matthew 11:28–30 mean to you?

🌿 Name a counselor better than Jesus to direct your life.

Mighty

Since we all were created to worship, we should choose to worship the mighty God. Jesus is that mighty God, and He is the very best object of worship. Why would anyone want to be under a different standard? Be wise! Don't let the world lead you into thinking that real life is outside Jesus' way.

🌿 John 1:17–18 is the Holy Spirit's description of the deity of Jesus. What do these verses teach you?

Everlasting

To have an everlasting Father is everyone's desire. When I received news of my daddy's death, I was in the process of making phone calls because of Loden's father's death. Loden bought me an airline ticket so I could be with my mother in Houston. I had time only to grab my purse and rush to the airport. As the plane began to taxi, I had a quiet moment to think, so I began the emotional acceptance of my daddy's death. I was 40 at the time, but still daddy's girl. I was devastated by my first reaction! *I am not my daddy's little girl any more!* Daddy was my rock in the sea of life. I had never worried about anything, because I knew my daddy would take care of me no matter what. And he had never disappointed me. Now I was going to be without that rock; it shook me to my deepest core. Losing my daddy was the turning point in my relationship with Loden. My husband had to become my earthly rock, and it made a difference in every aspect of my life. I had not truly left my father at marriage as I should have, and his death awakened me to that reality.

I had not truly left my father for my husband.

Jesus has promised to be your everlasting Father. That means forever and a day He will take care of your every need. Why would you not desire such a blessing and comfort? Who would ever want to lose that love and support? Dedicated to your everlasting Father, you will never be alone in life. You will always have a loving Father to look after you, listen to your prayers, and answer them in your best interest. You will live always with Him in heaven if you keep yourself under His banner.

 Look up 1 Peter 5:7. Write what it means to you.

 What promises does Hebrews 13:5–6 give to you?

Prince of Peace

Prince of Peace has a lovely ring, does it not? Jesus is the only one who has authority to give you peace, because He is Peace. Longing for peace is one of mankind's deepest desires. Jesus in that upper room spoke these precious words to His disciples: "Peace I leave with you; My peace I give to you; not as the world gives do I give to you. Do not let your heart be troubled, nor let it be fearful" (John 14:27).

The meaning of *peace* in this verse is the sense of rest and contentment consequent on one's relationship with Christ. A person feels complete and unafraid knowing that the relationship she has with Jesus is a unity like that between husband and wife. Only in Jesus can your soul find its resting place. French philosopher Blaise Pascal supposedly said that there is a god-like image in every man that only God can fill. How true. Man was created in the image of God, and only by living by God's standard will man's heart be in tune with God's. And only then is the heart of man at peace, at rest, and contented. It is not the peace the world knows, but it is the knowledge that no matter what happens, God will see that you are victorious.

 Make a list of things Romans 8:26–39 sets forth about being victorious and safe in the arms of Jesus. Circle the ones that mean the most to you.

 What does Jesus require of us to show our love for Him? (cf. John 14:15).

Your Building Standard

Rethink God's marriage law: "A man shall leave his father and his mother, and be joined to his wife, and they shall become one flesh (Genesis 2:24)." You and your husband are one for life. That oneness does not include children. They belong to God. You are to bring them up in the Lord and teach them to leave you, select a mate, and form a family unit. Give your children the foundation of a loving home so they will have the blueprints necessary to build their own home. This is your gift to them—an inheritance that will not only serve them in time but will also help them have a relationship which will take them into a joyful eternity.

Jesus laid down a profound principle at the end of His sermon on the mount. Read the parable (Matthew 7:24–29). You must make a choice as to what kind of builder you will be. No one can make that choice for you. There are only two ways to build, so choose wisely.

 Describe the two builders. Underline the builder you will be as you build your house of love? Every day, work on this project.

 Why are you wise to follow your Father's blueprint as you build your home?

Temptation: Choose Your Standard

Dear One, here is your hope. Jesus was tempted in all points as you are but was without sin (Hebrews 4:15–16). He knows how you feel. He is your great sympathetic High Priest. Through Him you can boldly come to the throne of grace and mercy and ask for help in time of need. The Father will always be open to your prayers through Jesus. You also have the aid of the Holy Spirit in your prayers. Your marriage will be blessed by your godly living, and you will have peace through Jesus when you live according to His commands.

> No temptation has overtaken you but such as is common to man; and God is faithful, who will not allow you to be tempted beyond what you are able, but with the temptation will provide the way of escape also, so that you will be able to endure it (1 Corinthians 10:13).

What a precious promise from our Father! You need to know, believe, and quote this verse often. It is your way to remain under the Father's protection. *Temptation* means "trials with a beneficial purpose and effect, divinely permitted or sent." Satan constantly uses any means available to defeat you just as he tried to defeat Job.

Just as Paul assured the Corinthians, he assures us that whatever trial we go through, it is common to man. In other words, we cannot moan and groan and lament about our trials. We can never say, "This has never happened to anyone else. I am alone in being beset with this!" Our Father allows negative happenings to teach us valuable positive lessons and make us aware of His protection. We learn patience, perseverance, and trust. We are tempted by Satan but God is faithful. He will be with us in every temptation. Next time you are tempted, rely on Him.

The hard part is to accept the "escape" God provides.

Another promise of 1 Corinthians 10:13 is that the Father will always provide a way to escape temptation. The hard part for you will be to accept the way He provides. You must overcome your pride and accept the way out without regard to personal consequences and temporary suffering. You will come to realize in time that God's way out is always the best!

Just as Satan tempted Eve and Jesus, he tempts us. Read 1 John 2:16. What are the three ways Satan tempts us?

a.

b.

c.

What did Paul say about the things he suffered? (Philippians 3:8).

Memory Verse

"No temptation has overtaken you but such as is common to man; and God is faithful, who will not allow you to be tempted beyond what you are able, but with the temptation will provide the way of escape also, so that you will be able to endure it."

1 Corinthians 10:13

My Take-Home

1. Re-evaluate your thinking toward your Christian life. Are you walking by faith or in your own way? How can someone walking in her own way correct her course?

2. Write a note to Jesus and tell Him how you feel and what your intentions are for the future. Tell Him specifically how you feel about following His blueprints for marriage. Tuck the note away and read it six months from now and then evaluate yourself.

My Homework

1. You and your husband have had a disagreement and he is angry. How will you respond to his tart comments? Proverbs 15:1 reveals God's way out for you. Write it down and meditate on it.

2. How do you defuse a volatile situation with your mate? Read Proverbs 25:15 and write your answer.

3. What does the Father want you to learn from James 1:2–8? Meditate on how you can have joy in such situations. Write your answer.

4. In order to grow spiritually, what must you be willing to do? (Matthew 7:3–5). What has this verse to do with a healthy marriage?

5. Quote the memory verse each day until it is seared into your heart.

6. Keep reading Proverbs and writing in your journal.

7. Get into the habit of daily Bible study. Buy a Bible that includes a calendar outline, designed for daily Bible study. Once you begin, the dates will help you form the habit of studying because your subconscious mind will urge you to keep up. I have practiced this mode of study for years and cannot skip a day without my conscience pricking me. Each year you will discover new knowledge you have overlooked in the passages you have studied many times. I keep a notebook, and each year I select a subject to study. As I read through the Scriptures, I write in my notebook the passages pertaining to that topic.

8. Begin a love letter to your husband. Do not rush to a conclusion, but keep adding to it as the weeks go by. When you have completed your epistle of love, plan some special event and present him with it all tied up in a pretty ribbon. You may never know how much this letter means to him. One young wife lost her husband not long after she had taken the course. When she opened their lock box at the bank, there on top of all their important papers was her husband's letter she had written him. Another older husband was so thrilled with his wife's letter that he framed it and hung it on the wall. In case you are wondering why, studies have shown that men are more romantically inclined than women give them credit for being.

Building Your House of Love

Called to Build: "The wise woman builds her house, but the foolish tears it down with her own hands" (Proverbs 14:1).

From the Father of the Bride: "Unless the Lord builds the house, they labor in vain who build it (Psalm 127:1).

Day 1

Foundation

Dear One, pick up your tool—the Word of God—and let us begin to build our house of love. Last week we discussed the importance of building on a foundation that would last through every storm of life. First Peter 2:4–8 tells us that Jesus is the cornerstone of His house, the church, and we must build upon Him.

Centuries of Builders

God commanded Noah to build an ark to save himself and his family. "Thus Noah did; according to all that God had commanded him, so he did" (Genesis 6:22). The Bible states three times Noah's obedience to God's commands to emphasize God's pleasure with Noah—a believer who followed the blueprints for the ark to the letter. Would the ark have floated if Noah had put two windows above instead of only one as God commanded? Because Noah was faithful, God used him to save the human race from terrible destruction.

Centuries passed and God erected another milestone on the road to fulfilling His promise. Abraham's descendants had to possess the land, so God raised up

Moses to lead them from Egyptian bondage, through the wilderness, and to the very door of the promised land. At Mount Sinai the Lord gave Moses blueprints for the tabernacle, including very minute details. Moses followed all the commands God gave him, and his obedience was of prime importance.

Under Joshua's command, the Israelites began to possess the land God promised to Abraham. David later became king of Israel. He was a man after God's own heart. David wanted to replace the tabernacle with a house of cedar. God honored David's faithfulness by giving him the temple blueprints so he could pass them on to Solomon. The blueprints were very exact for the construction of every inch of the temple and its furnishings.

The Romans later occupied the land because Israel had disobeyed the Lord, as was their habit. During the reign of Augustus Caesar, the time was right for God's Son to come to the earth to serve as the light of men and to fulfill the last promise given to Abraham—that all the nations of the earth would be blessed through his seed. Jesus said He would build His house, the church, upon the fact, the rock, that He was the Son of God. Jesus gave complete instructions for the laws, worship, and organization of the church, His bride. Those are found in His covenant with us, the New Testament.

Living Stones

Jesus' house is made of living stones (1 Peter 2:4–8). He left complete blueprints for each stone (child of God) to use to mold herself into a building block so as to fit perfectly in the structure of the house of God. These instructions are found throughout the New Testament.

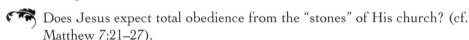 Does Jesus expect total obedience from the "stones" of His church? (cf. Matthew 7:21–27).

 What lessons do you learn from Jesus' words in Matthew 7:21–27?

What does the history of centuries of biblical builders have to do with your house of love? It has this basic principle: the Father created the institution of marriage. If He gave detailed blueprints for the ark, the tabernacle, the temple, and the church, how could He fail to give a complete set of blueprints for the most important human house ever created—the home, the human family? Nations come and go, cultures rise and fall, but the home endures no matter the country or the culture or the time. The home is the foundation of everything human, because every individual is born and reared in a family circle. Therefore, know that the Father has for you, His daughter, the blueprints for your love home, because His interest in you is pure love for your well-being.

Day 2

Feelings and Emotions

To understand the building material for your love house—which, by the way, is love—you need to understand the molecular make-up of love. Bible love is more than feelings, because feelings come and go with one's moods or circumstances. "I feel good today, but I felt bad yesterday." Our body organs experience sickness or health based on physical circumstances, but the fluctuations of our emotions are based on our thinking. But it is also true that the way my body feels may be due to my mental state, so we cannot base life on unstable feelings.

Cultures rise and fall, but the home endures.

Avoid the temptation to reduce thoughts, facts, and beliefs to feelings, because facts in and of themselves have no emotions. It takes a human to associate facts and feelings. In order to understand love, we must have the right relationship with the Father and Jesus because they are the source of true love. Love from God is not feelings but thinking. One believes the teachings of Jesus. He then acts upon them with feeling because of the mind's thinking. Listen to what God told His people:

> "Come now, and let us reason together," says the Lord. "Though your sins are as scarlet, they will be as white as snow; though they are red like crimson, they will be like wool. If you consent and obey, you will eat the best of the land, but if you refuse and rebel, you will be devoured by the sword. Truly the mouth of the Lord has spoken" (Isaiah 1:18–20).

God wants you to reason His way. Then you will obey His commands and benefit from all His promised blessings. For those who are not reasonable and choose instead the way of the world, death is the result (Romans 6:23). God's law says you reap what you sow, and your thoughts are seed. Jesus emphatically states in John 14:6: "I am the way, and the truth, and the life; no one comes to the Father but through Me." Notice the definite article *the*. How many ways does that word include?

What is the wise way for me to decide how to build my house of love?

Bury Your Sins

Jesus gives us the blueprint for becoming His child. It is the beautiful illustration of His death, burial, and resurrection. Read Romans 6—the entire chapter. Notice that baptism is the way you come into a relationship with Jesus.

Verse 4 relates the correlation of baptism to the death, burial, and resurrection of Jesus.

When a person is buried in a watery grave, the old man of sin is buried. Then just as Jesus was raised from the dead, so is the new man as he is raised from baptism (Romans 6:4). Verse 5 assures us that a union with Christ takes place in baptism, and just as Christ was raised with a new body, so is the old man dead and a new heavenly spirit is given to the new child of God. The new body is now free of sin, and the new child has the gift of the Holy Spirit (cf. Acts 2:38; Romans 8:9–17). What does this have to do with marriage? Everything!

When you act un-Christlike, you stink!

As a child of God you want to obey Him, and the marriage laws are as binding as any other laws God has given. You want to build your house of love based on God's blueprint. If you are not committed to following the way and the truth, then you will not be diligent in building your house as God wants it built. Many couples marry for the wrong reasons. They have no commitment to the marriage, so they try to protect themselves by making pre-nuptial agreements. Then they can feel confident in saying, "If it does not work out to suit me, I'm gone."

We should be dead to the old man of sin. In one of my classes a kindergarten teacher related the following: "After giving the account of Jesus' resurrection, I asked why Jesus had arisen from the dead in three days. A little tyke raised his hand and replied, 'Because if He had been in the grave four days, He would have stunk.' "

Of course we know this little fellow was thinking of Martha's statement about Lazarus. The point is that once you become a child of God, the old man of sin is buried forever. When you act un-Christlike—angry, jealous, or pouting—you are raising your old man of sin from the grave and you stink! I often have to look in the mirror and say, "Patsy, you stink. Get back into your grave! Do what Jesus wants you to do. Now!" Believe me, it works.

Write the message of Romans 6 to you, especially noting verses 13–18. What is your hope?

Only the Loving Are Loveable

Dr. Ashley Montague is a noted biologist and a professor of anthropology and anatomy. His book, *The Marriage of Marriages,* is in agreement with what God has to say on the subject. Dr. Montague says the notion that romantic love is an unreasonable yearning of the heart and loins is a myth, along with the false idea that marriage will reasonably solve all problems and conquer all contingencies. Most Americans believe they marry for love, but the truth is, many marry because of sexual attraction or the need for security. The latter group believes marriage cures loneliness and provides protection from abusive family members.

Genuine love is not a free gift, Dr. Montague says, but an earned achievement. It is not a state into which one "falls," rather it is an ascension through a process of growth and learning that begins at the very onset of life.

Here are some other definitions of love given by various authorities.

❧ Love is the total acceptance of another person. It is a relationship without "should" and "should not." When we are in love, we accept—period!

❧ Love is feeling safe and accepted, no matter what we do. We feel safe to be ourselves.

❧ Love is freedom from demands or expectations. The affirmation from this person is: "I accept you as you are and love you." Humans have the tendency to say, "I will love you if . . ." or "I'll love you but . . ." and put qualifications on their affection. Conditional love is not true love but a manipulative maneuver. It blocks the spontaneity of love as it turns into drudgery for the one trying to keep the loved one satisfied according to a selfish standard.

From these statements, can you not come to the conclusion that only the loving are loved and are capable of giving true love? It is as Jesus says in 1 John 4:19: "You love me because I first loved you" (paraphrase).

When did Jesus begin to love us? (cf. Romans 5:6–11). What do we learn from His actions?

We humans are to love others because Jesus' way is a way of love. Love others in spite of their faults! As they learn the way of Jesus, you allow them the freedom to grow in love and shed the faults. Your role as one who loves is to support, encourage, and praise. It is not to belittle, criticize, or demean. So be the loveable you that God created you to be, and be loved as God meant for you to be loved.

Day 3

Learn All the Loves

You have learned two things: God's words are the tools to use for building your house of love, and Jesus is your foundation. Now you can get started building the walls and the roof of your wondrous love home.

In English we have one word for adoring something—love! "I just love my cat"; "I just love to go skiing"; I just love my husband"; I just love to garden." On and on we go loving this and loving that in abandonment. We don't really understand the difference in intensity of our feelings.

To help us understand the various meanings of love, let's examine the Koine Greek, the common Greek in which the New Testament was written. This language has five words for love, and each of them has a special meaning. These are the building materials for your house of love: *epithumia, eros, storge, phileo, agape.* Their meanings are important because, together, they make the four walls and roof of your special abode.

The First Wall

Epithumia (ep-ee-thoo-mee'-ah), the first wall, is desire, craving, longing. Although the word is most often used in the Bible to express a lustful desire for the forbidden, we can use it to relate to our husbands in the way God intended.

The Song of Solomon emphasizes this meaning of love. When the Father gave Eve to Adam, He commanded them to "be fruitful and multiply and fill the earth and subdue it" (Genesis 1:28). The divine Father created the union of a husband and wife for pleasure and to produce children. *Epithumia* is a God-given gift, and you should cherish it. In the Garden of Eden, Adam looked upon his wife with love and adoration and appreciated her physical beauty with a pure heart. Remember the dress code of that day? What was it?

In the confines of your bedroom, allow your husband to have the same pleasure that Adam had with Eve. If you love your husband as God intended, he will think your body is the most beautiful in the world. He will truly see you through the eyes of love. Is that not one good reason to love him to the fullest and make him feel truly respected and adored as God intended?

Time will take a toll on your body, but to your adoring husband, you will always be beautiful if he feels he is your treasured head. That is one reason God commanded His holy women to dress modestly. Since the fall of Adam and Eve, man has looked upon the naked woman's body with *epithumia* in the evil sense, and that lust is a sin before God. Lust begins in the mind, so don't be guilty of contributing to any man's sin. Your body belongs to your husband and to Christ. Don't dishonor either by the way you dress.

The Second Wall

Eros (er'-os) was the Greek god of love, the son of Aphrodite. His love was passionate love, sensual desire, and longing. Wikipedia goes one step further in stating that *eros,* with contemplation, can become an appreciation of the beauty within the person loved. We use it to mean romantic love. Eros is the important second wall of your house of love.

Romantic Surprises

You must have the wall of *eros* to keep your marriage full of surprises and overflowing with a feeling of mutual cherishment.

Here are some suggestions. Send romantic cards and love notes to your husband at work. Put an occasional note on his pillow; prop one against a vase of flowers by his sink. Create novel ways to romance your love and show your appreciation of him. Give him a sense of value and the knowledge that you adore him every day. Your husband will forgive your many shortcomings if you communicate respect and adoration for him.

Never return a gift from your husband.

A few years ago Loden decided to do something special for me. His friend, a proprietor of a sign company, assigned a designer to help Loden create a special valentine for me. On the back were the words, "A Special Valentine Made by Woody Loden. 1995."

Each year for the rest of his life, Loden and the designer worked to make a valentine that topped the one of the previous year. After such a show of love, I had to come up with a novel way to surprise Loden, so I responded by giving him a glass heart with a note which read, "I give you my heart for one more year." The local paper featured our romance in a Valentine's Day article. The community began to look forward each year to seeing what the new valentine would be. A friend reported that when people asked her if we really were lovebirds or was it just a show, she replied, "Their love is genuine!"

None of us are shut away from the world. We can reach others and show them the way of love as God would have it. Romance your husband every day. Continual affection keeps your marriage from becoming a brother-sister type relationship.

Because of *eros*, you give flowers, valentines, and various kinds of affectionate gifts to the object of your affection. You must get into the habit of thinking of ways to romance your husband. When you find a small gift you know he will enjoy, take it home and give it to him in a special way. One of my treasured memories is a little bouquet of red clover Loden picked on the side of the road. And the bee that visited him there just added sweetness to Loden's gesture!

Romantic Planning

As the queen of the home, you are in charge of romantic planning, because a man will cease thinking of ways to romance his wife if she throws cold water on his burning love. Husbands tell me, "Why should I bother? She does not even acknowledge what I have done for her." Be excited over your husband's expressions of love, even the small ones, and he will keep finding new ways to please you. I never knew what surprise Loden would bring home to me from his daily travels. My gifts included an antique iron bed, pictures from the estate sale of a noted Memphis singer—not Elvis—and an iron kettle.

Be thrilled with whatever your husband bestows upon you and show him how grateful you are for his love and special attention. Most important, compliment him for his gifts in the presence of your guests. He is always pleased when you let others know he loves you, because that means you love him.

Keep the Gifts

Now, brand this rule on your heart. Never return a gift from your husband. He selected it because he liked it, and he thought it would be just what you wanted! If you return it, your actions will tell him he does not have good taste— that he cannot please you. Although your intention is good, your actions speak negatively about his choice. Find a way to use his gift and enjoy it! Then he will enjoy the gift also and take pleasure in having pleased you.

Once you begin doing romantic acts for your husband—sharing candlelight dinners, dressing for special events, or engaging in bedtime fun—he will begin to think of ways to be romantic and make plans of his own.

Always act in the best interest of your husband.

Loden and I daily enjoyed candlelight breakfasts and dinners. Eventually, he took it upon himself to light the candle. When I forgot, he reminded me that we could not eat until the candle was lit. He enjoyed bragging that his wife served him meals by candlelight. We do want to make our dear husbands proud, don't we?

You make the decision always to act in the best interest of your husband. When you don't feel like it, remind yourself that you can act your way into feeling the agape love you need.

Here is what one of "my girls" has to say about the importance of searing the motto into your mind so it will be ready to serve you when needed:

> I took the "Loving Your Husband" class from Mrs. Patsy several years ago. I still use a lot of the advice and teaching that I learned from that class. Here is the phrase I use often: "Act your way into feeling." There are many days when I don't feel like being cheerful or positive, but I try to act that way anyway. My husband is very grateful for this and compliments me for our happy home. He says, "When momma ain't happy, ain't nobody happy," but in our house that's not very often. Mrs. Patsy has shown me the tools from the Bible that I need to help our home be happy.

She told me she can hear my voice saying, "Act your way into feeling." I hope you too will repeat this motto over and over until it is tattooed on your brain. Handwrite the words and read them aloud so you will have the senses of touch, hearing, and sight to help your brain remember them.

The Third Wall

Storge (stor-gay') love is the natural affection between parents and children — family love. This love forms the third vital wall you must build to complete your love house. Every family member should back up to this warm wall every time they come home. It is acceptance, unconditional love, and honor. You express *storge* love to your husband as the head of the family. You accept this wonderful man unconditionally with warm affection. He knows he is safe in your arms; he feels loved for being himself. All our married life Loden and I told one another that "home" for us was within the circle of one another's arms.

Read Ephesians 5:33. We will discuss this in depth later, but just get used to this idea for guiding your *storge* love.

The Fourth Wall

Phileo (fil-eh'-o) is that warm hand that holds yours when you need a friend. Oh, what a vital wall this one is. Thayer says it means approval: to like, to sanction, to treat affectionately or kindly, to welcome, befriend. Its secondary meaning is to kiss, and its third meaning is to be fond of doing. Do you get the idea of what it means to have a fourth wall as the wall that gives you and your husband a bond the other three loves do not? You should be your husband's best friend, confidant, and source of strength in good times and bad. Don't ever let him down by publicizing confidential matters he shares with you, his best friend.

 What is Proverbs 17:17 teaching you?

The Roof

Agape (a-ga'-pay) love it not natural; it must be learned. It is the roof over your house of love. It will prevent the other four walls from crumbling when the rains of life fall. Natural love is selfish and you must learn to overcome such thinking. Remember, the old selfish woman was buried in the waters of baptism. You are a new woman of love; you will train yourself to think in those terms. Bible love is giving to another.

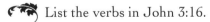 List the verbs in John 3:16.

John 3:16 describes agape love. It is giving. It is a very strong desire embedded in the choice of walking in Jesus' steps. Remember Gethsemane where Jesus prayed three times that the cup would be removed from Him? He made the choice to love mankind more than he loved His own feelings.

You see, no one had been separated from the presence of God as a sin-bearer. Jesus was about to have all the sins of the world, past and future, laid on Him—on Him who knew no sin. The thought of separation was almost more than He could take. He had never been a second away from His Father's presence and love. Aren't you thankful that Jesus had agape love for us? Aren't you glad He made the decision to obey His Father rather than to obey His own desires? Hebrews 12:2 says "for the joy set before Him" He decided to die for mankind.

This same promise is made to you. If you love your husband with agape love, the Father will see that joys will be set before you! Love not only your husband but also each person you meet. As God is love, so will you aim to become love. Agape love requires obedience to God and carries with it obligations to one's fellowman. Always remember it is a command of God in your best interest.

 Read 1 John 4:8. What active verb is in that verse? What tense is that verb? What does that teach you about love?

Love on Autopilot

Children of God must act in God's way, but what it His way? God is love, and so must we be (1 John 4:7–8). We must train our minds to think in terms of love—all five types. They must become our nature to the extent that we do not have to think in order to conduct ourselves properly. We just live always in the "is" tense. Trust me, it can be done. Practice, practice, practice. When you stumble, get up, dust yourself off, and say, "With your help, Father, I will do better." Few make a radical change overnight, but everyone can make many small changes over a period of time.

Growing into love takes a lifetime, because that old person constantly tries to resurrect herself. You must keep pushing her back into the grave. Also, know that you must act in the way of love, no matter what the actions of others are—including those of your husband. Nowhere does God excuse bad behavior. That Flip Wilson excuse of "the devil made me do it" may be true, but it carries no weight with the Father. "Act as My child in every situation," He would say if He were to speak to you directly.

 Read the first part of 1 John 4:8 and write its message about your actions.

To become love in a true sense, you must develop your total personality in the way God trains you to grow, and that is living like Jesus. He is your perfect example. You must develop the capacity to love your neighbor, which certainly includes your husband. Consistent love takes humility, courage, faith, and discipline. You must actively work each day to make your dream a reality. Love is an art, and like any art it must be practiced consistently until it is mastered. A devoted student first learns the theories of an art—music, painting, sports. Then she cultivates the expertise necessary to become a master.

What was Adam and Eve's day like? They did not know anything but love's way. They loved each other to the fullest and finished their day talking with their Father. About what? The garden and the various plants and animals there? Perhaps, but whatever it was, they entertained only love and positive thoughts because evil had not yet entered their love house. Life truly was ideal. As the builder of your home of love, you are the restorer of love's way in the life of your family.

False Love

Amnon's love for his half-sister Tamar is an example of the fleeting feeling of false love. Amnon "fell in love" with Tamar and pined for her day after day. His evil cousin Jonadab told him how to get Tamar to his side. Amnon feigned illness, and when their father came to see him, Amnon asked King David to send Tamar to prepare bread for him.

When Tamar came to Amnon's bedside with his bread, he grabbed her and said, "Come, lie with me, my sister." She begged him, "No, my brother, do not violate me, for such a thing is not done in Israel" (2 Samuel 13:12). She further told him David would give her to him as a wife, but he overpowered her and raped her.

Note the interesting way inspiration describes Amnon's feelings afterwards: "Then Amnon hated her with a very great hatred, for the hatred with which he hated her was greater than the love with which he had loved her. And Amnon said to her, 'Get up, go away!'" (2 Samuel 13:15).

You are responsible for your feelings.

Do you feel the action of our motto? By sinful deeds, Amnon acted his way into feeling hatred toward Tamar. The world will not help you to find happiness if you allow yourself to follow nature's way of selfishness instead of agape love.

A modern tale of Amnon was played out in a small town. A popular community leader had a dear, sweet wife. Her character was above reproach. But the husband thought he had fallen in love with an attractive sales representative. He left his wife and married the sales representative—his new love-wife. The community really was upset with the man.

However, within a few months, a look of sadness took up residence on the man's face. When dining in public, the newlyweds did not even look at each other, much less engage in conversation. Their faces showed scorn and disdain. They were no longer a happy couple. The honeymoon was over.

That sad tale is duplicated far too often in today's society!

You Can't Make Me!

You are responsible for your feelings, even though the world would have you believe otherwise. Have you ever heard anyone say, "I feel this way because I want to feel like this"? Don't we usually hear instead, "You made me angry"? Yes, but anger is a choice. A person is angry because he wants to be. Jesus says, "For the mouth speaks out of that which fills the heart." We think . . . we speak . . . Jesus teaches. We need to listen to Him. He will help us act our way into feeling instead of allowing our feelings to lead us into acting.

The nature of biblical love is based on deeds and facts; therefore, it is objective. Agape love is based on a responsible relationship with God, man (including our enemies), and ourselves.

Read Romans 5:3–5. What does this passage teach you? What does it teach about God's thinking?

Love Is / Love Is Not

Many aspects of love are set forth in 1 Corinthians 13. Read this chapter and list the ten positive traits of love and define their meanings:

1.

2.

3.

4.

5.

6.

7.

8.

9.

10.

Below, list the negative traits of love—"love is not"—and define their meanings:

1.

2.

3.

4.

5.

6.

7.

8.

9.

10.

11.

12.

Meditate on the aspects listed above and learn the way of love. Notice that the verb in each description is in present tense. Love always acts that way, and it is your training manual from now on. We can see from the verbs and their actions that they are "doing" words, not subjective ones. You have to will yourself to act in this way; you will not accidentally develop into the nature of God.

The world would have you believe that love is something you use or apply to yourself. Many ads have sexual overtones. Advertisers would have you believe if you use the right shampoo you will find love. However, God wants you to know that inner beauty comes from what you put into your mind, which takes it to your heart. Then love comes out in your words and actions.

The apostle John is a good example for the before and after ad God might have for the universe. John and his brother James were nicknamed Sons of Thunder. Their attitude was simple: Just wipe that whole village off the face of the earth, because an innkeeper denied us a place to stay for the night! (Read it for yourself in Luke 9:51–56.) In later life John was called the Apostle of Love. Love is the theme of four of his books, and we could certainly argue that God's love is the theme of his final book—Revelation. Jesus can do the same for you if you will work with Him.

Day 4

Love's Character

What is the character of Bible love? Care, responsibility, respect, and knowledge. Each character builds on another and makes love beautiful.

Care

Care is the active concern for the life and growth of the one we love. The book of Jonah sets forth good examples of both the positives and the negatives of this characteristic—God's love and Jonah's thinking, respectively.

Criticism is not a part of caring for your husband. It tears him down. Start now training yourself not to criticize. Period! Done with! Don't! We will study a better way than criticism in another week's study. Allow your love to grow and develop as you willingly give him the warm, nurturing air of your love house. Criticism makes for stale breathing and leads to poor health.

God Cared for Nineveh

God told Jonah to go to Nineveh and preach God's dissatisfaction with them and their pending destruction. Nineveh was the capital of Assyria, the empire that later conquered God's people Israel in the northern kingdom. The Assyrians were Jonah's mortal enemies. He had no intention of warning them about anything, so he turned from God's instruction and started for a destination in the opposite direction.

A large fish taught Jonah a valuable lesson: one cannot hide from God! Jonah finally went to Nineveh and preached. Then he positioned himself on a high hill so he could watch God destroy his enemy. Much to his disdain, the king of Nineveh led the people in repentance. He laid aside his regal garment, put on sackcloth, and sat in ashes. Next, he ordered a fast throughout the city, even proclaiming that the animals not be fed or watered.

God once again demonstrated that He was a "gracious and compassionate God, slow to anger and abundant in loving kindness, and one who relents concerning calamity." Jonah became very angry with God and asked that He kill him rather than let him see Nineveh spared. Jonah sulked, went to the top of a hill, and sat down in the heat of the blazing sun.

God prepared a gourd to protect Jonah from the sun. Then during the night God sent a worm to destroy the plant. He also sent a very hot west wind to test his prophet. Jonah was so hot and upset that he begged God to let him die. God asked Jonah if he had a good reason to be angry about the plant, and Jonah hotly replied, "I have good reason to be angry, even to death."

Next, God gave Jonah an object lesson in His goodness. He reminded Jonah that Nineveh was a great city, but 120,000 of its residents did not know their right hand from their left. He taught Jonah that the plant was not Jonah's doing, yet Jonah had greater compassion on the plant than on the many souls God spared. The lesson for Jonah was that a person labors for that which he loves, and he loves that for which he labors.

You have love and concern for your family, and because of the concern, you labor for them, and you labor for them because you have great love for them.

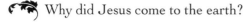 Why did Jesus come to the earth?

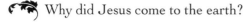 What does it mean to you to "care" for your husband?

Responsibility

This characteristic outflows from care and concern. You act in love toward your husband voluntarily. Jesus said, "You shall know the truth, and the truth will make you free" (John 8:32). Make you free from what? Let's ponder that freedom.

Every evil deed and thought that weighed you down before you became one with Jesus was your taskmaster. Anger, jealously, envy, evil speaking — they all controlled your mind. You did not control your thinking when you were engaging in sin; sin controlled you. Have you considered the life of a drug addict? He does not control the use of drugs; drugs control him.

You have no right to change another person.

However, you are free from those evil thoughts, deeds, and substances by the cleansing blood of Jesus Christ. You are free to act in love's way, so you can learn agape love and apply its principles! You are in control of love's way because agape love is the love of your thinking. You want the responsibility to take care of all the needs of your husband, from his sexual needs to his emotional needs — and even his stomach's need. That is why you can overcome any harsh feelings and act in a loving way even toward an enemy, just as the good Samaritan did.

Why did Cain kill Abel? Because he felt no responsibility toward him. When God questioned his jealous act, he asked, "Am I my brother's keeper?" Never forget that love always acts in a loving way; it can act in no other way. We cannot act contrary to our inner nature, so allow love to become your nature. Then you'll always act in the way of love without having to make a choice.

What does it mean to you to have the responsibility of caring for your husband?

Respect

Respect is the ability to see and accept another person as he is, acknowledging his right to be himself. The responsibility we feel for another can turn into a dominate nature if it is not tempered with respect.

Love your husband for who he is now. Did not Jesus accept you as you were and give you the freedom to grow in His love? He respects you as a free moral agent. You must give your husband and others the same freedom. You have no right to try to change another person; that is God's prerogative.

God gave you the responsibility to love, respect, and cherish your husband just as he is. You saw his strengths before marriage, and now you see the chinks in his armor. How normal! Are you perfect? No! Respect him the same way you want him to respect you. Will you practice using biblical love? Be kind, patient, and polite. Give yourself to your husband in every way. Living in an environment that is nurturing, cherishing, honoring, and respecting will give your husband the fertile soil to mature and grow into the man that God intends.

> Romans 14:19 is a command you must obey if you have respect for your husband and the Lord. Read it and write it down. How do you show respect to your husband in a responsible, caring way?

Knowledge

Knowledge is an essential addition for all three previous characteristics: care, responsibility, and respect. Your care and responsibility are blind without knowledge. And how can you respect your husband without knowing him?

Peter instructs the husband to dwell with his wife in knowledge, or understanding (cf. 1 Peter 3:7). The intent of his message applies to you as a wife as well. How do you gain this knowledge? Study your husband. What makes him tick? What are his likes and dislikes? Study his faults as well as his assets. Use your knowledge to enable you to take better care of his needs. Why should you administer to his needs? Because you are one with him. When you see to his needs, you are taking care of yourself!

Loden told me that I knew him so well I knew what he was thinking before he did. Wives need to guard against communicating an all-knowing attitude. If you anticipate your husband's actions and lord this knowledge over him, he will feel a loss of control. On the other hand, men also have an idea of women's reactions, but not in the intuitive feminine way. Do you think that is why God bestowed us with the privilege of being the caretaker of the home?

> Think of some ways you know your husband better, perhaps, than he knows himself. How can you use this knowledge positively?

Your Ministry

Some people will say, "I act the way I feel, and if I act in another way I will be a hypocrite." What does our Father say about this? Galatians 2:20 reminds us that we no longer live; it is Christ who lives in us. We must act toward all in a Christlike way. You are not a hypocrite when you love even your enemies and act kindly toward them just as Christ instructed.

So love your husband no matter how he conducts himself! The roof of your house of love is agape love, remember? Also think back to Jesus' teaching: when you give a cup of cold water to a needy one, you give it to Him. Jesus is the head of your husband, so as you minister to your husband, you minister to Jesus. Remember, act your way into feeling!

Day 5

Love and Appreciation

Where do we go to find wisdom about love? Most of us will answer quickly: "1 Corinthians 13!" Read these attributes of love aloud to yourself each day and practice, practice, practice until you become love. Reading out loud trains your hearing and seeing, even your touching. Imprint them on your heart. You will not change overnight, but you will change, and eventually you will become love because you think love. So give yourself time; practice each day so you will reach your goal. When you can act this way without thinking, you will reap the many rewards love promises you. I keep repeating this, but in repetition is learning.

Now, write your name on each blank below. Copy this sheet, and place it where you can read it aloud every day. You are training your mind and actions to be love.

_____ is patient.

_____ is not jealous.

_____ does not brag.

_____ is not arrogant.

_____ does not act unbecoming.

_____ does not seek her own.

_____ is not provoked.

_____ does not take into account a wrong suffered.

_____ does not rejoice in unrighteousness.

_____ rejoices with the truth.

_____ bears all things.

_____ believes all things.

_____ hopes all things.

_____ endures all things.

_____ never fails.

Learn to be appreciative. What do you accomplish by using words of appreciation to all you meet? You develop an attitude of gratitude and the mindset that focuses on good things, positive actions, and encouraging words. You present a gift of love to each person you encounter. As children of the Father, we must learn to be grateful. We need to show those around us that we are thankful—that we are positive thinkers. Your heart will thank you. Here are five exercises to help.

1. Close your eyes and picture some wonderful past blessing from the Father. Now say a prayer of thankfulness to Him.

2. Close your eyes once more and think of a wonderful act of love your husband gave you this past week. Thank him for loving you and for the act of love; tell him why it is important to you. I am continually thankful for things Loden did that really touched me. Sometimes, many years after a gift, I recall the pleasure it gave me.

3. Close your eyes and think of something your child, or some other child, did for you. Thank the child for this gift and tell why it is important to you.

4. The next time you go shopping, thank the clerk for some act of kindness. You may really have to work hard to find that compliment, but do it anyway.

5. Think of one good characteristic of your husband. Each day give prayers of thanksgiving for this trait and pray for the Father to help your husband grow in grace and truth. And don't forget to pray for yourself to become one of Sarah's daughters.

Memory Verse

"A new commandment I give to you, that you love one another, even as I have loved you, that you also love one another."

John 13:34

My Take-Home

Lesson sheet from teacher.

Letter to husband if you are in a class.

My Homework

1. Interview your husband. Set aside a quiet time and make it an enjoyable experience. Once I dressed up, put on a blond wig, and knocked on our den door. Was Loden surprised when he opened the door! If your husband says, "Oh, you know the answer to that question," you can reply, "Oh, but I want to hear what you have to say, so tell me."

These questions begin simply, with easy subjects to warm your husband to opening his heart, and then progress to those of a more personal nature. By the time you get to the personal questions, the ice has been broken, and he is comfortable talking about himself like never before. Never repeat anything he tells you in this interview. It is just for your learning experience. (The interview questions are listed below.)

2. Ask your husband each day: "What can I do to help you today?" Phrase it a different way each day. For example "I am going to town today. Is there anything I can pick up for you?" After a time your husband might pick up on this habit and begin asking you the same question without even realizing where he got the idea.

3. Pray daily for each family member, especially yourself, that you can learn to be love.

4. When shopping for cards, select some love notes. Mail one to your husband at his business. Let him have the joy of your love during a busy day.

My Husband's Interview

Jot down your husband's answers as if you were a reporter. File them and refer to them periodically. Ideally, you will make another interview with your own questions every year; then you will really know how your husband is growing. Question him on various topics so you can keep up with his thinking. Use this information to care better for his needs. The answers he gives to his feelings as a child are probably the same feelings he has as an adult.

1. What was your favorite toy as a child?

2. What was the game you most enjoyed playing as a young boy?

3. What was your favorite TV show when you were 12?

4. How were you punished by your parents? What did you do to get over the hurt of the punishment? Did you ever feel they punished you when you did not deserve it?

5. How did you feel about the punishment?

6. Who was your favorite teacher in high school? Why?

7. What characteristics do you look for in a friend? What act would you consider to be a breach of friendship? How would you respond to such a breach? How would you patch up the rift?

8. How did you take criticism? Did you ever feel you were unjustly criticized?

9. How did you get over the feeling of hurt when you were a teen?

10. What is your favorite food? Why?

11. What makes you angry? How do you get over your anger?

12. What dress does your wife have that you like to see her wearing? Why?

13. What is your favorite color for your wife to wear?

14. How do you like to make love? Why?

15. What are two qualities you really like in your wife?

16. What is the easiest part of being a husband?

17. What is the hardest part of being a husband?

18. What do you enjoy best about being a father?

19. What gives you the most stress in your job? How can your wife help you get over this stress?

20. What constitutes modest female dressing?

21. What makes a woman charming?

22. What are some characteristics in a woman that turn you off?

23. What is your favorite room in the house?

24. Describe the perfect dinner date for you and your wife.

25. What types of gifts do you enjoy giving your sweetheart?

26. What is your favorite gift to receive?

27. How can a couple modify their relationship to make their home more loving?

28. What is your most sought-after goal in life? How can your wife help you reach this mountain peak?

29. What is your favorite way of showing your wife you love her?

30. How can your wife best show her love for you?

Thank your husband for his answers and tell him what a terrific person he is to interview.

She Has Done What She Could

From the Father of the Bride: "Who can find a virtuous woman?"

Thought for the Day: "Make your ear attentive to wisdom, incline your heart to understanding. For if you cry for discernment, lift your voice for understanding. If you seek her . . . then you will discern the fear of the Lord and discover the knowledge of God. For the Lord gives wisdom; from His mouth come knowledge and understanding. He stores up sound wisdom for the upright; He is a shield to those who walk in integrity, guarding the paths of justice, and He preserves the way of His godly ones. Then you will discern righteousness and justice and equity and every good course, for wisdom will enter your heart and knowledge will be pleasant to your soul; Discretion will guard you, Understanding will watch over you to deliver you from the way of evil" (Proverbs 2:2–12).

From Sarah: Listen as Wisdom instructs you.

Day 1

My Journey

When I first sat at Dorothea's feet to absorb her wisdom, I thought I was such a good wife. I listened intently as she began to describe how I should build my house of love. But I arrogantly thought I had done a really good job; I thought my walls were straight and true. Instead, I found chinks in my house of love.

Take an imaginary journey with me and discover how I learned to refurbish my love house.

I eagerly stepped into my house of love to begin living the good life of love. Inside the entrance, mirrors lined the walls. When I looked at my reflection in one of the mirrors, I realized it was not an ordinary mirror; it was a mirror of my soul. What I saw horrified me!

Here was Patsy wanting to be the keeper of her house of love—but there staring back at me was a soul full of pride and anger. She had a sharp tongue, which in some cases was silent to punish her dear Loden; at other times it was used as a sharp knife to cut him to the bone. I saw horrible pouting and plotting of revenge. And, oh, I looked at the unforgiving spirit dwelling in that heart!

I was stricken because I knew such a soul could never be the queen of this house of love. Turning around in despair, I saw a door open to my right. In tears I walked through the door and realized it was a dressing room. A cross with nails in it was hanging on the wall. A beautiful, white robe of the finest cloth was hanging next to the cross. Suddenly, three lovely aged women walked into the dressing room and looked lovingly at me. One said, "I am Sarah, and I hope to be your mother." Another said, "I am King Lemeul's mother, and I hope to teach you the ABCs of being the wife you want to be for your Loden." The third introduced herself by these words: "I am Wisdom, and I hope you will take my words very seriously."

Sarah said, "Look at those nails on the cross. Do you remember that when you were baptized, you put off the old woman of sin and allowed Jesus to make of you a new creature? Why are you again wearing the old clothes of that worldly woman? You *are* wearing them, aren't you? Don't you remember that Colossians 3:8 instructs you to put aside all the filthy garments of your old self? Now, please take off those old dirty garments and hang them on the cross's nails, for Jesus said you must follow Him every day (Luke 9:23). See the beautiful, white robe? Jesus wants you to don it every day (Colossians 3:12–17). Read the verses in your Bible."

I read the verses and then looked at the new robe like every woman looks at a new dress. I gingerly took the beautiful robe off the hanger, ran my fingers up and down it, and enjoyed the feel of its fabric. Next I looked at the label: *From the House of Jesus.* Of course I had to check the rest of the labels. The robe was made in Heaven and the washing instructions read: *Prewashed in the blood of the Lamb.* The fabric content was one hundred percent holiness. I tried on the garment; it was a perfect fit.

Mother Sarah, Queen Mother, and Wisdom led me from the dressing room into the living room. On the wall was a portrait of a woman, so beautiful it took my breath away just to gaze upon her loveliness. She seemed to be looking directly into my eyes. Her smile made me feel loved. I walked over to the picture and looked at the brass name tag: *The Worthy Woman.* The artist's name in the right-hand corner—The Father. I stood there and wished somehow that I could be just half as beautiful as that woman. Her beauty came from her soul, not from her outward appearance.

Queen Mother came to my side and said, "I can tell that you are touched by her beauty. Would you like for me to tell you how you can become as beautiful as this Worthy Woman?"

I replied eagerly. "Of course! Will you please help me?"

Queen Mother said, "Come and sit with Sarah, Wisdom, and me. We will instruct you in the way of Wisdom, which is, as you know, God's Word. Listen to us, believe us, and practice what we tell you. Then you will become as the beautiful woman."

As the four of us sat on couches sipping tea, Wisdom began to teach me the "Be's" from Titus 2:4–5. "These have been passed down from generation to generation, and now it is your turn to learn them," she explained. "Be diligent to learn and practice them. Then you will please not only your Loden, but you will also give glory to your Father who created you to live this way."

I will now teach you what I learned about the "Be's" that are listed in Titus 2:4–5:

Be a loving friend to your husband.

Be in love with your children.

Be sensible or sober-minded.

Be pure.

Be a worker at home.

Be kind.

Be subject to your own husband.

Be a good name for God's glory.

These "Be's" are not multiple choices; they are laws from Jesus. Never forget His words, "If you keep My commandments, you will abide in My love; just as I have kept My Father's commandments and abide in His love" (John 15:10). Simply put, if you love Jesus, you will keep His commands. Isn't it wise to understand what each "Be" means? Let's delve into the richness of each trait.

Be a loving friend to your husband. You learned in Week Three how to love your husband, so we will just review by saying the five loves of your house are to become your way of life. You will practice until these five loves perform without thinking; they become who you are. The word used in Titus 2 for love is *philandros* which means fond—you are to be fond of your husband—and this word derives from *phileo* which means "friendship."

As a young wife you are to exhibit a willing and determined love that is not necessarily based on a husband's being worthy of your love. Your love is grounded in God's instruction and God's order for a healthy home. This means you use *agape* love, even if your husband is not conducting himself according to God's laws.

Be in love with your children. Not every woman who bears children is a loving mother. It takes maturity, patience, and much *agape* and *storge* love to rear children. You must learn to apply those loves to your children as well as to your husband. Proverbs 22:6 reads: "Train up a child in the way he should go, even when he is old he will not depart from it." *Train* means "to initiate or dedicate." After studying Bible passages—Proverbs and Ephesians 6:1–2, for example— we can understand that the Father wants His children to be reared in His way. And God does look upon your children as His own (cf. Psalm 127:3; Isaiah 1:2; Ezekiel 16:20; Mark 9:37).

The words, *in the way he should go,* mean "according to the tenor of his way." Individual children differ. Your role as a parent is to guide each child in the way of the Lord and to train him according to his talents. It is not wise to encourage a child to become a scientist when his heart and talents are encouraging him to be a football coach. If a child has a passion in life, that passion will mature but probably will not change substantially as he matures.

A mother is to be her child's advocate. No one can replace a child's mother in giving the love and attention the child needs to grow into a healthy adult. As a child develops, parental duties change. The art of parenting becomes an advisory and friendship relationship when children become adults, and oh what a dear relationship that is! You can share as best friends and not have the day-to-day responsibility of childcare.

Will your children say of you and your husband that you have taught them as Proverbs 4:10–15 describes? Write what you want your children to say about you when they are grown.

Be sensible. Self-control is a part of the fruit of the Spirit, and you must diligently work to maintain it (2 Peter 1:6). Faith, moral excellence, and knowledge are listed before self-control. The more knowledge you have of God's Word, the easier it will be to develop self-control. Self-control gives you mastery over your thoughts and actions in response to those of others. To be self-controlled is to be God-controlled, and that is His goal for your life.

Ask God for help in executing this "Be." Sensibility is the solution to many of life's problems. What is one thing I can do to have more self-control?

Be pure. Be chaste, modest, innocent, and blameless. Purity carries the idea of being clean in heart and mind. You are morally untainted; you are faithful to your husband and to Jesus, your bridegroom. Modesty refers to a healthy sense of shame in word and action. This includes dressing in a way that will not incite lust and will bring only a good report from the outside world to your husband. Both the church and the world recognize you as an ideal woman. Even strangers who see your dress, note your behavior, and hear you speak cannot help but conclude you are truly a lovely lady.

What does 1 Timothy 2:9–10 command you?

Read 1 Peter 3:3–4 and consider these thoughts. While it is not wrong to wear jewelry and go to the beauty shop, don't allow your outward appearance to be that by which people judge you; don't let that be all you think about! In New Testament times, rich women dressed in luxurious clothing and arranged their hair, decorating it with pearls and jewels. Then they paraded about the streets so all would know how rich their husbands were. The Father wants others to know you as His daughter and your husband's wife, not by the rich clothing and jewelry you wear, but by your inner beauty.

You must dress in a fashion so men will not leer at you. Your body is only for your husband's pleasure and viewing. Teach your daughters to be modest all their lives. You can't let them dress one way as little girls and then suddenly change their dress habits when they become delightfully aware that their bodies, in some strange way, are beginning to attract men and older boys.

You cannot keep "at home" if you go constantly.

A friend of mine asked her granddaughter, visiting from a Christian university, to speak to her teen girls' class. In preparation for the presentation, the granddaughter asked young men at the university for advice. They told her, "Tell them not to dress in a way that makes us lust." God will not hold you or your daughter guiltless if you allow her to dress in an impure way. This is a serious "Be" for you, my dear.

Critically view yourself in a full-length mirror. Are you modestly dressed? Consider your manners. Are they decent? Are you pure in heart?

Be a worker at home. In order to do that, you must be there—at home, I mean. You cannot keep "at home" if you are constantly on the go. The fast pace of modern-day living creates a hectic schedule for all of us, but some way you must find time to keep the home organized and running smoothly. It may mean eliminating activities. You cannot be all things to all people, so you must learn to say no. The mother's presence keeps the household running—whether smoothly or chaotically.

 How can I better train our children to help keep our home running smoothly?

Be kind. When the Bible uses *kind*, it means "that which is good in its character or constitution and beneficial in its effect." In the parable of the sower, the seed that fell into the good soil grew and gave much increase. Kindness is an attitude that always gives good, even if the recipient does not deserve it. Your kindness provides "good soil" to all who come in contact with you. Kindness nurtures. Jesus is our example.

 Write what Jesus says about Himself in Luke 6:35.

One of my teachers once said, "Manners are just behaving kindly toward others." Why should we teach our children manners?

Be subject to your own husband. This means to place yourself under his authority or headship. We will delve more deeply into this later. For now, just think upon the meaning of submission and ask yourself if you are willing to yield yourself to your husband.

 What does submission to your husband mean?

Be a good name for God's glory. God and Jesus are very proud of their names, and they do not want their children to act in a way that brings dishonor to them. If you do not practice each "Be," then the world will make fun of God, His Word, and even you for being a hypocrite. The world expects a person to live what he teaches. The Father does not want you to cause Him shame. After all, He gave His dear Son to redeem you from death at the hands of Satan, and He expects you to honor His sacrifice.

Dishonor means "to speak harm." In general, it means to bring ill repute and slander, defaming or harming one's reputation. Bad behavior on your part gives Satan an opportunity to tell the world, "God's way is not the best way, because His child does not believe it and acts in a worldly way." Your walk must match your talk. Your life is an advertisement for the Christian life and for a marriage made in heaven. Is your advertisement producing results?

Day 2

Promises of God

You will be complete if you abide in God (1 John 4:16–17). Those who love Him are in possession of His character. Post these verses so you can remember their promise. They will help you in those days when you lose your way and have troubles.

Note the four promises from God in the following texts. Learn them and store them in your heart. They will also help you on those days when life seems so "daily."

Promise One: Wait for the Lord

Do you not know? Have you not heard? The Everlasting God, the Lord, the Creator of the ends of the earth does not become weary or tired. His understanding is inscrutable. He gives strength to the weary, and to him who lacks might He increases power. Though youths grow weary and tired, and vigorous young men stumble badly, yet those who wait for the Lord will gain new strength, they will mount up with wings like eagles, they will run and not get tired, they will walk and not become weary (Isaiah 40:28–31).

How can we wait for the Lord? *Wait* in Hebrew means "to bind together." Ecclesiastes 4:12 teaches us that one who is alone can be overpowered, but two can resist being taken. Why? Because a cord of three strands is not quickly torn apart. When I bring the Father, the Son, and the Holy Spirit into my life, my rope of life becomes stronger. When a rope is lifting a heavy weight, its strands slip tighter and closer together, strengthening the rope. Not so with a single strand—even a light weight can break it.

Your walk must match your talk.

How can you face your problems? What will give you strength? How is your victory sure? Make sure your faith and hope are mingled with the three strands of the Godhead! Folly says, "Follow your own way," but Wisdom instructs, "Follow God's way." You decide.

Promise Two: You Are God's Own Possession

But you are a chosen race, a royal priesthood, a holy nation, a people for God's own possession, so that you may proclaim the excellencies of Him who has called you out of darkness into His marvelous light (1 Peter 2:9).

Isn't that an inspiring thought? When you were baptized into Christ, you became a part of the chosen race of Israel. You have the royal blood of Jesus flowing through your spiritual veins; you are a priest giving sacrifices of praise to Him. And this part is so beautiful, it will bring tears of joy to your eyes: You are a possession of God. The original language implies ownership and a surrounding.

The following illustration helps us understand *possession:*

Think of a large circle with a dot at the center. You are the dot, and the circle is God's love surrounding you. His love protects you from everything Satan can throw at you just as He protected Job during his trials. The only way Satan can get to you is by first going through God.

First Corinthians 10:13 promises that you are able to withstand any temptation. Why? Your Father will not allow a temptation that you cannot bear. What assurance! "I can do it" is your motto, because you wait upon the Lord. You can face trials without worrying and fretting.

Promise Three: God Is at Work in You

Work out your salvation with fear and trembling; for it is God who is at work in you, both to will and to work for His good pleasure (Philippians 2:12–13).

Isn't that challenging? Your Father wants you to realize that He gives you the freedom to work toward becoming like Christ. *Work* comes from the idea of miners struggling to extract every ounce of ore—or farmers cultivating a field to achieve the highest yield possible. Your Father wants you to know He is working with you when you intertwine your life with His.

Isn't it wonderful to know that you don't have to face life alone? You can be a woman of virtue. You must believe you can achieve this goal with God's help. God has all the answers for every problem. You do not have to go outside the scriptures to find help.

🌿 Do you believe you can become a woman like the Father wants you to be? How diligently are you willing to labor for this achievement?

Promise Four: You Are Not Alone

"Casting all your anxiety on Him, because He cares for you" (1 Peter 5:7). Never think you are all alone. Your Father, Christ, and the Holy Spirit are with you each day. Practice feeling the presence of the Godhead every minute of every day. If you think about these four promises, then you realize you are not living life alone! You have the greatest available power with you every step of the way, every day. Courage is yours; you can face anything!

🌿 Write in your own words what these four promises mean to you.

How do you intend to use this knowledge to help you grow into the woman of Proverbs 31?

Three Goals of Proverbs 31:10–31

To inspire women to fear God. This is the beginning of knowledge (Proverbs 1:7). If a woman fears God, then she will work to fulfill the role she was created to be—a help suitable for her husband.

To inspire those influenced by such a godly woman. Her goodness causes others, primarily her husband and children, to praise her ways.

To praise the godly woman for her wisdom. The opening verses of Proverbs promote wisdom. True wisdom implies knowledge of God. Proverbs ends with the personification of Wisdom as a spiritual woman. She is living proof that the knowledge of God is very much alive and available to every woman who wants to embrace it. Ruth was a real-life, Proverbs 31 woman. She is the only person described as being virtuous. Boaz and all of Bethlehem looked upon her as such. If you imitate this woman, you will be an excellent crown to your husband (Proverbs 12:4).

Cast all your anxiety on Him—you are not alone.

Day 3

The Rare Jewels: Proverbs 31

Let's go back to my imaginary house of love where Sarah, the Queen Mother, Wisdom, and I are having our tea.

The Queen Mother laid her hand gently on my arm and spoke softly. "I am here in your house of love to instruct you on the ABCs of being a good wife. You have worked very hard to build it, so do not be foolish and tear it down (Proverbs 14:1). I have been asked by Wisdom to instruct you from Proverbs 31. These basic lessons will enable you to live happily with your Loden and to train your son and daughter. Your son will know how to choose a wife, and Lisa will become the loving wife your future son-in-love will adore.

"Remember, I am describing the finished product. This wife did not start out perfectly. She had to learn her ABCs just as you must. God gives us the perfect example, and then expects us to grow into perfection. Jesus came to give you the exact example of how man is to live with God and man. This is the ideal pattern for you to follow to become the perfect wife for your man."

During the next three days, we will highlight Scripture from Proverbs 31:10–31. Why is this study important? These twenty-two verses describe the ideal wife—a worthy goal.

🅰 *"An excellent wife, who can find? For her worth is far above rubies"* (Proverbs 31:10). It is all about character! *Excellent* carries the idea of strength. In 1 Chronicles 12:8 the same word—*valor*—is used to describe great men of war. The Hebrew meaning is to be strong and valiant—to have many powerful resources like an army. In Judges 6:12 the angel of the Lord said to Gideon, "The Lord is with you, O *valiant* warrior." The same word is used to describe this *excellent* wife. She is strong in body and character and is very spiritually minded because she knows her strength lies in the Lord.

How many women have such character, especially young women entering into marriage? God created Eve to be at Adam's side, helping him with his work and life in the Garden of Eden. Today a loving wife must be at her husband's side to help him become victorious in life's battles.

Rubies are the rarest and most valuable of all jewels. When brides were purchased, a "ruby wife" brought the highest price. So what is an excellent wife worth? Her character is compared to a rare jewel. Who makes rubies? Only the Father. With God all things are possible—a mere rock can be made into a ruby!

🌿 Are you a ruby to your husband? If not, what plans are you making to become his ruby?

I keep asking, "Are you willing to become a woman of God?" If so, you must commit to intense study, prayer, and practice as God molds you. But the result will be worth the effort. How wonderful you will feel when you are truly your husband's rare ruby!

🅱 *"The heart of her husband trusts in her"* (Proverbs 31:11). Trust is vital to a relationship. Remember how Pharaoh made Joseph the number two man in all Egypt? Joseph took command of all the land to guide and plan for the coming famine. Should your husband be able to put all he has in your care and spend his time with his business affairs? Absolutely. He should never have to worry about the running of the house, the betrayal of confidence, exceeding the family budget, or any other hindrance to a smooth functioning household. He may help you, but you are his queen, and God gave you the home as your realm.

Trust is built over time, but from the beginning you should show your-self to be trustworthy. Throughout the Word of God we learn to trust only in the Lord for all our needs. God is your husband's spiritual help, and you are your husband's earthly helper. Your husband should find in you all he needs physically, mentally, emotionally, and spiritually. Give your husband the attention necessary to be healthy in all these various areas.

List some ways you can help your husband trust you.

"He shall lack no gain" (Proverbs 31:11). Fill your mate's soul with joy so that he does not have to find fulfillment elsewhere. Share your husband's goals in life, and help him to achieve them. You are strong and willing to shoulder the responsibility of running the home in a profitable way for him. He is rich because you are his. You become more precious to him every day. His investment in you will bring great returns. During famines in ancient times, men raided nearby villages to get grain to feed their families. Your husband should not need to make raids; family needs can be satisfied within your relationship.

Are you an asset or a liability to your husband? Name some of the ways you can be priceless to him.

"She does him good and not evil all the days of her life" (Proverbs 31:12). The worthy woman's husband is first in her life; she sees to his well-being in everything she does. There is no selfishness in her heart. His welfare means more to her than anything. She is committed to him and intends to see that his every need is met by her own hands every day. Is it any wonder that her husband looks upon her as his ruby? She has developed Godlike character; her mind dwells on good rather than evil. Only good thoughts and actions flow from her heart.

Women batter their mates much more today than ever before. The latest poll reports that 835,000 men in the United States are battered every year, but many such cases go unreported. Do women need to learn their roles from God? Definitely! How can God's beautiful, delicate, porcelain creation change into a battering ram?

Choose self-control to insure your good deeds, especially to your husband. You see every good and bad day he has, and yet do him good rather than evil. That takes a ruby of a woman!

🌿 Define the words *good* and *all.*

Day 4
Dedication to Family

🅔 *"She looks for wool and flax and works with her hands in delight"* (Proverbs 31:13). This woman's work ethic is diligent; she is not afraid to work with her hands. Work around the home is not demeaning to her, but an act of love. She is not lazy. She keeps her family clothed. Notice that she has a positive attitude — "in delight." It is our choice to make "home keeping" a chore or a gift of love. Your home can be a haven or a place of sorrow. As the queen, you decide.

🌿 How do you perceive the roles of a wife and mother? Why?

🅕 *"She is like merchant ships; she brings her food from afar"* (Proverbs 31:14). Making sure your family eats healthfully is your responsibility. This woman is willing to search for food to prepare the family's meals. Your family's diet is a great factor in their health. Fast food and packaged, processed food lead to poor health.

I fed Loden well and gave him all the right vitamins. I never thought he would have a heart problem, so when he had to have bypass surgery, I was shocked. The doctor explained that his genetic make-up was the cause: "Your serving him nutritious food kept his heart from having problems sooner." Study nutrition and love your man by seeing that he eats properly.

🅖 *"She rises also while it is still night and gives food to her household and portions to her maidens"* (Proverbs 31:15). Breakfast is the most important meal of the day, yet more people skip it than any other meal. Get up in time to prepare a nutritious meal for your loves. Children who skip breakfast usually end up with their heads on the desk sleeping. Adults often consume fast food on the way to work or at break time, clogging their arteries. Eating properly is far cheaper than paying medical bills.

🌿 How can you be sure your family is eating properly?

Great Entrepreneurial Keenness

h *"She considers a field and buys it; from her earnings she plants a vineyard"* (Proverbs 31:16). This woman *considers*. She does not rush into any project without counting the cost. Do you think she consults her husband before spending so much money? From the raw goods she purchases, she makes clothing for her family, purchases a field, and plants a vineyard. The money from the crops enables her to provide more for her family and to begin a manufacturing business as well. This woman is money savvy. She is confident of the future of her investment.

Why is it important to make a budget and to stick to it?

Why should you put aside money each month for emergencies and future use?

I *"She girds herself with strength and makes her arms strong"* (Proverbs 31:17). *Gird* means to prepare oneself for action. The wise woman fears, 'reveres,' the Lord. She knows God's law and is prepared to meet any trial or need that arises in her family. Her mental strength enables her to handle the mental, physical, and emotional traumas that come her way.

"She makes her arms strong." Not only is she prepared mentally to meet all necessities, but she keeps her body fit and able to perform all her tasks. She works at keeping her muscles toned and healthy. Medical studies now agree that mental and physical exercise are necessities for good health and successful aging.

Do you feed your soul daily from God's Word? If not, how and when do you plan to begin?

What steps will you take to make physical exercise a part of your health program?

K *"She senses that her gain is good. Her lamp does not go out at night"* (Proverbs 31:18). *Gain* means "increase." Profits from the sale of her products are good because of their high quality. She puts forth the effort to make sure her maidens produce good products. She does not quit at sundown; neither does she let her work cease at night. This verse carries the idea of keeping a lamp burning for emergencies. She has only oil lamps, but she makes sure light is available for arising at night. She thinks ahead to the possible needs of her family.

K *"She stretches out her hands to the distaff, and her hands grasp the spindle"* (Proverbs 31:19). Notice how often this woman's hands are mentioned. Her key quality is selfless service to her family. She is a good business woman and patient with her employees. Why? Because she knows each step of her business: buying, producing, weaving, and selling. One cannot teach what one does not know; excellence describes her in every way. She is goal-oriented.

Why should you have training in some profession outside the home?

Do you know enough about your husband's financial affairs to take over if needed? How can you better prepare yourself to look after your family?

L *"She extends her hand to the poor, and she stretches out her hands to the needy"* (Proverbs 31:20). Do you recall Jesus' teachings about Lazarus and the rich man? The rich man was sent to torment because he did not obey God's law of looking after the needy. All through the Bible God shows His love and concern for the well-being of the widows, the orphans, and the needy. One of the reasons the children of Israel were carried into captivity was because they did not help their needy; in fact, they misused them and cheated them. Not this woman! She works diligently with her hands to give to those less fortunate. She believes in a "hands on" approach in caring for the poor. Consider the largeness of her heart!

Does she open her arms to embrace the spiritually needy with love when they cry for solace or attention? The Father teaches us to help bear the burdens of the poor and those who fall into sin (Galatians 6:1–10).

The worthy woman probably takes her role of counselor very seriously. Does she weep with those who weep and rejoice with those who rejoice? Does she believe a hug goes a long way toward making one feel better? She is probably a mother figure to all, and oh, how the world needs such.

Why would this woman qualify to teach the "Be's" we discussed earlier?

How was she a comforter to others?

❧ *Day 5* ❧

Strength and Dignity

M *"She is not afraid of the snow for her household, for all her household are clothed with scarlet"* (Proverbs 31:21). The worthy woman's dominant characteristic is faith in God. She knows God will look after the needs of those who did their part. Jesus gives His bride this same promise (Luke 12:25–32). Worry is futile. Jesus admonishes us not to fear those who can kill the body, but to fear God who can cast both body and soul into hell (Luke 12:4–5).

Her priorities are in the right order: God, husband, children, others. She has no worry about the future; her faith is in God, and she prepares for the future as best she can. Her household is ready for winter! Scarlet clothing is double-dyed—very expensive. She has bought the best garments possible. Her family has coats for cold weather.

D *"She makes coverings for herself. Her clothing is fine linen and purple"* (Proverbs 31:22). How do you know how much to spend on clothes? Look at your bank account. Buy the best you can with your budget, and save for those items you know will be needed later. The rule is, don't spend more than you make. Debt is a millstone about your neck; it pulls the family down faster than anything. Financial problems are among the top ten aggravations that plague a marriage.

Dress so your husband is proud of you.

Dress yourself so your husband is proud of your looks. Too many mothers spend all their clothing allowance on the children, and then they wear any old slouchy thing. But that worthy woman dressed in fine linen and purple. In her day, linen was one of the most expensive fabrics, and to have it dyed purple showed that she wore the finest. In ancient times purple was associated with royalty. This woman wants to be a crown to her husband and dress like a queen. Your husband is judged by the way you dress and how you conduct yourself. Give him a good name. As your children mature, teach them to earn their own clothing allowance.

How do you budget for family clothing? How can God help you run your house as the worthy woman did?

How much thought do you give to your husband's tastes when you are purchasing clothing?

O *"Her husband is known in the gates, when he sits among the elders of the land"* (Proverbs 31:23). To sit among the elders is to sit in a high position. Her husband is wise. His position is similar to that of a councilman. Worthy Woman gives her husband a good name; she helps him to be financially sound so he can devote his time to helping run the affairs of state.

Today's corporate manager usually wants to meet the wife of a prospective employee. He knows her influence can affect changes in the company. In the church, a wife's behavior can influence her husband's ability as elder or a deacon. In any setting, a wife gives her husband a good name or a bad name. President Abraham Lincoln's wife was the source of much sorrow in his life, but he constantly defended her actions. He loved her very much. Wisdom teaches that an excellent wife is the crown of her husband (Proverbs 12:4). If your husband is king, then you are his lovely queen. Act like one!

Rate yourself from one to ten — poor to excellent — on the name you have given your husband. How would your husband rate you?

P *"She makes linen garments and sells them, and supplies belts to the tradesmen"* (Proverbs 31:24). Worthy Woman is a great business woman! She manufactures linen garments. Her products sell to the high end of the market; her profits are proportionate. She also makes belts for the tradesman, so she has income from every level of society. What a woman! Running a home takes diversified talent. A well-organized, well-run, well-loved household is not the result of a lazy and uncaring wife. Quite the opposite is true! The world looks on a housewife's profession as a very lowly position, but God looks on it as the kingdom of a queen.

Q *"Strength and dignity are her clothing, and she smiles at the future"* (Proverbs 31:25). Look at the worthy woman. She is self-assured, well-dressed, dignified, loving, and kind. You want her as a dear friend. She knows she is a child of God, and she acts accordingly. She represents her husband to the world, and she wants to give him a good name. Her most important clothing is her inner character; she dons strength and dignity in thought and deed.

R *"She opens her mouth in wisdom, and the teaching of kindness is on her tongue"* (Proverbs 31:26). To fear the Lord is the beginning of wisdom, and to have the knowledge of God is to have wisdom, so this woman is steeped in the Word of God. Is the Father by her side as her security and guide? Kindness is a law to her, just as it is a law to you, because love is kind (1 Corinthians 13:4).

🌿 Do you have the wisdom that is derived only from the Word of God? What is the law of your speaking?

🅢 *"She looks well to the ways of her household"* (Proverbs 31:27). This woman had no time to be idle. She is a diligent worker in her kingdom, her home. Her family is her main concern. Have you noticed that this woman always puts others before herself? She knew, even before Jesus said so: It is more blessed to give than to receive (Acts 20:35).

🌿 Over the past five years have you become more selfish or less selfish? What are you doing to become less selfish over the next five years?

🌿 As a homemaker, what one thing can you do to increase the happiness of your home?

🅣 *"Her children rise up and bless her; her husband also, and he praises her saying, 'Many daughters have done nobly, but you excel them all' "* (Proverbs 31:28–29).

This woman's well-trained children excel because they have a good foundation. They are wise, have good work ethics, and fear God. As a result they give their mother the honor due her. *Bless* in Hebrew suggests going straight, advancing, being with God. This woman's children know she is a woman of wisdom and love. They observe first hand what her character does for their family. The sons must be looking for wives with the characteristics of their mother, and the daughters probably realize what a happy home they can have if they emulate their mother's ways.

The woman's husband also pays her honor by declaring that he has the finest of the finest for a wife. She is a queen among queens. Her husband is one very blessed man because "a prudent wife is from the Lord" (Proverbs 19:14). Among men he is most fortunate, "for who can find an excellent woman?" He knows her price is far above rubies, and he knows how much she means to him as a suitable helper. He adores her.

I had become his ruby.

Years after I had begun my journey of love, Loden gave me one of the surprises of my life. He saved his money in order to honor me with a ruby ring on my birthday. How I wish I had a recording of each word he said when he presented the ring, because he was a man of few words. He was validating to me that all my efforts had molded me into the wife that pleased him—to him I had become his ruby. Later he diligently worked and saved his money to give me a ruby heart on Valentine's Day. Again his words brought tears of joy. I seldom take off my heart necklace.

Even though Loden is no longer here, the ruby heart and the ruby ring are constant reminders to continue to work, to love, and to refuse to allow my selfishness to turn me back into an ordinary stone. I learned those things because I was his ruby.

On a scale of one to ten, how would your children evaluate you as a mother?

Using the same scale, how would your husband evaluate you as a wife?

"Charm is deceitful, and beauty is vain, but a woman who fears the Lord, she shall be praised. Give her the product of her hands, and let her works praise her in the gates" (Proverbs 31: 30–31). Proverbs begins with Wisdom shouting in the streets for the sons of men to find her and treasure her in their hearts, because wisdom comes from the Lord (Proverbs 2:6). The book ends with Wisdom speaking for God and praising the worthy woman who has diligently sought wisdom and reaped the benefits. Her beauty is the inner part of a godly woman. Her husband and children laud her life. Everyone knows there is a treasure within their midst: a beautiful ruby from the Lord. That is ultimate praise.

Study Proverbs 31 and enjoy Wisdom's promises to those who learn her ways. Isn't it interesting that Wisdom is feminine? The Father gives a great blessing to a woman who fears Him and follows His way. She is truly the greatest treasure to be found, and she passes her wisdom on to following generations to insure that God's Word never dies in the human heart.

Memory Verse

*"An excellent wife is the crown of her husband, but she
who shames him is like rottenness in his bones."*

Proverbs 12:4

The bones are the dwelling place of life. There blood cells are made. When there is disease in the bone marrow, the body is in very serious trouble. A wife can give life to her husband or she can take life from him by her actions. God has put that marvelous idea into your heart. You can give your husband new life each day by the love you pour into his heart. You are the source of his having life! But on the opposite end of the spectrum you can bring disease into his life and cause death. Stress, anger, and constant turmoil will take their toll in the marrow of the bones: literally and figuratively. Studies have shown that more heart attacks happen on Monday. Why? Where have the men been all weekend? Yes, at home! Figure that one.

My Take-Home

What a chapter! List at least three areas in which you can improve. Then list some qualities in which you measure up to those of the worthy woman. Thank the Father for these traits He has helped you develop, and ask Him to help you grow to your full stature as a worthy woman.

List the areas in which you need to improve as a wife.

1.

2.

3.

List three areas in which you have improved as a wife.

1.

2.

3.

My Homework

1. *Practice contentment.* "Godliness with contentment is great gain" (1 Timothy 6:6 KJV). Remember, *gain* means increase. You will become far more valuable as a child of God if you are content. Why is this true?

   How will you incorporate the following traits to develop contentment?

   Control anxiety:

   Live with self:

   Give of self:

   Consider others:

   Get rid of anger:

   Learn to love:

   Accept reality:

2. *Learn the art of marriage.* Enjoy the following quote and the poem. The more you practice the poem, the more like a ruby you will become. A good marriage must be created. In your marriage the little things are the big things. Does this sound like the recipe for the ways of the five loves?

   Marriage is a privilege to be shared by two . . . not a convenience
   to be experienced by one at the expense of the other.

   —Author Unknown

   ### The Art of Marriage

   It is never being too old to hold hands.
   It is remembering to say I love you at least once each day.
   It is never going to sleep when angry.
   It is having a mutual sense of values and common objectives.
   It is standing together and facing the world.
   It is forming a circle of love that gathers in the whole family.
   It is speaking words of appreciation and demonstrating gratitude
       in thoughtful ways.
   It is having the capacity to forgive and forget.
   It is giving each other an atmosphere in which each can grow.
   It is a common search for the good and the beautiful.
   It is not only marrying the right person, but it is also being the
       right partner.

3. *Practice these daily habits:*

❧ *Kiss him.* We have studied love; we have learned how to be love; now let's practice one of love's sweet ways—kissing. This week kiss your husband a different way each day, and do make it a kiss he will remember!

❧ *Keep saying "thank you."* For different blessings you receive from your husband, thank him at least once this week for something he did, and tell him over and over again why it meant so much.

❧ *Keep asking each day, "What can I do for you today?"*

❧ *Never forget that you are in godly training 24/7.* If you do not practice being love daily, you will never be made into the image of Christ. Practice, practice.

❧ *Pray for courage to change what is needed and to strengthen the attributes of love that you already possess.*

May our Father's blessing be upon you as you continue to grow.

Week 5

The Training Room

From the Father of the Bride: "Work out your salvation with fear and trembling, for it is God who is at work in you, both to will and to work for His good pleasure" (Philippians 2:12–13).

Thought for the Day: Too often we believe our freedom rests on outward conditions or on other resources. Then without intending to, we become slaves to circumstance. We forget that everything begins within us. Instead of looking outward to others for our happiness, we need to find peace, prosperity, joy, and freedom of spirit within ourselves. True freedom is an inner state of awareness—an inside job—and it is available to everyone. It begins when we take up the reins of responsibility for our own lives. Gaining personal independence from all kinds of inner bondage will free the spirit (Ardath Rodale, *Prevention Magazine,* July 2008, 180).

From Mother Sarah: God provided the strength I did not have within me to conceive what He had promised to Abraham and me, a child of our own. He will give you the strength you need for the day.

> By faith even Sarah herself received ability to conceive, even beyond the proper time of life, since she considered Him faithful who had promised (Hebrews 11:11).

Day 1

Train in Righteousness

Last week I shared with you a pretend tea party in my house of love with Mother Sarah and the Queen Mother. This week we will return to the living room as the tea party is ending,

I sat and reflected on what I had learned. Proverbs 14:1 echoed in my mind, reminding me that the wise woman builds her house, but the foolish one tears it down with her own hands. I did not want to be foolish, so I knew I wanted to build my house of love on the strong foundation of Jesus and His teachings, and that I wanted to become a "ruby" to Loden and practice the "Be's" of Titus and the lessons from Proverbs 31.

As I sat in reverie, Mother Sarah spoke. I was surprised when she asked, "How much do you love your Loden?" Immediately, a scene from the past came into my mind as vividly as if it were yesterday.

We had just moved into our dream home. It was Saturday—bright, sunny, about ten in the morning. I was cleaning the kitchen. Telephone lines had not been run to that part of town, so I was surprised and curious when the doorbell rang. I opened the door. Charlie, a young man who worked for Loden, stood before me, a worried expression on his face. His words struck terror in my heart: "Loden's been hurt." When I asked how badly, he replied, "I don't know," a phrase often used when the victim is dead. "Come with me," he said.

I hurried to the bedroom to get dressed. *This house means nothing to me without Loden,* I thought as I rushed about. I had planned each brick and nail in that house; the house was my pride and joy. But at that moment I realized the truth of what Loden and I had told one another, "Our home is within each other's arms." Without him, the house was only a shell, and not a true home.

Thankfully, Loden was not dead, but his foot was almost severed. It was deftly repaired by a gifted surgeon. But I never forgot that feeling: without Loden there is no home!

I also remembered that funeral home in Eden, Texas, where I vowed that Loden would always know how much I loved him. I wanted him to know it every day we had together.

So I whispered softly to Mother Sarah, "He means everything to me. In fact, he is my life, but I still lack knowledge to show him this love."

She said, "That reply tells me that you want to be Loden's ruby, but you are rather puzzled as to how to begin. Let God's Word teach you how to exercise your body, mind, and heart so you will become the love you want to be for your Loden. Come with us to the Training Room. We want you to meet your Trainer. You must be willing to use the Training Room each day to become truly the worthy wife."

We set our teacups on the table, arose, and went down a corridor to the Training Room.

Imagine a training room containing various types of equipment for physical workouts. Centered on the back wall is a large picture of Jesus. He is your ideal; you are striving to exercise to become like Him. He has promised that you, beholding as in a mirror the glory of the Lord, are being transformed into His same image, from glory to glory (2 Corinthians 3:18). You must do a daily workout to abandon your own image and to be fashioned into Jesus' image.

You must keep Jesus' image ever before you, looking only to Him as you pursue your special goals. Brother Paul said it this way: "One thing I do; forgetting what lies behind and reaching forward to what lies ahead, I press on toward the goal for the prize of the upward call of God in Christ Jesus" (Philippians 3:13–14). Again, "be imitators of me, just as I also am of Christ" (1 Corinthians 11:1). Each day Paul looked toward Jesus and worked to become like Him, forgetting yesterday. He never took his eyes off that goal.

Here is your final fitness test: Do I look like Jesus? Exercising will remake you into the ideal wife. When your husband sees you, he will be very pleased by your new look!

He Will Guide You

Who is your Trainer? When Jesus returned to heaven to reign, He left His apostles with these words: "The Helper, the Holy Spirit, whom the Father will send in My name, He will teach you all things, and bring to your remembrance all that I said to you . . . and He will guide you into all truth" (John 14:26; cf. 16:13).

So it was the Holy Spirit who guided those men as they wrote the only true Training Manual, the Bible. The Holy Spirit uses that same manual to train us in all righteousness! His lessons will instruct you and show you how to be like Christ. When you are trained, you will have the same loving marriage that Christ has with His bride, the church.

The house meant nothing to me without Loden.

You will begin training each day with the deep-breathing exercise of *self-control*. Without breath control, your body will not work effectively; neither will your mind receive the necessary oxygen to function at its finest. Likewise, your spirit needs the exercise of self-control.

Next, *lift your mind*. The weight lifting of anger gives you great freedom to love. Then pay special attention to your *lip exercises*. They will tone your words from negative to positive. Follow up with attitude weights, loving-arms workouts, and walking-in-love exercises. Don't neglect your *heart exercises* that will ensure a warm, loving home. You will even do *mental flips* for thought fitness.

After your daily workout, it's time to get dressed. You will learn how to dress properly for your husband.

These exercises are necessary to develop your body, mind, and soul. When you have mastered them, the image in your mirror will be that of Jesus and not your own. Only when you see Him will you know you have successfully trained in godliness and have put on the teachings of "How to Live in Love with Your Husband." Stay tuned for the same kind of training in "How to Live in Peace and Love with Your Other Half."

How can you totally remake yourself so that the outcome is far more beautiful than any surgeon can sculpt with his scalpel? Go into the Training Room every day with your Training Manual.

I have outlined the daily exercises below. You can become a totally new and exquisite woman if you follow the Trainer's workout.

Exercise One: The Breath of Self-Control

Manual Directions: "I run in such a way, as not without aim, I box in such a way, as not beating the air; but I discipline my body and make it my slave, so that, after I have preached to others, I myself will not be disqualified" (1 Corinthians 9:26–27).

Just as your physical breath determines your body's abilities to achieve, so you must control each spiritual breath to determine your spiritual actions. How do you learn this?

> In the knowledge of God and of Jesus your Lord; seeing that His divine power has granted to us everything pertaining to life and godliness, through the true knowledge of Him who called us by His own glory and excellence (2 Peter 1:2–3).

As you breathe in knowledge from the Word, your spiritual breath is strengthened in faith. Your faith develops into moral excellence which in turn leads to your self-control. Allow the Word of God to direct your every breath, and self-control will become as natural as breathing. Why? Because God's Word directs your every thought.

When you are truly led by the Spirit through His Word, you will eat of His fruit. Self-control is part of the fruit of the Sprit. Without it you are at the mercy of Satan and his servants who have as their goal distracting and leading you from your training goal of becoming like Jesus.

How much self-control do you have at this time? How can you learn to have more self-control?

How will self-control help your marriage?

Exercise Two: Daily Mind Lift

Manual Directions: "If anyone wishes to come after Me, he must deny himself, and take up his cross daily and follow me" (Luke 9:23).

Wow! This one will be difficult, but with practice, everything can be accomplished because you will say to yourself, "I can do all things through Him who strengthens me" (Philippians 4:13).

Put yourself daily on the cross and follow Jesus. What did the cross represent to everyone who saw it from the streets of Jerusalem during the days of Christ? It meant a horrible, terrible, humiliating death for the worst criminals. Such were you before dying with Christ and becoming a new creature by His blood in baptism!

Jesus became a new creature after His death. He still looked the same to those who saw Him, but He ascended into heaven in His heavenly body. Similarly, in your old life you were guilty of your terrible sins and should have died the death of a criminal, but His blood washed you clean. You resurrected from that water-grave a new heavenly being, although still clothed in human flesh.

Unlike Christ, who entered heaven after dying to become your Savior and King, you remain on earth. Since you can revert to a worldly life, do a spiritual exercise every day. Put yourself on the cross and die mentally to the world. Look to Jesus each day and dutifully follow Him.

Follow expresses union, likeness, and a way—one going in the same way. The word is used *77* times in the Gospels. The purpose of this daily exercise is to remind you of God's desires for you:

> The grace of God has appeared, bringing salvation to all men, instructing us to deny ungodliness and worldly desires and to live sensibly, righteously, and godly in the present age, looking for the blessed hope and the appearing of the glory of our great God and Savior Christ Jesus who gave Himself for us to redeem us from every lawless deed, and to purify for Himself a people for His own possession, zealous for good deeds (Titus 2:11–14).

When you truly reflect Jesus, you will be ready to work at your marriage. That is part of your goal of working out your own salvation with fear and trembling. You have the grace of God, the salvation of Jesus; now you must do your part by "working out" to develop into Christ's image.

Remember to allow your Trainer to be with you constantly as you perform these exercises to build your spiritual body. Post the words from His Training Manual all around you. When you have mastered them, your spiritual body should be classed as a ten. The Father's will is for you to be perfect as He is perfect (Matthew 5:48). *Perfect* here means complete. When you master these exercises, your spiritual body will be complete.

🌿 Considering the number of times *following* is used in the New Testament, do you think it is important to Jesus for you to learn to die to self and follow His way and only His way? How do you intend to learn to do this?

Day 2

Get Rid of Anger
Exercise Three: Lifting Anger

Manual Directions: "Lay aside the old self . . . be renewed in the spirit of your mind, and put on the new self, which in the *likeness of God* has been created in righteousness and holiness of the truth . . . Be angry, and yet do not sin; do not let the sun go down on your anger" (Ephesians 4:22–26).

Dr. Charles D. Spielberger, distinguished research professor at the University of South Florida and specialist in the study of anger, describes anger as "an emotional state that varies in intensity from mild irritation to intense fury and rage." Colossians 3:8 has long taught us when one becomes angry, that anger accelerates into wrath if it is not checked. Wrath brings loss of control merging with malice, which resorts to violence. Do you see why self-control must be exercised and why the exercise of dying to self is so necessary? When do you become angry? Usually when your rights, as you see them, have been violated. Anger is the strongest of all the emotions. In and of itself, anger is not a sin; God has righteous anger with the wicked (Psalm 7:11).

However, look into the life of Jesus. You will find that the Bible only one time says that Jesus was angry (cf. Mark 3:5). Was it because of something done to Him? No. It was because of the bad attitude of the Pharisees when Jesus wanted to heal the man with a withered hand on the Sabbath day. Even at the first cleansing of the temple, the only emotion ascribed to Jesus was zeal. At the second cleansing, no emotion is stated (cf. Matthew 21:12–13). Does this tell you something very vital about your peace and health?

Medical research has recently found anger to be the most destructive emotion. Just think, the Trainer knew this all along! Studies have found no end of diseases caused by anger, including heart trouble, ulcers, and high blood pressure. Finally, all bodily functions are hurt by constant anger. Consider these expressions: "As bitter as gall," "This is killing me," and, "This is eating me up!" They are not just old sayings. They are true! Anger is as bitter as gall and as deadly as poison. Dr. Bernie Siegel, an oncologist, says when he knows you, he can usually predict what type of cancer your body will have, if you develop it.

Get Rid of It

What are you to do about anger? The answer is given by your Trainer, the Holy Spirit. "Do not sin in your anger; do not let the sun go down on your anger." Did you hear what the Manual said? Do not let the sun go down before you handle anger in the proper manner. How? The ideal way is just to get rid of it. Poof! It is gone forever. "Let all bitterness and wrath and anger and clamor and slander be put away from you, along with all malice" (Ephesians 4:31). If you do not handle it before sunset, it is likely to have grown by morning—perhaps from a molehill to a mountain. Can anger be cast aside? Very definitely yes! You too will accomplish this confidence through your exercises.

No one can make you angry without your permission.

I once had a temper that flared quickly when I was not getting my way, and much sin ensued. When I began to practice the exercises of the Spirit, I learned to control my anger, and I finally let it go completely. Do I ever become irritated? Yes, but I am learning even to let that go. Most people behave the way they think is best. I am learning to reply to them in love. I find it's a better way of handling every explosive situation.

When I realized my anger was a sin, I began my efforts to keep Loden from making me angry. That was my first mistake! Remember this: no one can make you angry unless you choose to let them. I read that in a book and it changed my life. Think about it; you will see it's true. Your husband can say something one day that angers you, but the next day you might find the same statement humorous.

React or Respond?

Each of us decides how to respond to life. Act your way into feeling—respond, don't just react. I would ask Loden, "Are you trying to get on my wrong side?" Of course he did not want to ruffle my feathers. Our husbands know they will suffer when they make us angry—we see to that.

I kept practicing my anger control and started saying to Loden, "What you just did makes me erase a Brownie point." When he did something good, I gave him Brownie points; I actually marked the air to make sure he knew he made good points. When I wished to subtract points, I would raise my hand and pretend I was erasing a coveted Brownie point. My antics worked well. In fact, we continued to use the Brownie point system, and Loden went about telling every husband, "All I want to do is earn Brownie points with my wife."

As I grew spiritually and realized that anger was a waste of time, I began using humor. I'd tell Loden, "I am going to punish you for that action!" Then I would make his "punishment" something that was very, very pleasurable to him. Soon he was asking what he could do to be punished! When I truly grew up, I would just look at him and say, "If you are trying to rile me, forget it; I know you too well." Then I would laugh and give him a hug and kiss. Such behavior helped us to respect each other in sensitive areas.

What Does Anger Profit?

Dear One, nothing in this world is worth getting angry over except wickedness. Life is too short, love is too wonderful, and peace is too divine to allow anger to have even a corner in your life. It accomplishes nothing. In fact, if you look at your Training Manual you will find the following instructions:

> For it is because of these things that the wrath of God will come upon the sons of disobedience, and in them you also once walked, when you were living in them. But now you also, put them all aside: anger, wrath, malice . . . (Colossians 3:6–8).

> But I say to you that everyone who is angry with his brother shall be guilty before the court; and whoever says to his brother, "You good-for-nothing," shall be guilty before the supreme court; and whoever shall say, "You fool," shall be guilty enough to go into the fiery hell (Matthew 5:22).

 Why was anger such a serious topic to Jesus?

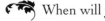 When will you make a vow to yourself to learn to get rid of anger, as you are commanded to do?

Anger is a very selfish response to any situation. It solves nothing; it robs you of reason. Without reasoning ability, you are not responsive to seeking a solution.

Anger enslaves. You cannot act in a loving way when you are angry. Anger dictates how you will act, and it is always in a negative way. The Holy Spirit assures in His Training Manual that when we learn self-control (which is essentially mind control), and learn to think of pleasing others first, anger will no longer show up in our lives.

When you are free of anger, you are free to love in the special five ways of loving. Jesus taught, "You will know the truth, and the truth will make you free" (John 8:32). When your heart is free of all negativism, then you make the wise choice of only being loving, kind, and full of compassion. You will react to life's problems in a loving, positive way, and that brings peace to the heart and home. The day I kicked anger out of my life was a day of rejoicing. I truly felt liberated! Anger accomplishes nothing but pain.

Make a Choice

My sister had to make a choice early in her marriage. Tom was in the Navy and was gone for months at a time. In addition to learning to be content without Tom, Sue had to make all the family decisions. And then when Tom came home on leave, he came home to a frustrated wife. Sue expressed their reunions this way: "I learned I could either spend the short time with him in anger, or I could spend it in joy. I chose the latter, and I have never regretted it."

Tom developed a very debilitating disease (ALS) which robbed him of the use of his legs. As the disease wore his body down, it was heartwrenching to see him struggle to make each step on his walker.

She was all he ever wanted in a wife.

During that time Tom decided to buy a special gift for Sue. He parked his pickup and walked a block to the store. The owner winced inwardly when Tom struggled up the lane to her shop, but he was not content to let her select the gift. He wanted to do that personally and then have it beautifully wrapped. After all, Sue was the woman of his life, and he had to show his love to the one who was making his life complete.

Not long after that time, Tom left this world. His last act of love was to buy online a special gift for Sue—an antique coffee pot. It arrived four days after his death. When his dear Sue opened the package, it was a very poignant moment. Until Tom's last breath, he worked diligently to take care of Sue's every need. Why? Because she was all he ever wanted in a wife.

I hope you will make the same wise choice in your life: totally love and respect that man every day!

❧ Does Jesus want you to learn a better way of responding to life's situations than by anger?

❧ Are you willing to give up anger as a response to your not getting your way? What new ways of communication will you use?

❧ What is meaning of James 1:19–25?

Day 3

O Be Careful, Big Mouth

Exercise Four: Lip Exercises

The Training Manual gives us five exercises for the lips. Each one must be mastered before you will speak as Jesus.

"Let no unwholesome word proceed from your mouth, but only such a word as is good for edification, according to the need of the moment, so that it will give grace to those who hear" (Ephesians 4:29). *Unwholesome* (corrupt) is defined as bad, putrid, or rotten. Words that do not build up the receiver are forbidden! They are like feeding the hearer rotten garbage. Is the message of Ephesians 4:29 a command or a suggestion? The above verse says to me, "What do you not understand about no? Do you fully realize that *edification* means the act of building a house?"

The words you speak to your husband will either build up or tear down your house of love. The words you speak to others either build your relationship or tear it down. *Need* is "that which bestows or occasions pleasure, delight, or causes favorable regard." Every word you utter should help build your relationships—especially with your husband.

Your goal is to make each word positive, not negative. Later when you learn to buffet your body and keep it in subjection, you will use good words to solve negative situations. Remember, your Manual has the answer for every problem. But for it to influence your life properly, you must take the time to turn to the right page.

Does Ephesians 4:29 instruct us to use our words to give people what they need? Absolutely. Perhaps a person has done wrong, but she realizes her mistake. She does not need more negative or condemning words or words of put-down! She needs words of encouragement and assurance of forgiveness, words of building up and words of comfort. Our Trainer admonishes us to love others as we would like to be loved; it is called the royal law (James 2:8).

"Do not lie to one another, since you laid aside the old self with its evil practices" (Colossians 3:9). Read carefully and practice faithfully! This "lip instruction" reminds us that lying is an evil practice of the old sinner. We should practice using our lips only for the truth! Truth is positive and lies are negative. You must use positive forces so your body will be healthy. Negative forces make one ill and unbalanced.

In modern times medical researchers have learned much about the correlation between mind and body. The Father knew all along that nothing will harm a relationship more than lies. Eve believed a lie and it caused every one of her children to suffer untold agony. Does not this verse say: "do not lie"? Is that plain enough for you to grasp and obey? Truth-telling is not an option for the

Christian; it is a command! Obey it to be successful in remaking yourself into the image of Christ."

 Read Ephesians 4:25. This is the second time you have read this direction. What does it mean?

 How do you not ever lie?

 What does Hebrews 6:18 teach you about self-control in telling the truth. What does the adjective *impossible* mean?

"Do not lie to one another." Is that plain enough?

"Put them all aside: anger, wrath, malice, slander, and abusive speech from your mouth" (Colossians 3:8). The two-lip habits of slander and abusive speech are destructive to your health. Slander is a no-no. Never be guilty! It will make you sick. Practice exercises that will build up your spiritual health, not tear it down. Never talk negatively about anyone, especially your dear husband.

The Training Manual prohibits abusive speech. Use only words that build up. You do not want to tear down your house of love by the misuse of your lips. Criticizing is a negative use of the lips. Never allow critical words to come from your mouth. Did you read that? Use of the lips to criticize is harmful to the human soul.

There are better ways of handling situations that need changing. Criticism does two things:

It creates a feeling of superiority in the critic. "I am the standard maker" is the idea. The one who does not measure up to that person's ideal is wrong. But we know that only God has the right to make the standard for a person's conduct.

It inspires feelings of inferiority. It sets up negative thinking in the brain of the person being dressed down. In the criticizer, it sets up a negative idea of that person in the brain. The world is cruel enough to each of us. We do not need to hear negative judging from anyone, especially from those we love the most!

Often those who should love us the most are the ones who talk the ugliest to us. They tell us how superior they are and how inferior we are. However, our Manual specifies that the lips are to be used only for sweet talk. Examine yourself and answer truthfully.

❦ How much do I criticize my husband?

❦ How do I feel when I am criticized?

❦ Why do I need to criticize? When am I going to start exercising my self-control to stop criticism from escaping my lips? How will I learn how not to use this harmful way of speaking?

❦ How will it profit me to begin to kiss, hug, and say I love you many times a day, starting today?

"May he kiss me with the kisses of his mouth! For your love is better than wine" (Song of Solomon 1:2). The Shulamite bride uttered these words about her lover Solomon. Can you say the same about your lover? She was eager to kiss his lips. In one study on the power of the kiss, it was found that husbands who were kissed good-bye before work and when they came home from work lived longer and healthier lives than those who were not kissed. Is it any wonder that the Father gave the lips for such an enjoyable exercise? You can never kiss your husband too much. Practice, practice, and enjoy!

❦ How much do I really kiss my husband? How can I vary the way I kiss him?

❦ Do I allow him to kiss me when he desires? Why or why not?

"I love you" are three of the most precious words you can utter. Early in our marriage, Loden and I began the practice of verbally expressing our love for each other. Over time we developed a language all our own and used a form of "I love you" many times during the day. An example of such is, "Do you?" "Yes" was the answer. "How much?" The answer varied day to day. Or I would say, "I need to hear it." And back he would come with "I love you."

Dear One, women use about 24,000 words per day, while our husbands speak about half that many, so we have to initiate such heart-warming lip exercises. The more you affirm your love for each another, the easier it is to work through the rough times.

"Pray without ceasing" (1 Thessalonians 5:17). The most powerful exercise your lips can practice is that of prayer to your Father. The Trainer put this in His Manual as a total answer for the soul: "Be anxious for nothing, but in everything by prayer and supplication with thanksgiving let your requests be made known to God" (Philippians 4:6). Don't stop yet; keep reading: "And the peace of God, which surpasses all comprehension, will guard your hearts and your minds in Christ Jesus" (Philippians 4:7).

Negativism is not permitted in our Training Room.

In every situation, we can have confidence of this peace of God as a result of prayer, supplication, and thanksgiving. Isn't this a comforting thought? All our lip exercises are wonderful, but prayer is by far the most blessed. Practice knowing that the Father, Christ, and the Holy Spirit are with you. Talk to God all day long. When you need help, call on Him. When you are happy, sing praises to Him, for He says, "Through Him [Jesus] let us continually offer up a sacrifice of praise to God, that is, the fruit of our lips that give thanks to His name" (Hebrews 13:15).

Why is prayer so important to my spiritual health?

How can I learn to practice the presence of God in my life?

Day 4

Attitude Determines Altitude
Exercise Five: Heart Exercises with Attitude Weights
Service Weights

Fill in the blank: The greatest among you is your _____ (Matthew 23:11). Jesus described Himself to His apostles, "I am among you as the one who serves" (Luke 22:27). Work on the service attitude daily. How can you know what Jesus meant when He told you to take up your cross and follow Him? How can you have a greater appreciation for His great sacrifice? Add the servant qualities of Philippians 2:3–4 and the servant attitude of Christ to your life.

❧ Have humility of mind.

❧ Esteem others as more important than yourself.

❧ Look out for the interests of others.

❧ Have this attitude in yourselves which was also in Christ Jesus, who . . . emptied Himself, taking the form of a bond-servant . . . in appearance as a man, He humbled Himself by becoming obedient to the point of death, even death on a cross (Philippians 2:5–8).

I learned by this exercise that it is far better to think of others than to think of myself. As Jesus taught, great happiness comes from giving: "It is more blessed to give than to receive" (Acts 20:35). I personally experienced an increase of problems when I did not put Loden and others before me. When I began to master this exercise, positive feelings increased. Attitude weight-lifting is a profitable exercise for heart health!

🌿 How can I learn to put others before myself?

🌿 I will memorize the following Scripture to help me learn to put my husband first. (Write your favorite one on this subject.)

Kindness Weights

Your Training Manual is specific about this attitude weight: "Be kind to one another, tender-hearted, forgiving each other, just as God in Christ also has forgiven you" (Ephesians 4:32). The Holy Spirit teaches us that kindness is a way of life from now on. So what is kindness? It is an action of love or service needed, not necessarily what I think is needed. So we must know our husbands well. We need to show them kindness even when they do not deserve it! Kindness in the face of adversity is Christ's way.

Tender-hearted means to be compassionate. The Gospels report several occasions that Jesus looked upon the needy with compassion and performed a wonderful act of love. You must look upon your husband with compassion and seek ways to make his life better and happier.

A gentle touch of the hand is very powerful. Touch your husband at every opportunity. You cannot touch enough. The more you touch your husband, the more you will feel connected to him, so get rid of anger. Anger resists touching.

What is your most treasured gift from Jesus? Forgiveness of sins! Therefore you must forgive others, especially your husband. Forgiveness is for you as much as for the other person. An unforgiving heart causes many health problems. Most important, God has decreed the law given in Matthew 6:14–15. Write it down and remember it.

Peace Weights

Your manual instructs, "Pursue peace with all men, and the sanctification without which no one will see the Lord" (Hebrews 12:14). What does that mean? What is peace? It is harmonious relationships between humans. Don't start a quarrel with anyone, especially your husband. Live in such a way that you feel serenity and calmness no matter who surrounds you. People will be able to feel the love that radiates from your heart and soul. "If possible, so far as it depends on you, be at peace with all men" (Romans 12:18).

One of the greatest gifts you can give yourself and your family is a peaceful, loving home where all members are cherished. Compare a peaceful scene with a quarreling and bickering environment. You can look into a man's face and tell much about the status of his home. Many men have told me, "I'll buy my wife two copies of your book," and then sheepishly claim they were only joking. Were they truly?

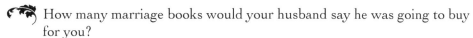 How many marriage books would your husband say he was going to buy for you?

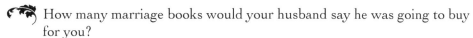 How important is peace to the health of the body and soul?

Exercise Six: Mental Flips
Control Your Thoughts

Manual Directions: "Whatever is true, whatever is honorable, whatever is right, whatever is pure, whatever is lovely, whatever is of good repute, if there is any excellence and if anything worthy of praise, dwell on these things" (Philippians 4:8).

Thinking correctly is the secret to changing your image into Christ's image! New discoveries in medical science reveal that negative thoughts create harmful chemicals in the body.

What do you notice about this list of mental exercises? All are positive! By now I am sure you have noticed that negativism is not permitted in our Training Room. Jesus wants us to look upon the Son, not on the dark side of the moon. He is called the Morning Star and requires us to shine as lights in this world by reflecting His light as the Son. If everything you say is to build up the hearer, you must think only of good. Look on the plus side of situations, problems, and people. That applies especially to your husband. Look for good and not bad.

Rejoice, Pray, Be Grateful

Develop your self-control muscle by showing this attitude: "Rejoice always" (1 Thessalonians 5:16). How is that possible? Continue reading verses 17 and 18: "Pray without ceasing; in everything give thanks; for this is God's will for you in Christ Jesus." When you have a prayerful attitude of gratitude, your spirit responds in joy. "Rejoice always" is not a lofty command when you practice prayer and gratitude.

I wrestled with this concept for a long time. After much thought and prayer, I reached a conclusion. Not everything in this life is good, pleasant, or healthy for me. The only constant in my life is a relationship with the Godhead. God promised to be with me and protect me. Satan can put nothing on me without God's permission. He knows what I can stand. Remember Job's trial.

My joy and thanksgiving come from the assurance of my salvation in Jesus. He will return and take me home as His bride. I have come to realize, as did Paul, that nothing in this life is worth anything but Jesus. Whatever I must suffer is nothing compared to the joy of a future life with Jesus in heaven. Why shouldn't I live with thanks on my lips and praise in my heart? I am part of the bride of Christ; I own the greatest gift from Jesus—my salvation.

Overspending creates unnecessary tension.

It was my privilege to be a help suitable to my Loden. In every situation "we know that God causes all things to work together for good to those who love God, to those who are called according to His purpose" (Romans 8:28). Notice the word *all*. What does that leave out? I will receive good from God in the long run if I look for it. And so can you!

Prayer is vital to the life of your spirit. Learn to live in the presence of God. Feel Jesus leading the way daily after you have put yourself on the cross. The more you pray, the more you will feel the presence of the God in your soul. Prayer helps to control your mind. It helps to screen your words, protecting the ones you love most.

Something for God to Do

Is there anything that will help you to establish peace, rely on prayer, and stop worrying? Many women have benefited by a "Something for God to Do" box. This is a box that you set aside for prayers. Write your prayer request on a slip of paper, date it, put it in the box, and forget about the problem. Put the box in a prominent place, and every time you pass it, put your hand on it and say, "Lord, I have faith that you are taking care of this situation, and the answer will be far better than I could do." Every few months, go through your box and see how the Lord has been gracious to you. If the prayer has not been answered, have patience. We are on God's timing, not ours. Look for a special box; when you see it, you will know it. We must trust God to keep His promises to take care of us and help us through our trials.

David said the Lord was at his right hand (Psalm 16:8). His presence will help you make good choices.

Day 5

Walk This Way
Exercise Seven: Walking

Manual Directions: "Therefore be imitators of God, as beloved children, and walk in love, just as Christ also loved you and gave Himself up for us" (Ephesians 5:1–2). Brother Paul gives us our walking instructions and stresses: "If we live by the Spirit, let us also walk by the Spirit. Let us not become boastful, challenging one another, envying one another" (Galatians 5:25–26). Walking in love is a lifelong exercise. Refresh your memory:

> Love is patient, love is kind and is not jealous; love does not brag and is not arrogant, does not act unbecomingly; it does not seek its own, is not provoked, does not take into account a wrong suffered, does not rejoice in unrighteousness, but rejoices with the truth; bears all things, believes all things, hopes all things, endures all things (1 Corinthians 13:4–7).

How can you learn to choose to walk in love?

How can you always give your husband the benefit of the doubt instead of misunderstanding him and always having your feelings hurt?

When we walk in love and bestow kindness on others because we honor them above ourselves, and when we are gentle in spirit and treat others with gentle words and deeds, then we truly reap good rewards and have the assurance that our marriage was made in heaven. Think of Eve. While she lived in the Garden of Eden, she knew only the way of love in her treatment of Adam. Only after she allowed Satan to deceive her did she begin to behave in unloving ways. You were created to be love just as God is love (1 John 4:8). In fact, if you don't walk in love, you don't even know God. That's what the Manual says!

"Above all, keep fervent in your love for one another, because love covers a multitude of sins" (1 Peter 4:8). That's not a suggestion; it's a command: "keep fervent" in our love for each other. Do you think our spiritual "walking in love" covers our negligent spiritual behavior?

Exercise Eight: Contentment Stroll

Manual Directions: "Not that I speak from want, for I have learned to be content in whatever circumstances I am" (Philippians 4:11).

Contentment is the secret to being able to have a good walk in confidence with what you have, where you are, and who you're with. Brother Paul carries the idea still further when he admonishes,

> Godliness actually is a means of great gain when accompanied by contentment. For we have brought nothing into the world, so we cannot take anything out of it either. If we have food and covering, with these we shall be content (1 Timothy 6:6–8).

Hebrews 13:5 holds both a command and a promise from the Father. "Make sure that your character is free from the love of money, being content with what you have; for He Himself has said, 'I will never leave you, nor will I ever forsake you'" (Hebrews 13:5).

Having a contented heart prevents hurtful lusts and painful mistakes in your marriage. Overspending creates unnecessary tension between couples. Excessive desire for things gets countless marriages into deep and disastrous financial situations, even before families realize it. Learn to budget and keep your wants within your earnings. Contentment also keeps envy and jealousy at bay. If left unchecked, these two evils will eat your heart away, so avoid them like the plague! Trying to keep up with the Joneses is deadly. Don't contaminate yourself!

Avoid Complaining

If you are walking contentedly, you will avoid complaining. God gives you two commands for your daily workout.

- "Do all things without grumbling or disputing; so that you will prove yourselves to be blameless and innocent, children of God above reproach in the midst of a crooked and perverse generation, among whom you appear as lights in the world" (Philippians 2:14–15).

- "Nor let us try the Lord, as some of them did, and were destroyed by the serpents, nor grumble, as some of them did, and were destroyed by the destroyer" (1 Corinthians 10:9

These words are very straight and plain; you should have no problem understanding them. God does not like complainers; neither does your beloved husband. How can the good seed of the word sprout in a complaining heart, much less grow? Whining about what you don't have, about what your husband lacks, and about another's behavior shows great disrespect to Jesus and to your husband. It is contrary to every idea listed in your Manual.

Negativism has its roots in Satan's work. Do not let him deceive you as he did Eve. She was in total paradise, both figuratively and literally. Then Satan came to visit. How did he get her attention? Why did she desire to go against the command of God? Because she suddenly became discontented with what God had provided. A complaining heart leads to envy and jealousy, but a contented heart is free.

Don't fall into the quicksand Satan has devised for complainers. I can attest to its dangers first hand. I was a natural-born complainer and excelled in it as I grew older. My poor Loden could never do anything right. I felt superior to him, and that feeling allowed me to generate a disrespectful attitude toward him. When he left shaving gear on the sink, I fumed.

God does not like complainers; neither does your husband.

One day after studying God's way for me, the truth hit me: *You must stop complaining and criticizing Loden and others!* I decided that day that everything I did from then on would be because I *chose* to do it. I would act from the love of my heart. Bingo! Life changed dramatically. When Loden left something out of place, I lovingly picked the item up and thought: *How wonderful it is to have such a great man to serve.* My respect for him grew along with my love. I learned later that he considered himself very tidy! We all think what we do is okay, or we would change it. So each of us has to give to others the respect we desire from them. I learned if there was something I really, really wanted from him, I would tell him, "It would really help me if you would —," and he was always happy to oblige me. Is that not better than nagging?

Reflect on yesterday. How much did you complain? Does complaining ever make things better?

How much better is the clothing you will now be wearing?

Get Dressed

The last exhortation from our Manual tells us to dress in the proper exercise clothes. What are we to wear?

> Put on the new self who is being renewed to a true knowledge according to the image of the One who created him. . . . Let the peace of Christ rule in your hearts, to which indeed you were called in one body; and be thankful (Colossians 3:10, 15).

What type of apparel will you wear to perform your daily exercises? When you have dressed yourself in the white, pure clothing of a child of God, walk over to the special mirror on the wall, look at it, and ask, "Mirror, mirror on the wall, do you see Jesus in me at all?" Then look at your reflection, and your heart will answer truthfully. The truth lies in the choices you make every day.

A Healthy Soul

The Trainer encourages you by always being with you in heart. He helps you in your prayers (Romans 8:26). At last I had the tools to finish my house of love. I understood my mentors' instilling in me this thought: "By wisdom a house is built, and by understanding it is established, and by knowledge the rooms are filled with all precious and pleasant riches."

You are ready now to gain the knowledge needed to fill your rooms with precious and pleasant riches to give your husband. As you leave the training room, be joyful. When I left, I joyfully sang a verse from a song I heard in my childhood:

> You've got to accentuate the positive,
> Eliminate the negative,
> Latch on to the affirmative,
> And don't mess with Mr. In-Between.

Summary

Jesus commanded us: "Love your neighbor as yourself" (Matthew 22:39). In this chapter we have learned how to love ourselves by training to be like Jesus, whose number one goal was obeying His Father. You must also learn to master yourself and train in holiness to be in perfect harmony with Jesus. Only then can you have true self-love and a pure heart to minister to your beloved husband. God, Jesus, husband—that will always be God's ordained order for you (cf. 1 Corinthians 11:3). The sooner you understand God's command given for your protection, the sooner you will begin to grow and develop into a loving wife. Surely our pursuit of peace includes the attitude found in the home of a woman who fears the Lord and wants to please Him.

Memory Verse

"Pursue peace with all men, and the sanctification, without which no one will see the Lord."

Hebrews 12:14

My Take-Home

Goal: *To learn the exercises given by the Trainer.* List the exercises on an index card. Work every day to make them a part of your being, and eventually you will function automatically in the way of the Spirit. Don't forget: it takes up to six weeks to learn a new habit, so don't become discouraged. When you make a mistake, admit it, pray for help, and keep your eye on the goal of becoming like Jesus. You will be so proud of yourself when you overcome negative thinking and actions!

A *Truth:* *Commitment leads to real freedom, in any area.* "This is particularly true in relationships of all kinds, for you can only be intimate to the degree that you can be vulnerable and open your heart to the degree that you feel safe — because if you make yourself vulnerable, you might get hurt. Commitment creates safety and makes intimacy possible" (Dean Ornish, M. D., *Love and Healing,* Harper-Collins Publishers, 141).

Assignment: *Make a commitment to yourself, to Jesus, and to your husband to love, honor, and serve in order to experience real freedom and contentment.* Without commitment, you will flounder and give up your quest at the first obstacle encountered in your relationship with Jesus and your husband. Commitment does not tolerate giving up and leaving! Rather, it creates a desire to work harmoniously to solve all problems. That will be a win-win situation for you and your beloved.

My Homework

1. Examine yourself.

    _____ Are you writing your love letter to your husband?

    _____ Are you striving each day to compliment him?

    _____ Are you asking him each day how you can help him?

    _____ Are you praying for God's help each day and thanking the Father for helping you learn how to be a better lover?

    _____ Are you kissing your husband each day in a way that tells him he is very special to you?

2. Practice touching your husband. The object of this exercise is to learn to touch your beloved each time you cross his space. Touching produces powerful energy, and it is very healing. It connects in ways we do not even understand physically. Just do it. List seven non-sexual ways you can

affectionately touch your husband. (Example: caress the back of his neck and kiss it as you pass his chair.) This example does not count for one of the seven, but it is a nice one to make number eight.

_____

_____

_____

_____

_____

_____

_____

3. Fill in the blanks: "If_____, so far as it depends on _____, be at _____ with all men" (Romans 12:18).

Week 6
God's Marriage Covenant

From the Father of the Bride: "Because the Lord has been a witness between you and the wife of your youth . . . 'For I hate divorce,' says the Lord, the God of Israel, 'and him who covers his garment with wrong,' says the Lord of hosts. 'So take heed to your spirit, that you do not deal treacherously' " (Malachi 2:14–16).

Thought for the Day: "Love is ineffable. Intimacy is not just about love. It is also about peace. We talk about inner peace, but what is inner peace? It is that sense of being completely open—with nothing else needing to happen, including curing or healing. It's a total willingness to be at peace right now with things as they are. To me, that is synonymous with love, and synonymous with intimacy, and synonymous with the highest wisdom and courage" (Dean Ornish, M.D., *Love & Survival,* HarperCollins Publisher, 1998, 185).

From Sarah Your Mother: "May the Lord judge between you and me" (Genesis 16:5).

Day 1

God's View of Marriage

Let's continue our pretend "tea party" scene from my house of love with Mother Sarah and the Queen Mother:

As I left the Training Room singing my little ditty, I remembered to call Loden so he could join us in learning about how to love one another.

When Loden arrived, we went into the living room and I introduced him to Mother Sarah and Queen Mother. Queen Mother turned to Loden and asked two unexpected questions:

Is it better to live in a desert land than with a contentious and vexing woman?

Are a constant dripping on a day of steady rain and a contentious woman alike? (Proverbs 21:19; 27:15).

Loden thought a minute and then replied, "I know I speak for most men when I say, 'We do not like contentions; we want peace with our wives.' "

Queen Mother smiled and said, "Well, you do agree with the wisest man who ever lived! So Patsy, I think you should listen to these wise men and think about your role in making your relationship with Loden a peaceful unity."

Mother Sarah nodded in agreement. "Yes, you see, marriage was intended to be the perfect solution to two problems: Man was lonely and needed a suitable companion.

"We plan to instill in both of you an understanding of your marriage covenant. What laws make up the covenant? Do you know that God is the authority for the marriage covenant? When you made vows to one another, God became a witness to your marriage, He bound it, and only He can release you from its bonds."

The Marriage Covenant

When Sarah was desperate for a child, she decided to take things into her own hands instead of waiting on God's time. She gave her servant Hagar to Abraham so she could bear a child for Sarah. However, when Hagar became pregnant, she became haughty and gave Sarah much sorrow. Sarah quickly brought the matter to Abraham. Was she afraid he would divorce her and take Hagar as his number one wife? Sarah explained the situation to her husband and concluded, "May the Lord judge between you and me" (Genesis 16:5).

Was Sarah reminding Abraham of their marriage covenant? It was binding; he was not to put Hagar before her. God had made the covenant; He would judge Abraham if he divorced Sarah for Hagar. Abraham told her to do as she wished with Hagar. He truly did honor the marriage covenant. Abraham loved Sarah as his only true wife.

You are going to learn respect for the marriage covenant and the laws governing your marriage. To be pleasing to your Father and Jesus, you must obey their commands (cf. John 14:15).

God instituted marriage because Adam needed a counterpart as did every other creature. Marriage was made in the Garden of Eden. It was to be as perfect as the rest of creation. After Eve was created, the Godhead exclaimed, "It is very good!" We still have marriage.

We women are the "very" of creation! Life is as it should be when we function in the way we were created—as suitable helpers. Marriage, like the rest of creation, was set up with laws. All creatures instinctively follow God's laws except man. Only man was given the choice to do good or to do evil; to follow God or to follow the devil; to sow good seed or bad seed. This freedom of choice will, until the end of time, be the unchangeable law of God.

Marriage Is a Divine Institution

1. Genesis 2:18: *"Then the Lord God said, 'It is not good for the man to be alone; I will make him a helper suitable for him.'"*

   What was God's purpose in creating woman?

2. 1 Corinthians 11:8: *"For man does not originate from woman, but woman from man."*

   What truth do you learn from Paul's words? How does this knowledge affect your relationship with your husband?

3. Genesis 2:24: *"For this reason a man shall leave his father and his mother, and be joined to his wife; and they shall become one flesh."*

   What does it mean to be joined to his wife?

4. Genesis 3:16: *"To the woman He said, 'I will greatly multiply your pain in childbirth, in pain you will bring forth children; yet your desire will be for your husband, and he will rule over you.'"*

   Desire in Hebrew means "longing." The Father placed within each woman a deep longing to have her husband be her head and protect her. In a household with the wife as "head," unhappiness and unrest prevail. There is no peace. No one knows his place in the family.

   What do you think of this verse? Is not this "desire" an umbrella of protection the Father gave His beloved daughter Eve and her daughters? Adam had not stepped forward to protect and save Eve from Satan. God cursed the serpent and Adam, but He did not curse Eve. I believe that God her Father wanted to protect her from Satan's snare in the future. The Father put within each woman a reminder of her identity, of her role in life. He did not want her to be deceived again in her innocence by Satan's craftiness, so pain would be present as a thorn in the flesh to remind her to let God's grace rule in her life. Does this remind you of Paul?

> For this reason, to keep me from exalting myself, there was given me a thorn in the flesh, a messenger of Satan to torment me—to keep me from exalting myself! Concerning this I implored the Lord three times that it might leave me. And He has said to me, "My grace is sufficient for you, for power is perfected in weakness." Most gladly, therefore, I will rather boast about my weaknesses, so that the power of Christ may dwell in me. Therefore I am well content with weaknesses, with insults, with distresses, with persecutions, with difficulties, for Christ's sake; for when I am weak, then I am strong (2 Corinthians 12:7–10).

5. Matthew 19:6: *"So they are no longer two, but one flesh. What therefore God has joined together, let no man separate."*

What is Jesus teaching you in this verse?

6. Romans 7:1–2: *"The law has jurisdiction over a person as long as he lives . . . the married woman is bound by law to her husband while he is living; but if her husband dies, she is released from the law concerning the husband."*

Does this law also apply to a husband? How long is marriage to last?

7. Ephesians 5:23: *"For the husband is the head of the wife, as Christ also is the head of the church, He Himself being the Savior of the body."*

What does it mean for Christ to be the head of the church? What does it mean for the husband to be head of the wife? What influences your decision to allow your husband to be the head of the family?

As you can deduce from reading these scriptures, the Father and Christ have the final authority in marriage. It is a covenant—a divine institution. If we are children of God and love Him, we obey. It is that simple, that binding, and that complete. Are you willing to obey Him?

There is no place for common-law marriages, trial marriages, living together, same-sex marriages, or any other departure from God's law. It is God's prerogative as creator and ruler of the universe to set the boundaries for His entire creation; and He did create marriage.

Day 2

Marriage Establishment and Laws
God Established Marriage in a Covenant Agreement

Yet you say, "For what reason?" Because the Lord has been a witness between you and the wife of your youth, against whom you have dealt treacherously, though she is your companion and your wife by covenant. But no one has done so who has a remnant of the Spirit. And what did that one do while he was seeking a godly offspring? Take heed then to your spirit, and let no one deal treacherously against the wife of your youth. "For I hate divorce," says the Lord, the God of Israel, "and him who covers his garment with wrong," says the Lord of hosts. "So take heed to your spirit, that you do not deal treacherously" (Malachi 2:14–16).

A great sin of Israel was divorce. Men divorced their wives for any reason and broke the covenant of their youth—a covenant that was binding until the death of one of the participants. A covenant is the most serious and binding agreement made between two parties. What was the law of covenant? The one who broke the covenant suffered the penalty.

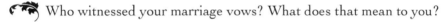 Who witnessed your marriage vows? What does that mean to you?

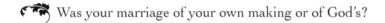 Was your marriage of your own making or of God's?

Read Genesis 15. Discuss the strangeness of these rites God used in making a covenant with Abraham.

Deuteronomy 28 dictates the curses Israel would endure if she broke the covenant made with God at Sinai.

So all these curses shall come on you and pursue you and overtake you until you are destroyed, because you would not obey the Lord your God by keeping His commandments and His statutes which He commanded you (Deuteronomy 28:45).

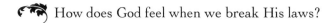 How does God feel when we break His laws?

Marriage Laws

The Bible teaches, "A wife is bound as long as her husband lives; but if her husband is dead, she is free to be married to whom she wishes, only in the Lord" (1 Corinthians 7:39).

 How does the Lord define the duration of marriage?

Only means alone. What does "only in the Lord" means to a Christian widow?

Read Matthew 19:1–12 and apply it to a discussion of the following.

1. Marriage was created by God in Eden when he brought man and woman together. There is no such thing as a homosexual marriage in God's Word.

2. The newly married couple is to separate from their parents' headship and begin a new family unit with the groom as the head of the union.

3. "Be joined to the wife" refers to the sexual union. This is the act by which the bride and groom are transformed from "I, me, and mine" to "we, us, and ours."

4. In their sexual union, God joins the male and the female in one flesh.

5. No one has a right to divide what God has joined together.

6. From the beginning God intended one man for one woman for life. That means "when it was created it was so, now it is so, and in the future as long as there is a world it is so." That is God's decree.

7. Jesus' new covenant allows divorce and remarriage only in the case of immorality. Immorality carries with it the idea of any type of sexual relation with anyone or anything other than one's mate. Christ is faithful to his betrothed bride, the church, and He commands the same loyalty in His children.

8. The apostles said it was better not to marry if one could not divorce. Christ replied that the saying is only to those to whom it is given. He said there are three reasons one is a eunuch: by birth, by man, and for the sake of the kingdom. Let us reason this out for understanding. If one is a eunuch for the kingdom of heaven, it means that one does not have sexual relations by

choice. Read Mark 10 for a repeat of this law. Does Christ mean what He is teaching?

Day 3

What Does Jesus Want?

When a woman or man is in a harmful marriage, the Lord says one may leave but not remarry. We may think this is a harsh law, but as children of the Father, we have to trust that He is all-wise and that His law is good for us. Ours is to obey, not to question.

If you leave your husband for any cause except adultery, you must remain unmarried. How binding is this law to Christ?

> But to the married I give instructions, not I, but the Lord, that the wife should not leave her husband (but if she does leave, she must remain unmarried, or else be reconciled to her husband), and that the husband should not divorce his wife (1 Corinthians 7:10–11).

Sociologists have finally concluded that monogamy is the best marriage relationship. Second marriages are less likely to survive than are first marriages. Marriage survival is less likely as the number of marriages increase. Many have confessed: "I would have been much happier and better off if we had worked out our problems." Did the Father know this all along? Is that why He wants us to work on problems before they become so great they overpower us? Is that the reason Paul said "do not let the sun go down on your anger"?

Satan works in favor of divorce. He wants you to give up on your marriage and justify your actions by saying, "Divorce is the only answer!"

Satan works in favor of divorce.

Divorce is worse than the death of a mate. It brings disturbing inner conflicts which are never truly expunged. A man, now single and trying to recover from two failed marriages, told me in very emphatic terms: "Tell women the importance of handling their differences every day; do not let them escalate until there is no desire in either heart to remain together." He is a very caustic man, even though his marriages have been dead for years. So take heed!

The husband and wife owe each other sexual release. Only when there is mutual consent—and then for a good reason—is abstention acceptable. Even then abstention must be for a short time so Satan will not tempt them for their lack of self-control. And he will certainly try (cf. 1 Corinthians 7:1–5).

🍃 What is Paul's message to the wife who constantly says, "Not tonight, I have a headache"?

🍃 How can you and your marriage benefit if you "act your way into feeling" during a "headache" moment?

A wife is to be under the authority of the husband. "Wives, be subject to your own husbands, as to the Lord" (Ephesians 5:22).

🍃 How are you to be subject to the Lord?

🍃 What is the meaning of *subject*?

A husband is to love his wife with the love Christ has for His church. "Husbands, love your wives, just as Christ also loved the church and gave Himself up for her" (Ephesians 5:25).

🍃 Love in this verse is *agape*. Describe the love Christ has for His bride.

🍃 What should your husband's love be toward you?

Children are to obey and honor their parents. "Children, obey your parents in the Lord, for this is right. Honor your father and mother (which is the first commandment with a promise), so that it may be well with you, and that you may live long on the earth. Fathers, do not provoke your children to anger, but bring them up in the discipline and instruction of the Lord" (Ephesians 6:1–4).

🍃 These verses explain the law for the family. Relate what God expects from children and parents in the home.

Be faithful to your mate. "Or do you not know that the unrighteous will not inherit the kingdom of God? Do not be deceived; neither fornicators, nor idolaters, nor adulterers, nor effeminate, nor homosexuals . . . will inherit the kingdom of God" (1 Corinthians 6:9–10).

🌿 How important is marriage purity to God?

Day 4

Marriage Created for Happiness

"Then the Lord God said, 'It is not good for the man to be alone; I will make him a helper suitable for him' " (Genesis 2:18).

🌿 Why was woman created? Why do you feel it an honor to be created for the purpose of fulfilling your husband's needs?

"Let your fountain be blessed, and rejoice in the wife of your youth" (Proverbs 5:18).

🌿 *Fountain* has to do with the sexual aspect of marriage. What is your role in providing rejoicing for your husband?

"How blessed is everyone who fears the Lord, who walks in His ways . . . Your wife shall be like a fruitful vine within your house, your children like olive plants around your table" (Psalm 128:1–3).

🌿 What does the fear of God have to do with happiness?

"He who finds a wife finds a good thing and obtains favor from the Lord" (Proverbs 18:22).

🌿 Why is finding a wife a good thing for a man?

"House and wealth are an inheritance from fathers, but a prudent wife is from the Lord" (Proverbs 19:14).

🌿 *Prudent* in Hebrew means "to cause to act wisely, understand." In what sense is a prudent wife from the Lord?

"Enjoy life with the woman whom you love all the days of your fleeting life which He has given you under the sun, for this is your reward in life and in your toil in which you have labored under the sun" (Ecclesiastes 9:9).

 What does the word *fleeting* teach you about enjoying each day with your husband?

 How is happiness a reward from God?

"A joyful heart makes a cheerful face, but when the heart is sad, the spirit is broken" (Proverbs 15:13).

Dr. Jon Kabat-Zin, founder and director of the Stress Reduction Clinic at the University of Massachusetts Medical Center, has this to say about meditation, intimacy, and healing:

> A sense of compassion can allow you to see things without having them have to be a certain way. You can see the situation more the way it is, because you've gotten away from your own insistence that it has to be a certain way. And that can be profoundly healing, because your heart opens—it actually sees, feels, is intimate with and directly knows the heart of the other person. There's desire to do no harm, a desire to really nourish the well-being of that heart, that person, whether it is a child, parent, or lover (Dean Ornish, M.D., *Love & Survival*, HarperCollins Publisher 1998, 176–177).

This man hit on the very heart of God's teaching: joyfulness, peace, and oneness with God, man, and especially your husband is healing to your soul and overall health! Is creating a peaceful home worth the effort? Note the words of the apostle John: "Beloved, let us love one another, for love is from God; and everyone who loves is born of God and knows God" (1 John 4:7).

"All the days of the afflicted are bad, but a cheerful heart has a continual feast" (Proverbs 15:15).

When you are love as described in 1 Corinthians 13, then you are free to love. Life is a continuous love feast because you look upon everyone as someone worthy of love—not of hate or anger. Life becomes one love bite after another, especially with your beloved. You constantly feed one another love bites and bestow touches of love in word and deed.

 What is the main source of your past painful experiences?

What brings you the most joy in life? Do these have any connection to your loving others?

Day 5

Selected for Submission

Washington Irving stated this axiom: "Great minds have purposes, others have wishes." To purpose means to aim, intend, resolve, or plan, while to wish means to long, want, desire, or crave. Do you have a purpose in life or only wishes?

Read Ecclesiastes 3:1–8. Notice the appointed times at the beginning of the chapter. Faith in your Father must play a large part in your reaching your goals. I trust having a happy, loving marriage was foremost in your planning. Understand that your Father is in control of your life—if you so choose. He will help you work life out for your good (cf. Romans 8:28; Philippians 2:12–13). He has put longings in your heart to help you, such as the desire to be protected by a loving husband. Not only did he make everything appropriate in its time, He has also put eternity in your heart (Ecclesiastes 3:11).

How did Christ accomplish submission? 1 Peter 2:23

You have the responsibility of passing your godly knowledge to young women coming after you, so the chain of godly wives directing the home will not be broken, and God will continue to bless your country (Proverbs 14:34).

Your husband and children are to follow in the way of the Lord under your influence. "Every man who eats and drinks sees good in all his labor—it is the gift of God" (Ecclesiastes 3:13). Your home will be a blessing to each family member who reaps what is sown. These are all gifts from God to you! Pass them on to the next generation.

Commit and Submit

In order to make a commitment to your marriage, let's define it fully. To *commit* means to bring together; give in charge or trust; deliver for safe keeping, pledge; bind; engage. Read 1 Peter 2:21–3:18 before you go any further.

Focus on Christ's example to us. Verse 21 uses the word *purpose*: "For you have been called for this purpose, since Christ also suffered for you, leaving you an example for you to follow in His steps." God has selected you to be in submission to your husband, just as Christ was in submission to His Father. Notice how Jesus accomplished this great deed: "While being reviled, He did not revile in return; while suffering, He uttered no threats, but kept entrusting Himself to Him who judges righteously" (1 Peter 2:23).

Here is the answer for Christ's victory and for your victory in being a ruby of a wife! When Jesus went into the Garden of Gethsemane to pray, He told His apostles, "My soul is deeply grieved to the point of death; remain here and keep watch with Me" (Matthew 26:38). Jesus prayed as no one before or since that dreadful night. He asked three times for the Father to remove the cup of His crucifixion, but instead the Father sent an angel to strengthen Him for the ordeal ahead. He left the garden as the sin-bearer, ready to be crucified for the sins of the world.

How did He do that? Christ committed Himself—"entrusted Himself"—to His Father (1 Peter 2:23). He forgot self, counted self as nothing, and allowed His Father to use Him as He would. As a result He became the Shepherd and Guardian of our souls (1 Peter 2:25). The very next verse (3:1) commands that "in the same way, you wives, be submissive to your own husbands."

We must commit ourselves totally to the headship of our husbands, just as Christ did for His Father, trusting them to do what is best for us. Total commitment must be your purpose in marriage! As a result you will have the privilege of becoming a ruby to your mate. You will help in being a guardian to keep his soul in the Great Shepherd's care.

Write your definition of commitment to your marriage.

Are you hesitant to commit yourself to the headship of your husband? Why or why not?

Make sure that your character is free from the love of money, being content with what you have; for He Himself has said, "I will never desert you, nor will I ever forsake you," so that we confidently say, "The Lord is my helper, I will not be afraid. What will man do to me?" (Hebrews 13:5–6).

What would the words "I will never desert you, nor will I ever forsake you" mean to your husband in showing your commitment to the union?

What effect do the above words have on your psyche relative to your commitment to your marriage?

Summary

Loden and I truly learned our lesson from Mother Sarah and Queen Mother. We agreed that divorce would never be an option for us. That commitment helped during the early years when I didn't know how to be content. I had to find ways other than divorce to resolve my inner turmoil. You too will find safety in your inner being by doing the following:

❧ Make a commitment to your marriage.

❧ Work to make happiness your goal.

❧ Keep your covenant of love with your beloved.

❧ Obey God's laws of marriage.

Everything God designed for us is for our well-being. He never intended us to know sin and the pain that accompanies yielding to Satan. Remember daily the life God planned for Adam and Eve in the Garden and work at making His plan your goal in marriage.

Memory Verse

"Commit your way to the Lord, trust also in Him, and He will do it. He will bring forth your righteousness as the light, and your judgment as the noonday."

Psalm 37:5–6

My Take-Home

Goal: *To make a mental and emotional commitment to my marriage.* Commit yourself to Jesus to be used as He sees best. Write your purpose of commitment and your vow to Jesus below:

🌿 The purpose of my commitment to my marriage:

A Truth: "One of the most important things we can do to keep our relationship strong and healthy is to build the bond of affection. It starts as a thin cord and grows ever thicker and stronger. When the inevitable stresses of life befall us in the form of differences and disappointments, the cord can become frayed. Gradually, with conscious choice, commitment, and intention we can repair the connective cord with sincere acts of consideration, generosity, and kindness on a daily basis" (Linda and Charlie Bloom, *101 Things I Wish I Knew When I Got Married*, New World Library. 2004, 4).

My Homework

1. Continue writing the love letter you began in the first week.

2. What compliment did I give my husband on Tuesday of last week? (Did I catch you on that one?) Remember at least one a day, and it has to be a new one. You want to keep your eyes focused on the good things he does for you. The more compliments you give, the more you will have to compliment. Remember to "cast your bread on the surface of the waters, for you will find it after many days" (Ecclesiastes 11:1).

3. How often did you pray for your marriage this week?

4. Keep up the kissing, touching, eye contact, and good deeds to feed him properly.

5. Make this week's "doing exercise" a special meal for your family. Get the children involved in setting the table. Use your best dishes, silver, and cloth napkins; please do not forget the candle. How else will your family know how to enjoy the better side of life? The Father is preparing a wedding banquet for His Son, and you want to know how to eat properly. Make this a habit. If you cannot do it every week, at least have a special meal once a month. You can even have a planning session with the family to decide on the menu.

6. Also, require that dress be more than casual. Our society has lapsed into sloppiness, and when we dress, think, and act sloppily, that becomes our character. What actions follow a sloppy character? Dressing up, acting politely, and talking gently breeds a gentleman and a lady. These physical actions reflect a spiritual truth: your Father demands your best!

7. Exercise each day by lifting yourself on the cross, dying to self, and committing yourself into the hands of your loving Father, who is Shepherd of your soul. You will find blessed peace and happiness when you turn yourself over to Christ. You will live a bountiful, healthful, contended life and bring joy to the man of your heart, as well as to your children—the physical signs of your love for one another.

Week 7
Mother to Daughter

From the Father of the Bride: "Your adornment must not be merely external—braiding the hair, and wearing gold jewelry, or putting on dresses; but let it be the hidden person of the heart, with the imperishable quality of a gentle and quiet spirit, which is precious in the sight of God. For in this way in former times the holy women also, who hoped in God, used to adorn themselves, being submissive to their own husbands; just as Sarah obeyed Abraham, calling him lord, and you have become her children if you do what is right without being frightened by any fear" (1 Peter 3:3–6).

Thought for the Day: "It's worth repeating that men yearn for, first, their mothers' acceptance, approval, and appreciation, and then their wives'. When they get those three A's, they'll do just about anything to please their wives" (Dr. Laura Schlessinger, *The Proper Care and Feeding of Husbands*, Harper Collins Publisher, 2004, 174).

From Mother Sarah: "Look to Abraham your father and to Sarah who gave birth to you in pain; when he was but one I called him, then I blessed him and multiplied him" (Isaiah 51:2).

Day 1

Crown of Creation

Join me again for another imaginary "tea party" where faithful Mother Sarah instructs on holy living for women:

Mother Sarah invited me once again to come into our house of love and sit at her feet for more guidance toward becoming Loden's ruby. I entered the living room as Mother Sarah took a seat beside the lovely Queen Mother. How blessed I felt that they loved me enough to teach me the way of God! As we sipped our tea, Mother Sarah began speaking.

"When the Lord called my husband Abraham, He promised he would be the father of many children; all the nations of the earth would be blessed through him. Abraham was seventy-five and I was sixty-five; we had no children. Abraham believed the Lord and answered His call to leave his home in Haran and go where the Lord led him. I also embraced the Lord in faith and our lives changed drastically. From that day to our deaths, we were led by the Lord's Word.

"The promise of children came true in our son Isaac. Through him came many children. In the fullness of God's time, another special son was born in the lineage of Abraham—His name was Jesus. Through Him all the promises of God culminated.

"When you were born again through baptism, you became a child of God. Also, through the promise to Abraham, you became Abraham's child (Galatians 3:29). Now listen closely while I tell you another truth. You can become my daughter if you do what is right without being intimidated (1 Peter 3:6).

"The purpose of your being here today is to earn the right to be my daughter. I am going to teach you lessons so you can emulate me and become my blessed daughter. Society looked down on me because I had no children. I held dear the promise of a child. I treasure each of my daughters in Jesus and I wish to continue to teach them. I desire that every married woman who is a child of God may live as my daughter and reap the blessings of our heavenly Father.

"Listen closely as I instruct you in the way of holy living with your husband. Then you must train yourself to live this way. It is your duty to train the women who will come after you. This is a mother-to-daughter inheritance— you must not fail me."

Queen Mother joined the conversation.

"Yes, you must allow the Father to make you Loden's ruby. Not only will you be his jewel, but you will also be the Father's most precious daughter! He promises that you will be precious in His sight, if you will develop yourself with the Spirit's help (1 Peter 3:4). Isn't it a great joy to know that if you allow the Spirit to make you a ruby, you will be treasured by the Father, by Sarah, and by your husband? What greater honor could any woman have than to be called the crown of her husband and be called *mine* by the Father (Malachi 3:17) and have Mother Sarah say, "My daughter, I am proud of you!"

Are you willing to make changes to become a daughter of Sarah? Let's study now as mother to daughter.

Will you please stop and pray to the Father to give you a willing heart and patience to learn Sarah's way?

Leave and Cleave

A wife must be willing to leave father and mother and cleave to her husband. Sarah lived in Ur, an urban city. She had all the comforts and luxuries that city life afforded her. She probably had her network of friends, merchants, and perhaps even a beautiful garden tended by her staff. Sarah was willing to leave everything behind, go with Abraham, and never look back. What did Sarah give up to follow Abraham's call from God? Everything! She lived as a nomad the rest of her life.

Her tent was not as austere as modern camping tents. In fact, it was probably quite beautiful, but it was still not a home where she could put down roots with permanent fixtures to give her relaxation and beauty. Today many husbands cannot get ahead in their chosen fields because their wives are not willing to leave home. Don't forget. When you marry you become one with your husband. It is your privilege to make a home for him wherever his work carries him. It is your choice: make him the center of the home, or suffer the consequences of having a husband who is squelched by your selfish desires.

Each stage of life is precious.

It is not easy to move about, but many successful, happy wives find it an adventure. Each new city is a learning experience! There is opportunity to meet wonderful people and to do much work for the Lord all over the world.

Why Did I Marry Him?

Everywhere Abraham and Sarah went, they honored the Lord. So let it be with you. Many military families and business people have planted churches where they settled. You must encourage and support your husband in pursuit of his dream. After all, it is his work that keeps bread on the table. Allow him the time he needs to attain his goals. Many successful men work more than forty hours a week.

I have never been jealous of another woman, but I was jealous of Loden's business. He worked ten to twelve hours a day, six days a week. But when I complained to him about it, he simply said, "You don't mind spending the money I make." His statement pricked my conscience and gave me a new way of thinking.

I began to find productive ways to occupy my time. Then I began to feel the blessings of his work. After all, one of the reasons I married him was because he was ambitious.

This Too Shall Pass

When the children were small and sleep was precious to me, Mrs. Loden often reminded me: "These are the most precious years of your life." I thought, *You have to be kidding! If these are the most precious times, I'm not sure I want to go on.* However, every stage of life is precious if we look on it as such. Once you get on the other side of parenthood, you look back and say, "I can't believe how fast that went." So when you're weary, pray for strength for the day and remember, "This too shall pass." The rewards are worth the effort.

A very successful high school coach was also a faithful Christian. His wife was also a teacher; she was totally involved in her husband's coaching. Many young men on his team had a poor home life. She was a mother to them: she served as a cook, private tutor, and counselor. She never missed a ball game. As soon as the last whistle sounded, she was on the field at her husband's side. They worked together to teach the team Christian values. How do you think the coach felt about his ruby? She embraced his life and his dreams as her own. Everyone could see love flowing between them. What a tremendous effect their love had on those young athletes!

 Do you keep your husband from his life's goals?

 If so, how can you change? If not, how can you help him more?

Stop Complaining

Sarah's life was not easy after she left Haran, the first stop on their journey with God. Just think of the difficulties of trying to run your home with no water—unless you could dig a well. Imagine packing and moving just when the tent was set like you wanted. Sarah's only permanent dwelling was the cave in which she was buried!

Did she have a woman friend in whom she could confide? Did she have a garden? Probably not. Yet, no matter the circumstances, she never complained. Abraham was her focus. She provided his every need to the best of her ability.

A woman who babysat me and my siblings gave my mother an axiom: "Men don't like complainers." How true! Complaining is an extremely bad habit! And it is a habit! Can habits be broken? Absolutely! Children of God are to radiate positive attitudes. Complaining is negative—a sin in God's eyes!

> Nor let us try the Lord, as some of them did, and were destroyed by the serpents. Nor grumble, as some of them did, and were destroyed by the destroyer. Now these things happened to them as an example, and they were written for our instruction, upon whom the ends of the ages have come (1 Corinthians 10:9–11).

Look for the Whistles and Fleas

We have a choice. We must choose to take action instead of complaining. Bear the negatives with patience and be grateful for the good things in life. Work to change negatives into positives.

Have the attitude of the woman who went to pay her final respects to the meanest man in town. Everyone knew she always spoke good, never evil, of everyone. Neighbors stood near the casket waiting to hear her comments to the family. As she looked into the face of the deceased, she hesitated and then proclaimed, "Well, he sure could whistle!" So look for the whistles in your dear husband and count him as a blessing in every way.

Complaining is a sin in God's eyes.

My daddy was a man of few words, so when he met my sister Sue's husband-to-be, he simply said, "Tom, I can tell you one thing about Sue. She sure can whistle." That settled it then and there; Tom was hooked. To this day, Sue can surely whistle and delights us with her ability.

Two sisters were in a German concentration camp. One was complaining about the fleas that infested their living quarters. Her sister said, "Thank God for the fleas; they keep the Germans from coming into our quarters." So be grateful for the fleas in your life. Perhaps they serve a purpose you have not considered.

Living Sacrifice

One of Sarah's most important qualities was her willingness to follow Abraham and leave her idols behind in order to serve the living God (cf. Joshua 24:2). She supported him in obedience to all the commands of God, and she cherished the promises given her husband, especially the one about his being the father of many children. Her barrenness was a daily grief for her to bear.

Sharing faith in God is the most important element in fully cementing your marriage. When two people are committed to obeying God, they will work to fill the potholes on life's road. Living for God is one continuous journey into faith and more faith. Abraham and Sarah grew in their love for God each day. Everywhere Abraham went, he built altars that remained as testimonies to God. So we must offer ourselves daily as living sacrifices to God (cf. Romans 12:1) and be a reminder to all that we are a living image of Christ our Savior.

Prayer was vital to him. His talks with the Lord were intimate and faith-building. So must husbands and wives pray daily together, asking the Father to help them to be a living example of the love Christ has for His bride. What better teaching can you give your children than a living example of what God expects in marriage?

Loden and I had daily devotions with our children. We used *Hulbert's Children's Bible Stories*. Loden's mother had read that book to him. As our children grew, we let them take turns reading the Bible events.

Teach your children to pray at the table and in your devotions. However, do not allow them to take over the family's prayers. When children do all the praying, they might think prayer is something they will outgrow. Let them hear you pray. Daily devotions will bring your family close together and help your faith grow. Faith is developed through word and actions. You must supply both in your journey of faith.

List one way you can help yourself and your husband to grow in faith.

Do you have a daily devotion with your family? If so, how does it help your family? If not, when and how will you begin it?

Day 2

Mistakes

Did Abraham make mistakes? Of course! Did Sarah bring them up to him in rebukes, chidings, or ridicule? I don't think so.

You will recall one mistake. When a famine hit Canaan, Abraham took his family to Egypt for relief (Genesis 12). As they approached the capital city, he asked Sarah to say she was his sister. Why? Sarah was extraordinarily beautiful even to those of her own culture, and Abraham knew she would have a great appeal to foreign men.

In those days, a man would kill to take another man's wife. However, they respected a man's protection of his sister. Those desiring her were legally obligated to pay a bride price. When Pharaoh's officials reported that a beauty was in their midst, Sarah was taken to Pharaoh's harem. Pharaoh paid Abraham a rich bride price for her.

Abraham and Sarah both must have prayed the Lord would save them as 1 Peter 3:5 reveals: "The holy women hoped in God." God brought great plagues on Pharaoh, who identified Sarah as the source of his misery. He severely reprimanded Abraham and sent him away.

Abraham's faith was not as strong as it would later be, so he repeated the "sister" mistake. Once again the Lord rescued him. God was truly looking after him, but King Abimelech gave Abraham a much-needed rebuke for duping him and almost causing Abimelech to sin against God (Genesis 20:8–14). Adultery was a sin even in ancient times.

Millstones or Stepping Stones?

Sarah did not cause Abraham grief by constantly reminding him of his lack of faith. She allowed God to work on Abraham. Through his mistakes he was learning and growing in wisdom. When Edison was chided for his hundreds of light-bulb failures before his success, he responded, "Well, I learned what did not work." He invented many things because failures to him were stepping-stones, not millstones.

Likewise you must allow your husband to make mistakes. I can assure you, he beats himself enough without your joining in, so comfort him: "You did what you thought was the best with the information you had. I am proud of you for making a decision and admitting it was not the best. What did we learn from this?" Notice the "we." You are putting yourself with him in this decision. Does that not sound better than "I told you it would not work!"

Everyone makes mistakes. Usually, they are honest errors. We, like Edison, learn what not to do! One woman would not let her husband forget a bad business decision he had made years before. She reminded him often that she would not have made such a mistake. How did he patiently endure this time after time? Who was showing the most patience and tolerance in that case? By observing the actions of women like that, the Father enables us to have the wisdom to make the choice of handling negatives properly. Turn them into positives and learn what does not work. It is your choice! Choose wisely with the Father's help.

Allow your husband to make mistakes.

Why should you allow your husband to make mistakes?

How can you help him when he feels bad about a "deal gone wrong"?

To Sir with Love

The Father wants us to emulate Sarah in her obedience to Abraham—she called him lord. Dear One, He is revealing Sarah's action as an example for us. *Lord* means "sir" or "master" denoting the giving of respect and obedience. Understand her example: the Lord wants you to call your husband lord. The word *submit* is a six-letter word with a four-letter reputation. Young women sometimes tell me, "If the loving class is going to tell me I have to submit to my husband, I am not interested in attending." Shame, shame, and more shame for such an attitude.

Most despise the idea of submitting, but it is my prayer that when you finish this study, you will be so thankful to the Father for giving you a protective covering that you will repent of any ill thoughts you've had and rejoice in the freedom it gives you. When you have earned your husband's trust, you will be amazed at the freedom he will give you. I was continuously thankful to Loden and often told him, "One of the greatest blessings you have given me is my freedom."

Submission carries with it the idea of rank. To be submissive, someone must be over you. We easily understand the importance of having rank in the military, business, and government, so why should the home be any different? The husband ranks over the wife, though they are joint-heirs in Christ (1 Peter 3:7) and equal in the church where there is neither male nor female (Galatians 3:28–29).

However, there is rank in the church: elders, deacons, ministers, saints (Philippians 1:1–2). Although we are one, the elders rule, and we must obey (Hebrews 13:7; 1 Timothy 5:17). Jesus gives this simple but profound statement in John 14:15: "If you love Me, you will keep My commandments." It is the same with your husband; if you love him, you will keep his commandments.

Burden or Blessing

Consider this reasoning: Jesus has said obeying Him is proof of your loving Him, and He has commanded you to submit to your husband, so if you do not submit, you do not love Him. Until you submit to His commandments, He can do nothing for you because you refuse to allow Him. Our Father told us through John: "For this is the love of God, that we keep His commandments; and His commandments are not burdensome" (1 John 5:3).

Submission is not a burden but a blessing. Your husband is over you, just as Christ is over His church. Until you submit to His authority, He cannot love you and bless you in the way His Father intended. Your lack of submission may cause your husband to disobey Jesus also, for Paul said, "But I want you to understand that Christ is the head of every man, and the man is the head of a woman, and God is the head of Christ" (1 Corinthians 11:3).

For a better understanding of allowing your husband to be your head just as Christ is his head, let's follow the thread the Holy Spirit weaves. Read 1 Peter 2:1–3:18.

Peter begins chapter 2 by referring to their new birth through baptism—the result of their believing and obeying the Word of Christ. As newborn babies in Christ, they needed training to be Christlike. (Back to our Training Room—remember?) The new Christian offers herself to Jesus, who uses each Christian as a building block in His spiritual house. Each Christian becomes a priest in this spiritual house. What are the priestly duties? To offer up sacrifices—the body as a living sacrifice—and praises to Christ.

Bond Servants

Christians are to submit to the powers of government, "for such is the will of God that by doing right you may silence the ignorance of foolish men" (1 Peter 2:15). What does that mean? We are to obey the laws of the land!

A Christian missionary working in his native Poland told the Minister of Religion: "You should not fear Christians doing anything against your law because we work under the law of the country where we live. We will be your best citizens." As a result, the minister gave him almost everything he wanted; the official learned to trust him to keep the law.

Verse 16 reads, "Act as free men, and do not use your freedom as a covering for evil, but use it as bondslaves of God." Jesus promised, "You will know the truth, and the truth will make you free" (John 8:32). A child of God does not use this freedom to do evil but to love his fellowman and to bring him to Jesus (Romans 13:8). Here we have twice been told to submit to government and to "honor all people, love the brotherhood, fear God, honor the king" (1 Peter 2:17).

Submission becomes natural to a Christian.

Verse 18 is a slave's command to be submissive to his master with all respect—the bad and the good master—"for this finds favor, if for the sake of conscience toward God a person bears up under sorrows when suffering unjustly" (1 Peter 3:19). God is pleased when His children bear unjust treatment with patience. He taught submission to the Christians who were slaves to men. Peter instructed them to serve their masters faithfully and please God. The free, as well as the slaves, must submit to someone.

Our Calling

For you have been called for this purpose, since Christ also suffered for you, leaving you an example for you to follow in His steps, who committed no sin, nor was any deceit found in His mouth; and while being reviled, He did not revile in return; while suffering, He uttered no threats, but kept entrusting Himself to Him who judges righteously (1 Peter 2:21–23).

We have been called for the purpose of submitting to God, to government, to one another and to those who employ us. (Although we are not slaves, we are under "masters" in business.) Submission is a way of life; it becomes natural to a child of God. Why? Because we put ourselves to death in our self-sacrifice to Christ, and we work in His stead to be a beacon of His Word and love.

Entrusted is sometimes translated "committed." In the Garden of Gethsemane when the Father let Jesus know there was no other sacrifice, Jesus turned Himself over to the Father. He allowed the Father to make of Him the perfect sacrifice to save man from sin. From the time Jesus made that commitment, He said nothing for Himself. He endured all the pain, humiliation, and indignity of the cross because He trusted His Father to do what was best for Him and mankind—perfect trust, perfect submission, perfect glory!

> He Himself bore our sins in His body on the cross, so that we might die to sin and live to righteousness; for by His wounds you were healed. For you were continually straying like sheep, but now you have returned to the Shepherd and Guardian of your souls (1 Peter 2: 24–25).

> *Righteousness* means "right action." In the writings of Paul, the Spirit defines it as that gracious gift of God to men whereby all who believe on the Lord Jesus Christ are brought into right relationship with God. This righteousness is unattainable by obedience to any law, or by any merit of man's own, or any other condition than that of faith in Christ. . . . The man who trusts in Christ becomes "the righteousness of God in Him" (2 Corinthians 5:21); that is, he becomes in Christ all that God requires a man to be, all that he can never be in himself. Because Abraham accepted the Word of God, making it his own by that act of the mind and spirit which is called faith, and as the sequel showed, submitting himself to its control, therefore God accepted him as one who fulfilled the whole of his requirements (Romans 4:3). (W. E. Vines. *An Expository Dictionary of New Testament Words*, Oliphants LTD 1966, 298–29).

Christ totally submitted Himself to God's control and was rewarded by being given the title King of kings and Lord of lords; He sits at the right hand of God and is the Shepherd of your soul.

Now pay close attention to the following scripture:

> In the same way, you wives, be submissive to your own husbands so that even if any of them are disobedient to the Word, they may be won without a word by the behavior of their wives, as they observe your chaste and respectful behavior (1 Peter 3:1–2).

 What does "in the same way" mean?

Precious in the Sight of God

Christ gave us the example of entrusting Himself to His Father without any restraint. Just as He committed Himself to His Father, so you must entrust, commit, and submit to your own husband.

> For in this way in former times the holy women also, who hoped in God, used to adorn themselves, being submissive to their own husbands; just as Sarah obeyed Abraham, calling him lord, and you have become her children if you do what is right without being frightened by any fear (1 Peter 3:5–6).

What is the fear we are not to have? It is fear for ourselves. God is asking us not to look at the man (husband), but to look to Him in trust. Obey your husband as Christ obeyed God—totally. In submitting to your husband, you submit to God. How does our Father regard this spirit of submission?

> Your adornment must not be merely external—braiding the hair, and wearing gold jewelry, or putting on dresses; but let it be the hidden person of the heart, with the imperishable quality of a gentle and quiet spirit, which is precious in the sight of God (1 Peter 3:3–4).

Wise Solomon put it this way: "An excellent wife is the crown of her husband, but she who shames him is like rottenness in his bones" (Proverbs 12:4).

Jesus was crowned as the King because of His submission to His Father. Likewise, you will be the crown of your husband if you are excellent in strength of mind and body.

Now back to your Training Room for more exercise! To the world, a wife is the sign of her husband's authority. The world will look on you as a beautiful jewel while giving your husband the respect due a king—all because of your submission to him. But best of all, you will be very precious to the Father. The Father, the Son, the Holy Spirit, your husband, your children, and the world will look upon you as a woman to be loved and admired. What more could you desire?

Submission is of your own free will.

Two-Headed Oddity

In spite of this promise of glory, the question often asked by women is, "If I obey my husband, he will take advantage of me, and I am my own woman. It is not in my best interest to allow myself to be totally under someone else's control, much less my husband's. I am as good as he and often smarter." Back to the Training Room, Dear One!

Remember that order, function, and commands are the best way for a home to be run: husband, wife, and children in that order of command. Submission is of your own free will. If your husband forces you, that subjugation is against God's law. Just as you freely submitted to the will of God and Christ, so must you willingly put yourself under your husband as your head. You know that no two-headed living thing is normal, so how could your home be normal with two heads? The two of you are one; therefore, one of you must submit to the other, or you will be a two-headed oddity! God says your husband is the only head.

❧ What do you have to fear from submission to your husband?

What do you have to gain by obeying God's will?

Do you feel God and Christ have made you less than a human, put undue pressure on you, or demeaned you by asking for your submission? Your husband has that same request for submission from his head, Christ (Ephesians 5:22–33). He has to love you as Christ loved the church and tenderly see that you live in an environment which will allow you to grow into your full stature in Christ. He is to be willing to die for you, he must set you apart for his own, he must nurture you so he can present you back to Christ pure and holy, not having a spot or blemish. He is to love you as he does his own body. He must nourish and cherish you as well. Quite an order, isn't it? God really puts submission in perspective, doesn't He?

Respect His Role

The Father built into man the desire to love and cherish his wife and family. In order to satisfy his longing to protect them and take care of their needs, the husband must have reassurance that his wife willingly puts herself under his protection and care. Remember the thought for the day? Acceptance, approval, appreciation!

Appreciation is what Christ wants from you; He suffered for you. Lack of thankfulness was a big downfall of the Israelites. They were not thankful for anything God did for them. All they did was complain, grumble, and worship other gods. Your husband was made in the image of God, so he has the same desires for you as God had for His wife Israel. Christ has these same feelings for His bride, the church. Your husband wants you to respect his role. Then you can have whatever you want.

A submissive wife has so much control over her husband that it is scary. In a popular movie, a mother tells her daughter: "Your father may be the head, but I am the neck which turns the head." That is so very true. Therefore, as righteous wives we are very careful how we use our power over our men.

Think of Jezebel. She was so dominant that she reduced King Ahab to a sniffling little boy who took to his bed and turned his pouting face to the wall when he did not get Naboth's vineyard (1 Kings 21). Jezebel took control and committed murder to get Ahab's desire.

Jezebel was so frightening that Elijah, God's faithful and powerful prophet, was terrified of her. He fled her presence and begged God to let him die. She is the opposite of what Sarah was to her Abraham.

Being submissive to Jesus gives His bride, the church, great power:

Ask, and it will be given to you; seek and you will find; knock, and it will be opened to you. For everyone who asks receives, and he who seeks finds, and to him who knocks it will be opened. . . . How much more will your Father who is in heaven give what is good to those who ask Him! (Matthew 7:8–11).

🌿 Write out James 4:10. What is the Father telling you?

Lift Burdens

Learning to be submissive can bring you great joy. You will look to your husband as your head, talk everything over with him, and accept his decisions as final. It will take many burdens off your shoulders. Your husband will lovingly take your thoughts and desires into his decisions and try to do his best for you and the family.

Even if your husband is not loving and kind, you must still submit to his headship. By your loving, Christlike way, he might learn God's way. Remember Nancy? Her husband never became a loving, caring husband, but she became a more loving wife and experienced a deeper joy in Christ. Eventually, she overcame being frightened of her husband. She was able to nurse him all his days, and his children rose up and called her blessed because they appreciated her endurance. Your submission to your husband will determine his standing in the church and the community. A man is judged by his wife. Give your husband a very good name, Dear One.

🌿 Are you willing to commit yourself totally to your husband's care? What are your thoughts about submission to your husband now?

Day 3

Soothe, Don't Seethe!

Sarah allowed Abraham to run his own business. She did not try to involve herself in his decision-making. When Abraham graciously gave Lot first choice of grazing land, Sarah trusted Abraham and his God. Lot took the lush green pastures, but she knew by now that Abraham and God would see to her needs. When Abraham left her and took 318 of his trained servants to rescue Lot, Sarah did not complain—she knew what he had to do. She trusted God and was not afraid to stand alone while Abraham was away.

Allow your husband to make plans which have to do with the welfare of the family. Talk over all situations, needs, and problems with him and help him make his decisions. Trust him to do the right thing. As he gets used to making decisions, he will learn to trust God, pray for guidance, and take time to ponder important decisions. Praise him for his efforts and do not condemn his mistakes.

We women often think we are perfect, but so many times we are wrong! I used to seethe over Loden's decisions, but guess what? Most of them proved to be correct.

Thankfully, I did not reveal my feelings or I would never have finished asking his forgiveness, but I did learn to trust his judgment. I know that he was usually crossing home plate while I was standing out in left field. I began to feel with him like I did with my mother when I was a child, "I just wish one time you would be wrong!" Mother usually was not wrong, and neither was Loden. Always remember that the Father knows best, and trust your husband's judgment.

Who Knows Best?

Sarah received some strong teaching on decision-making. Like Eve, Sarah decided she knew better than the Father and Abraham. She had the perfect solution to her barrenness. She planned to have a child by her handmaid. Abraham went along with her plan (Genesis 16:2). What an example of the power of a submissive wife!

Sarah had sway over Abraham's better judgment, but Hagar, when she became pregnant, despised Sarah. Sarah realized her mistake and was terrified! Abraham might divorce her and realize God's blessings through his new wife Hagar. Sarah was seventy-six years old and Abraham was eighty-six. In an insecure moment, did Sarah think that youthful Hagar had more appeal to him that she did? She confronted Abraham with her pain, and like many of us, blamed him for her trouble: "May the wrong done me be upon you. I gave my maid into your arms, but when she saw that she had conceived, I was despised in her sight. May the Lord judge between you and me" (Genesis 16:5). Sarah pled with her husband to remember their covenant, honor it, and not put her away.

Women often lay aside reason and lead with emotion.

Husbands have not changed through the ages. Abraham loved Sarah, and he told her, "Behold, your maid is in your power; do to her what is good in your sight." Abraham showed his love by yielding his authority for Sarah's security and contentment. Sarah dismissed Hagar and sent her away, but the Lord honored Abraham's seed by sending her back, requiring that she submit — there is that word again — to Sarah. Hagar did.

Sarah took Hagar back, knowing now that her marriage was solid. She tolerated Hagar and Ishmael, a son whom she now had no desire to call her own.

Send Him Away!

Fourteen years after Ishmael's birth, Abraham and Sarah celebrated the birth of a long-promised son. Her maternal instincts took over and she demanded of

Abraham: "Drive out this maid and her son, for the son of this maid shall not be an heir with my son Isaac" (Genesis 21:10). Her demand distressed Abraham for he loved Ishmael. God came to Sarah's aid and told Abraham He would bless the boy and give him twelve sons, so Abraham sent Hagar and Ishmael away. Had Sarah known the pain she would bring to her son Isaac and his descendants —and that pain continues today—she probably would not have made the choice she did. Later, Ishmael's descendants would carry Joseph, her great-grandson, to Egypt in chains to be sold as a slave.

God put woman under man's head for a reason. Men use reason more than feeling. We women often lay aside reason and lead with emotions! Talk over your decisions with your husband and get his input. Loden's critiques of my ideas and plans have saved me a lot of misery. Remember, your husband is the head; you are the neck! Trust him. Trust in the Lord and pray.

Name a bad decision you have made that you failed to discuss with your husband.

Does God have a good reason for every command He gives us? How do you know?

Day 4

Nothing's Too Hard for God

Sarah's journey of faith began with her covenant marriage to Abraham in Ur of the Chaldees. When God called them to leave Haran, He promised them land, children, and a blessing to the entire world through them. Abraham was seventy-five and Sarah was sixty-five when they left Haran.

The Lord made a covenant with Abram and changed his name to Abraham, "father of a multitude," and Sarai became Sarah, "princess." (All her daughters are of royal blood, so act like a princess!) The Lord told Abraham, "She shall be a mother of nations; kings of peoples will come from her" (Genesis 17:16–17). Abraham fell on his face and laughed, saying, "Will a child be born to a man one hundred years old? And will Sarah, who is ninety-nine bear a child?"

Later, the Lord, on his way to Sodom, visited Abraham. Sarah laughed when she overheard Him tell Abraham she would have a child. The Lord asked Abraham why Sarah had laughed and questioned, "Is anything too difficult for the Lord?" (Genesis 18:14). The Lord rebuked her and assured her that by that time next year she would hold a son in her arms. God told them to call him Isaac, 'laughter.'

Had this couple sat idly by and waited for a baby to fall from the sky? No, they believed God would strengthen their bodies, and they acted in faith to bring about the natural process of procreation, trusting the Lord to fulfill His promise.

> Without becoming weak in faith he contemplated his own body, now as good as dead since he was about a hundred years old, and the deadness of Sarah's womb; yet, with respect to the promise of God, he did not waver in unbelief but grew strong in faith, giving glory to God, and being fully assured that what God had promised, He was able also to perform (Romans 4:19–21).

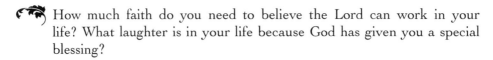 How much faith do you need to believe the Lord can work in your life? What laughter is in your life because God has given you a special blessing?

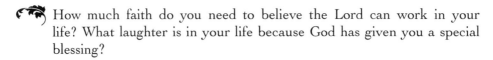 Since the Bible teaches nothing is too hard for God, how do we make that a part of our faith?

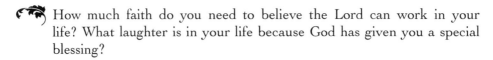 Write down a special request you have of the Lord. Begin praying for it, remembering that when you pray in accordance with the Lord's will, what is best will be done. Continue to ask God to fulfill your desires according to His will.

Tell Your Husband

We have learned that it is not wrong to question our husbands about our fears and feelings. Sarah went to Abraham with her feelings of humiliation regarding Hagar. She explained her problem very well and suggested a solution. Fourteen years later she confronted him again, and he sent away the child he deeply loved. For Abraham's sake, God took care of Ishmael and Hagar.

We should have courage to go to our husbands with any problem and allow him to help us find a solution. However, sometimes we don't need a solution. I told Loden many times, "I don't want you to fix anything. Just hold me tight and tell me everything is going to be okay." After his hug, things were on their way to being okay, and I could pray for the Father to give me the strength I needed. So, you see, we have our husbands and our Father to help us over life's bumpy roads.

In a study about disagreements, Dr. Mark Stengler wrote,

Keeping quiet didn't seem to upset the men, but for women, the study's finding about this so-called "self-silencing" was astonishing. During the decade-long studies, wives who habitually suppressed their feelings and held their tongues during arguments were four times more likely to die [prematurely] than were the women who spoke up (Dr. Mark Stengler, *Bottom Line*, "Good Relationships Are Very Good for Your Health," September, 2008, 7).

Stengler further noted that people who were lonely or in unhappy marriages had more health problems, including depression, anxiety, and fatigue. Dr. Stengler advises that we accept differences, think positive, be appreciative, and be understanding.

Aren't these the very things you learned in the Training Room? We should try to appreciate, not try to change, our husbands. Always think positively, and understand everyone's differences. Respect their views. This is Jesus' teaching!

Therefore if you are presenting your offering at the altar, and there remember that your brother has something against you, leave your offering there before the altar and go; first be reconciled to your brother, and then come and present your offering (Matthew 5:23–24).

Is putting your relationship at peace with your brother more important than worshiping God? Jesus said to leave the gift at the altar and go make things right with your brother. Sarah was not at peace with herself or Abraham until she went to him and straightened out their relationship. It is far easier than you think. Your husband wants to be at peace with you and does not like confrontation. He wants very much for you to be happy and contented.

Pleasure and Procreation

Did Sarah enjoy her sexual life with Abraham? When she overheard the Lord promise Abraham that she would be holding her child within a year, she laughed and asked the question to herself, "After I have become old, shall I have pleasure, my lord being old also?" (Genesis 18:12). The sexual union of a man and a woman is one of the Father's greatest gifts. He gave it for His children's pleasure and not just for procreation. Sex was one of the first commands given when God blessed the first couple: "Be fruitful and multiply, and fill the earth" (Genesis 1:28).

After Eve's creation, God's first comment on the creation was "very good." Don't forget! You are the *very* of creation, so live up to God's idea for you.

How can you enjoy the sexual union more with your husband?

❧ *Day 5* ❧

Adopt Sarah's Personal Traits

Sarah took care of herself. Two kings desired her as a wife because of her beauty. *Mrs.* does not mean "Miserable Rut of a Slob." Your husband appreciates your keeping fit, attractive, and well dressed. How you present yourself reflects on him and his standing.

Tale of Two Men

Once there was a man with a highly visible and responsible job that required wisdom and mature thinking. However, he was the laughingstock of the community because of his wife. She was like a bulldog, a smoking one at that, and when she charged into the grocery store, everyone got out of the way! About five paces behind her was her husband, his head hanging low. The scene was that of a mistress dragging her dog along. There was no need to ask if she was in subjection to her husband. She ruined the respect he should have had among his peers.

On the other end of the spectrum was a married couple in their mid-forties. They were obviously very much in love. In the ticket line at a movie, they were oblivious to others. With great intensity and a special gleam in their eyes, they chatted happily, hanging on to each other's every word. As they walked toward the popcorn stand, he put his arm about her waist. Once again they looked into one another's eyes as they made their choices. I just had to walk over to those strangers, embrace them, and tell them what joy their mutual devotion had given me. The man looked me in the eyes and said, "I love her more than anything on earth." His wife beamed. Do you think she objected to submitting to his love and going to him with her problems and needs?

Money Attitude

Sarah was a very wealthy woman, probably one of the most well-to-do women in her area. However, we find her cooking dinner for Abraham's three strangers who happened by on the way to Sodom. She did not have servants prepare the food. Had she not been willing to cook for the strangers, she would have missed the wonderful blessing of hearing the Lord promise her a child within a year. We never read that Sarah put on airs or paraded her wealth. Her wealth lay in following the Lord alongside her husband who looked for "the city which has foundations, whose architect and builder is God" (Hebrews 11:10).

Sarah knew her wealth lay in her son Isaac and in her faith in following God's way. The Father knows we need money, and He has promised to bless our labors. He is not a stingy Father; He wants us to have nice things in life after we give Him His share.

Do you think the Father is proud to be called your God? How do you help others with your wealth?

Where is true joy found in having money to spare? (cf. Ephesians 4:28). What is the principle God is teaching you in this verse?

Hospitality

On a very short notice, Sarah gave her visitors the best. In the Lord's church, an elder must be hospitable. Who makes hospitality possible? The wife, of course. Having guests in your home makes your husband feel important and teaches the children how to mix with people of all ages. Opening your home to visiting preachers and missionaries is one of the most precious gifts you can give your family. Think what a great blessing Mary, Martha, and Lazarus must have had in being hospitable to Jesus. We are commanded to do likewise: "Be hospitable to one another without complaint. As each one has received a special gift, employ it in serving one another as good stewards of the manifold grace of God" (1 Peter 4:9–10).

I have been very selfish in wanting to house visiting preachers, because then they are captive and we can discuss Bible questions. Our family has fond memories of visiting with many great men of faith up close. Think of the influence this hospitality has on a family! Our visitors' deep faith and missions helped guide us on our journey of faith.

Think of the influence of hospitality on your family!

Invite the young people of the church into your home. There they learn good manners—how you serve, and how you live. You get to know them, and they will feel free to ask for your help when they need counseling, because you have earned their love, respect, and trust.

How often do you have others over for an evening of pleasure?

How are we accountable to be judged according to 1 Peter 4:9–10?

A Mother's Sense of Destiny

Sarah was an excellent mother. When Ishmael began to threaten Isaac, she removed that threat without hesitation. She must have worked diligently with Abraham to instill in Isaac that he had a destiny from the Lord—to carry on the covenant Abraham had with God. We see the result of this training when Isaac willingly became a sacrifice to God. He could have overcome Abraham and run away, but he calmly allowed himself to be placed on the altar just as Jesus allowed Himself to be put on the altar for the sins of the world.

Sarah knew her future and the world's future lay in this special son. She was such a loving mother that Isaac was not comforted after her death until he married Rebekah. Note this tender scene: "Then Isaac brought her into his mother Sarah's tent . . . and he loved her; thus Isaac was comforted after his mother's death" (Genesis 24:67).

After your place as a wife, your most important role is to be a good, loving, godly mother.

Grandmother Loden

My grandparents were dead when I was born, so Loden's "Grandmother Loden"—Vera Pope Loden—was my dear, darling grandmother. She was widowed at an early age.

Grandmother Loden's husband, the first Fernando "Nando" Woody Loden, died young from a ruptured appendix and left her with two sons: Woody II (Loden's father) and Dee. She lost a two-year-old daughter prior to Dee's birth. Grandmother owned property in Hamilton, Alabama, where she and the boys lived until Woody reached college age. Not many children went to high school, much less college, but Grandmother sent her boys to boarding school, and then she sold enough land and timber to move to Oxford, Mississippi, so her Woody could attend pharmacy school.

Dee wanted to be a mail carrier, so she sent him for the appropriate training. Grandmother lived with Woody II and his wife Valeria. When their son James left for college, they moved to Batesville, Mississippi. My Loden was their first-born, Woody III.

Uncle Dee brought Grandmother to Jackson, Mississippi, and built her a small house behind his. When our children were about five and three, we rode a train to see Grandmother. She pulled out photographs—there she was at thirty, with goodness radiating from her lovely face. I asked her, "Grandmother, why didn't you remarry? You were so beautiful!"

He answer became my creed: "Well, Nando was not a Christian, and I determined in my heart that I would devote myself to seeing that my boys were Christians." I sat there and thought to myself, *That is what I will devote myself to—rearing our children in the Lord!*

I am thankful to say that both of Grandmother's sons were elders in the Lord's church. Also, her grandson Woody was an elder, and her other grandson

James died at fifty-nine, a deacon in the church. Loden and I tell our children often, "The greatest gift you give us is to be faithful children of the Lord."

Rear your children with the knowledge of who they are (children of God), why they are here (to prepare themselves for eternity, to teach God's word to others, and to do good deeds), and where they are going (to heaven). Here is a charge from the Lord: "Fathers, do not provoke your children to anger, but bring them up in the discipline and instruction of the Lord" (Ephesians 6:4).

Is Ephesians 6:4 a command? What responsibility do you have in obeying it?

What are you and your husband doing to rear your children in the Lord?

Sarah's Good Pride

Sarah's strength cast out any fear of traveling with Abraham. She faced the trials of being taken as a wife by two kings. She worked beside Abraham and his vast holdings of livestock and servants. She fulfilled her duties as a wife without complaining. She bravely faced pregnancy and childbirth in old age. She protected Isaac and looked after him for thirty-seven years. She faced the future with the same strong faith that Abraham had, and she lived in a way that her God honored her as the mother of all Christian women. What a woman!

Good pride was one of Sarah's characteristics. She was honored to be chosen as Abraham's partner in his covenant with God. Her real pride came at Isaac's birth when she exalted, "Who would have said to Abraham that Sarah would nurse children? Yet I have borne him a son in his old age" (Genesis 21:7).

Take pride in your husband, his mission in life, bearing his children, and bringing them up in the nurture and admonition of the Lord. Be proud of your position as a Christian wife. The Father wants you to have pride resulting from obedience—not a selfish pride based on what you have or where you have been or how smart you are. No matter how good you are, someone is higher than you, and someone is lower. So what does it matter to the world? Jesus' pride was that He always did the will of His Father; He urged everyone in the world to follow in His footsteps. Your only lasting monument is the inscription of your name in the Book of Life. What more could you ask?

What is wrong with having selfish pride?

❧ What does the parable of the foolish man teach you? (Luke 12:16–21).

Summary

I hope you have benefitted from this mother-to-daughter talk. Please live so you are considered a member of Sarah's very special "daughters" list—to enjoy the blessings the Father gives you as His special ruby, as well as the wonderful love you will receive from your husband. You will find that the more you grow into God's woman, the more you will find peace in the middle of storms, contentment in dire circumstances, and love beyond measure from your beloved. I felt proud when Loden boasted, "Patsy takes care of all my needs." I always felt, "My job is well done." May you have the same joy and pride I had in my fifty-one-year journey of faith with Loden. God bless you, my dear, as you try to imitate our beloved mother, Sarah.

Memory Verse

"Therefore be imitators of God as dear children. And walk in love, as Christ also has loved us and given Himself for us, an offering and a sacrifice to God for a sweet-smelling aroma."

Ephesians 5: 1–2

Bones represent the life of a person; marrow is where the body rebuilds itself with blood. If you are not Sarah's daughter, then whose daughter are you? There is only one answer: Satan's. Is that clear and important for you to understand? There's no middle ground, no gray area. Either you are or you aren't Sarah's daughter.

My Take-Home

Goal: *To learn what submission truly means and to commit myself to being submissive to my husband.* A strong commitment automatically solves many problems because your husband will not have to try constantly to establish his position. You will respect him as God commanded. You will continue working on yourself to become the daughter of Sarah and to wear her name with pride. You will learn to have a positive attitude and not allow negatives to drag you down.

Some Truths: Sarah's life teaches us truths about marital intimacy. The following is one man's summary of the five levels on the path to intimacy:

❧ *Speaking in clichés:* The small talk we have at the beginning of our marriage.

❧ *Sharing facts:* There is no controversy, just daily happenings of each of you.

❧ *Sharing opinions:* Once you begin to share your opinions, concerns, and expectations, you both are at greater risk for starting an argument. Opinions are the ground where battles break out, but there are skills that can overcome differences. If you have not learned how to handle arguments at this level, you are at risk for developing one or all of the four divorce factors.

❧ *Sharing feelings:* By this level, you feel safe and can share every care, every dream, and every opinion because you feel safe with one another. You discuss differences and agree on win/win solutions. Conflicts reveal that a person's feelings and needs are not being understood or fulfilled.

> (Patsy's comments: By this stage, both of you should have the desire to please each other more than yourselves, because you will have developed agape love. One young wife told me toward the end of the course, "Since I have been in this class I have said 'I am sorry' more than I ever did in our thirteen years of marriage." You learn to cherish your husband, and you want him to have peace and contentment, so you work toward giving him the love to achieve this level. And Dear One, it is so nice!)

❧ *Sharing needs:* Level five is different from the previous levels. This is where you feel safe to share your own deepest needs. You feel safe, secure, and intimate with each other.
—Gary Smalley, *Secrets to Lasting Love*, Simon and Schuster, 240

My Homework

1. Continue to pray for the Father and Spirit to work in your life to mold you into one of Sarah's daughters.

2. Continue to write your love letter.

3. Have you had your date?

4. Keep learning how to caress your husband by your touches, kisses, words, and actions.

5. This week's "doing" exercise is to sit and look at yourself. What you see in your husband is what you judge in yourself. As Sarah said, "May God judge between you and me." What we judge negatively is often characteristic of our own lives. Spend this week reflecting on negatives you hold against your husband, and see if they are in your inner being. Work on removing them. Your goal is the total acceptance and appreciation of your dear husband. Pray the Father will help you in this exercise of self-exorcism of your "little

demons." Through His word that pours into your soul, the Spirit will help you to sweep your house clean. Refurnish it with good deeds.

Marriage Bill of Rights

Just as we enjoy the protection of our Bill of Rights, those in a marriage should have certain rights granted to them. They are as follows:

The right to good will from the other.

The right to emotional support.

The right to be heard by the other and to be responded to with courtesy.

The right to have your own view, even if your mate has a different one.

The right to have your feelings and experiences acknowledged as real.

The right to clear and informative answers to questions that concern what is legitimately your business.

The right to live free from accusation and blame.

The right to live free from criticism and judgment.

The right to have your work and your interests spoken of with respect.

The right to encouragement.

The right to live free from emotional and physical threat.

The right to live free from angry outbursts and rage.

The right to be called by no name that devalues you.

The right to be asked respectfully rather than to be ordered.

—*The Verbally Abusive Relationship* by Patricia Evans, page 122

Will you say amen to these? Give them to your husband as you would want them given to you. They follow biblical principles. Don't ever forget Ephesians 2:10: "For we are His workmanship, created in Christ Jesus for good works, which God prepared beforehand so that we would walk in them." You were created to be your husband's suitable helper; that is where you will find your joy and peace. Your marriage is the best "good work" you can have, so realize that its success is the most wonderful accomplishment you can desire.

Week 8

Wife to Wife

From the Father of the Bride: "So then we pursue the things which make for peace and the building up of one another" (Romans 14:19).

Thought for the Day: "All I ever wanted in life was someone to love me." This statement came from a young husband in a marriage with an unloving wife. Would your husband feel the same? Just because you think you are a good wife does not make it so in your husband's eyes. Ask yourself often: "If I do not follow the way of Sarah, then am I a loving wife?" The result is a higher standard of conduct.

From Mother Sarah: How do you think I felt on the day I stood at my tent door and watched Abraham go away with my precious Isaac to offer him as a sacrifice to God? Do you think I knew my husband well enough to know something profound was about to take place? Do you think I had the same faith he had that the Lord would raise Isaac from the dead? Do you think I shared some of the feelings Mary had at the foot of the cross when her Son was being offered as a sacrifice for the world? God's command was designed to test my husband, but it tested me as well.

From Wisdom: "By wisdom a house is built, and by understanding it is established; and by knowledge the rooms are filled with all precious and pleasant riches" (Proverbs 24:3–4). You will not only build your house of love, but you will furnish it according to the way you treat your husband. Your home will be a peaceful castle filled with love, laughter, and peace, or it will be a cavern filled with echoes of fear-producing, disturbing sounds and unknown pitfalls.

From Queen Mother: "She does him good and not evil all the days of her life" (Proverbs 31:12).

Day 1

Little Foxes

Join me once again as we step into our imaginary house of love. Loden and I wanted to discover how to furnish our home with happiness and peace.

We walked hand-in-hand into the living room. Wisdom, Queen Mother, and Mother Sarah were there to greet us. But who was the lovely vision of beauty in the fourth chair? Mother Sarah introduced us: "Patsy, meet Solomon's wife Shulamith, 'Peace.' How do you feel about the significance of her name?"

Wisdom, Queen Mother, and Sarah left the room so Shulamith could instruct us in filling our home with precious and pleasant riches. We eagerly hung on to every word.

Catch the Foxes

Now it is your turn to receive instruction from Shulamith. In order for each room of your home to ooze with love, peace, and joy, you must desire each quality; they are jewels for your furnishings. Young Shulamith learned from her wise husband Solomon, who penned the saga of their love story, Song of Solomon. Just as Shulamith's name means peace, so you should desire peace with your husband. This peace is not achieved overnight; you must work at it daily.

Think of your own house of love. Imagine that when you open the door, a horrific sight greets you: the bedclothes are shredded, the curtains hang in tatters, and the chair legs are broken and beaten. Pillows have been ravaged and thousands of feathers float from the ceiling. Why? Because little foxes are running about barking, gnawing, and making havoc of everything their teeth can tear.

Problems in the bedroom? —Problems throughout the house!

"Catch the foxes for us, the little foxes that are ruining the vineyards while our vineyards are in blossom" (Song of Solomon 2:15). Solomon's words apply to your home. It is your vineyard. You are the vines, and your love is to blossom and produce fruit.

In Solomon's day, these little foxes sneaked into his vineyard, burrowed under the vines, and ate the roots. Then the vines withered and died—fruitless! So it is in your marriage. If you don't remove the pesky little foxes, those negatives will undermine your love; your marriage will not grow and flourish. Which walls are at greatest risk? Romantic and sexual love walls are easily threatened. You do not want to live in a lop-sided house, do you?

Often it is the little things in life that cause us the most problems. The little foxes represent irritations, squabbles, and differences of opinions. Think of challenges that interrupt your family's peace: money issues, discipline of children, sexual concerns, career choices, housing decisions, spiritual responsibilities, and personal habits. If these small foxes are not faced and conquered, your peace will be broken and your love flow will become static.

Sarah taught us to stand together and be one, but these little foxes can destroy the most intimate of all your rooms; they will break your life. You see, if there are problems in the bedroom, there are problems throughout the house. Don't let these foxes run loose in your love house! Learn how to settle your differences in a loving way.

If you don't get rid of the foxes, the walls of your house will be gnawed away and you will be left without a roof over your head. Little foxes can eat your heart, and you won't even realize it until you wake up one day devoid of feeling! Then how will you lavish love on your adored mate?

 What are some little foxes in your relationship with your husband?

Selfishness

What are some common little foxes? And how can we eliminate them? *Self-centeredness* is the lair of all little foxes. Your house of love will crumble if you allow selfishness to gain a foothold. After all, marriage is no longer about "I" but "we."

 What does Matthew 6:23 teach about self? Contrast that passage with Galatians 2:20?

When we die to self and start living to please our husbands, we are far happier. Philippians 2:1–16 gives this principle. Meditate on verse 2. How does it apply to your marriage?

What is the command of Philippians 2:3–4? (Notice it is a command, not a suggestion.)

🌿 What was Christ's attitude in Philippians 2:5–11?

"Work out your own salvation with fear and trembling" (Philippians 2:12). "Work out" means to gain the most from one's work. A miner works his lode until he has extracted all the ore. A farmer works his field for maximum yield. So you must work to be the best you can be for Christ. By absorbing scripture, you are allowing the Holy Spirit to create you anew in the image of Christ (2 Corinthians 3:18).

Six Truths from Philippians 2

Die to yourself every day. Crucify your selfishness and follow Jesus. (Notice this is to be done daily or we will slip backward.)

Eliminate selfishness totally. The word *nothing* means exactly that: not one thing should be done from selfish motives. My actions reflect my husband's wishes.

Make sure your husband is your number one—your most important person. You do have personal interests that you should follow—health, rest, personal appearance—but he is to be primary.

Follow the example of Christ's emptying Himself to do the work His Father sent Him to do, to seek and save the lost. Will I empty myself so my primary work will be a suitable helper of my husband?

Work with the talents God gave you. Work to become like Christ. Your old self has died, and He is to live within you. Give Him glory and honor! God derives pleasure from your life.

Do everything from a heart of love and gratitude. Don't complain, grumble, or dispute with your husband. You will be like a star shining in heaven—a glimmering ruby. As a star and as a ruby, you reflect the light of the Son of God!

Day 2

More Little Foxes

Anger

Anger is one of the worst foxes in a marriage. In Galatians 5:20 anger is listed as a work of the flesh.

Luke's ever-present smile served him well as a volunteer greeter in the local emergency room. While on duty one day, an ugly scene was being played out just a few blocks away. Faces contorted with screaming anger and biting words filled the air. A kitchen knife flashed in the ray of sunlight streaming through the window. The screaming stopped! Then the wail of an ambulance cut through the stillness.

When the EMTs wheeled the gurney into the emergency room, Luke witnessed a terrible sight. A knife in the victim's eye was protruding from his mouth. What strong man had inflicted this dastardly deed? The victim's wife! Terrified, she called for help. She was arrested while her husband fought for his life.

That same week, the newspaper told of a husband who forced his children to gaze upon their mother whom he had just shot to death. These are two extreme cases of anger gone wrong. The relationship between these two couples deteriorated and ended in death, because the little fox of anger was not driven from the vineyard.

Ephesians 4:26 tells us to be angry without sinning—neither should we let the sun go down on our anger. Don't give Satan any opportunity to get his little foxes into your life. Sometimes anger is justified, but love covers a multitude of sins (1 Peter 4:8). Is it better to get angry and spout words of ill will or to address an issue calmly and reach a mutual agreement? Which gets rid of the little fox in a loving way?

 Give an instance of a situation in which anger is the best solution. What is the best way to handle damaged emotions?

Anger usually results when my rights, as I see them, are violated. Therefore, I have a right to be angry and lash out as I see fit, to discipline the one who has dared cross my path. How many times do you count the words *I* and *my* in that statement? Do these words sound like an ego trip? How many times do the Gospels record occasions of Jesus' anger? You will find the answer in Mark 3:1–6. Try to find another.

Anger is Satan's way of handling a problem. Love's answer is far different, much gentler. No one can make you angry without your permission. Remember that truth from another lesson? Don't forget it.

 How will Ephesians 4:29 help you handle your anger?

Lying

There is never an excuse for lying to your husband. Lying is one of the sins that will keep us from heaven (Revelation 21:8). Lying was first on the list of impurities that a child of God is to lay aside (Ephesians 4:20–25).

Once you have lied to one who trusts you, it is very difficult for that person to regain trust. A lie not only kills the body, but it also kills the soul. It is far better to suffer the consequences of truth than to destroy a relationship with lies.

Forgiveness is available if we confess our faults; isn't that far better than lying to evade the truth and then being caught in a web of deceit? To live in truth is to live in peace; you do not want to do or say anything to jeopardize your husband's confidence in you. Truth does not need a good memory; lies do.

Have you ever been caught in a lie? How did you feel? Was it worth the lie?

Selfishness, anger, and lying are common little foxes. Name some others.

Day 3

Help "Suitable"

In Song of Solomon we read the lovers' descriptions of each other. The lover describes Shulamith in man's terms; on the other hand, she praises him in a woman's way. Men and women definitely see things from different perspectives.

Shulamith teaches us to go back to the beginning to understand our roles of husband and wife (Song of Solomon 4:1–16; 5:10–16). We learn to recognize the differences between the sexes. Understanding our husband's purpose helps us to eliminate little foxes before they ruin the home.

Go to the scriptures and examine God's intent for humanity. Man was the creation of the Godhead. Man (including woman) was created in the likeness of God for companionship (1 Corinthians 11:7–12). God came into the Garden of Eden in the cool of the evening to commune with Adam and Eve. Adam's divine place was the head of the home. His tasks included ruling over and naming the animals, keeping the garden, and directing the spiritual affairs of the home (Genesis 1:26–30; 2:8, 15, 19–20).

Before Eve's creation, all living things were made from dust, but she was created from the very body of Adam! God gave her a special place in creation and in Adam's mind.

> The woman was created, not of dust of the earth, but from a rib of Adam, because she was formed for an inseparable unity and fellowship of life with the man, and the mode of her creation was to lay the actual foundation for the moral ordinance of marriage. As the moral idea of the unity of the human race required that man should not be created as a genus or plurality, so the moral relation of the two persons establishing the unity of the race required that man should be created first, and then the woman from the body of the man. By this priority . . . the man, and the dependence of the woman upon the man, are established as an ordinance of divine creation. This ordinance of God forms the root of that tender love with which the man loves the woman as himself, and by which marriage becomes a type of the fellowship of love and life which exists between the Lord and His church (Ephesians 5:32) (*Keil & Delitzsch Commentary on the Old Testament*, 89–90).

Notice that after each day of creation God declared, "It is good," but after the creation of Eve, He said, "It is very good!" That should show us how delightfully unique the Godhead considered woman. She was the crowning act of creation, very special to both man and to God. Don't allow anyone to teach you that God holds women inferior to men. All through the Bible the protection of widows was uppermost in the Father's mind. Israel's sin of neglecting and misusing widows and children was one of the reasons He destroyed that nation. In New Testament times, the early church was charged to practice "pure religion," seeing to the needs of widows (James 1:27). God esteems women highly.

Glued Together

Eve was to be everything to Adam that he lacked in himself. She was to be his companion, his sex partner, the mother to his children, and his helper in tending the garden. She was to give him what he could not give himself, just as God gives us what we cannot give ourselves and provides protection for our weakness.

When Adam saw Eve, he excitedly exclaimed, " 'This is now bone of my bones, and flesh of my flesh; she shall be called Woman, because she was taken out of Man.' For this reason a man shall leave his father and his mother, and be joined to his wife; and they shall become one flesh" (Genesis 2:23–24). This truth was repeated by Jesus in Matthew 19:4–6 and then by Paul Ephesians 5:31. Is it important to God?

The law of marriage was given by God from the beginning and, as Jesus says in Matthew 19, it is the law that will stand until the end of time, "From the beginning" regulates all marriages—past, present, and future until the end of time.

Marriage was meant to be the union of a man and woman into one, *Cleave* means "to cling, stick, stay close, and follow closely." It carries the idea of two sides becoming one by gluing them together so they no longer are two but one unit. So when we say "I do" in the wedding ceremony, it is no longer I, but we! The woman's role was to be under man's arm for her protection and guidance, and to give him strength when he needed help and loving care. Each was to feel the need to nurture and protect the other at all times and to supply lacking qualities, thus complementing one another.

"From the beginning" regulates all marriages.

His and Hers

When Adam and Eve sinned, both failed in their God-given roles. As a result, death came to both body and soul. It was not until Jesus came that man's sin was blotted out, and once again man could become a son of God as was intended in Adam's creation.

Eve stepped out of her role of looking to Adam as her head and her religious guide. Adam failed to give Eve the protection and strength she needed to repel Satan's lie. Adam allowed Eve to believe the lie and eat the forbidden fruit, and he partook with her rather than using his God-given authority to steer her clear of Satan's lie. He knew what he was doing, but Eve was deceived.

🕊 Read 1 Timothy 2:9–15. What are you being taught in these verses?

Appreciating your husband's God-given role and your special role should be a blessing. Your husband will keep you in a loving way if you truly respect him as your head. A head does not mistreat its body but takes care of it and nurtures it. So be thankful for the special place the Father has given you—at the side of a loving husband to help him in the ways he cannot help himself.

God allotted three main roles to husbands: headship of the home, religious leader of the home, and providing for the physical care and nurturing of the wife and children.

🕊 Read the following scriptures: 1 Timothy 5:8; 1 Timothy 2:8; Ephesians 6:1–4 (pay special attention to verse 4); Ephesians 5:22–33; 1 Peter 3:7. Outline a clear picture of the husband's role and how he is to lead.

🕊 How is a husband to love his wife?

God allotted four main roles to wives: a helper to care for the husband's needs, the main caretaker of the home, a child bearer, and a coworker with the husband to rear the children in the Lord.

🕊 Write a truth from 1 Timothy 5:14.

Why Men?

I had to grow into accepting Loden as my head. But once I did, I found life more peaceful, more loving, and more secure. I certainly had far fewer worries!

Why did God give the lead to men? The differences in the make-up of men and women are part of the reason. The male and female are different mentally, physically, and emotionally. Men tend to be left-brained, dominated with strength in math, physics, and engineering. They tend to choose work which uses the large muscles and careers that use reasoning. Women are generally right-brained, leaning toward social work, teaching, art, music, nursing—occupations that require emotion. The physical make-up is also quite different. Heart rate is different, blood flow is different (as is its make-up), and muscle is different. Bone structure is different. Even artificial knees and hips are designed differently for men and women.

Physical stamina is greater in men than it is in women, but women endure pain better; they are more caring and have more patience. Their brains are wired differently. The logical approach is provided by the father, and the emotional approach is provided by the mother—complementary characteristics in the rearing of children.

About Children: Stand Firm and United

When our children were near age ten, they began to argue with me. They no longer wanted Momma telling them what to do. I requested that Loden begin to counsel them in their decisions. We women can take from one second to ten days to decide if something is okay. We have to weigh everything and then analyze it for all the pros and cons before making a decision. However, Daddy can make up his mind by the time the question "May I—?" is out of their mouths.

You will have much rest and peace of mind when you learn to allow your husband to be the decision-maker. It won't be long until the children come and request, "Talk to Daddy so he will let me—." Then you must stand by your man; whatever Daddy says is what you say. I learned not to answer the children until I had cleared with Loden what he had told them.

Dear One, trust him, trust him, trust him. You do not know how boys think or how to control them, and Daddy has been there. This puts a peaceful atmosphere in the home, and it takes a very big burden off your shoulders.

Confrontational questions do not help solve problems.

Therefore, the rule should be, "Whatever Daddy says is it." Later if you want to talk about his decision—notice I said talk, not argue—do so privately. Say something to the effect, "I am so thankful you make these hard decisions easily. It is more difficult for me to think through them so quickly. Your logic will help me to grow more in my reasoning ability. Usually, I can read your mind, but not this time. I did not catch why you made that decision for the children. Please explain it so I can help them understand if they question me about it."

Confrontational questions and charges against your husband do not help solve problems. "Why did you do that?" "I can't believe you made such a decision!" "How dare you make that decision without consulting me!" How would those questions make you feel? If you want your husband's strength to shield you, be gentle and ask for help; do not berate or challenge him. Your every word must build up and give grace to the hearer. The children will test you to see if you will break, so at all cost, keep a united front for their sakes.

When They Kick and Scream

Children need to know that you are their anchor and that you won't change even when they kick and scream. I discovered this firsthand when Lisa came home from college for the summer. She asked if she could go with her boyfriend to a weekend social club meeting. "Talk to your daddy about it," I said, "but I don't think he'll go for it. Besides, a proper young woman does not go off alone on a weekend trip with her boyfriend. And I don't think you want me to go as your chaperon!" We talked about what would take place when it was time to retire for the night. She finally looked at me and said, "Oh, Mother, I didn't really want to go. I just wanted to see what you would do."

Keep a firm grip on what is proper, and do not give in to your children's foolish desires. You will regret it for the rest of your life if you give in and something unforeseen happens to your precious child. If you bend when your children test you, they will be disappointed in you. We told our children to use us as a shield and say, "My parents would be very sad if I did that."

My friend is very protective of her teen daughter. She always meets her daughter's friends and their parents before she allows her child to visit them. She says, "Our girl is too precious for us to take a chance on any bad thing happening to her." What a mother! How much better it would have been for Eli, Eli's sons, and Israel had Eli said, "No, my sons, you will no longer sin against the Lord." The Lord held Eli responsible for his grown children's conduct because he did not chastise them for their sins. Children do not usually die from hearing the word *no*.

Two Halves Make One

It is as Adam exclaimed: it takes two of us to make a whole! You and your husband have different talents, different tastes, different desires, different aims in life, different family types, and different friends, but putting the two together makes for a better whole than the two halves acting individually could ever be.

It is not that one gender is superior to the other! We are joint-heirs with Christ. The two of you blending and recognizing that one is more apt in a certain area makes for a solid marital base. Use that base to the advantage of the whole; don't be jealous or bitter because you do not have a certain ability. Many marriages are marred by jealously between mates. It should not be so. Victory should be felt by both when one is victorious. A marriage based on God's principles cherishes the talents that each brings to the union. Each partner gives the other the freedom to develop talents for the good of the relationship. Each cheers the other on, encourages the other, and is honored when the other achieves a goal. As you blend together, there are no longer two but truly one.

In some points the man is superior, and in other points he yields to the superiority of his wife. Loden always thought my book knowledge to be far superior to his, and he used that to his advantage. I knew he was way beyond me in the business world, so I definitely deferred to his knowledge and felt blessed to have him by my side.

Husbands and wives learn to predict each other's actions. Each knows what pleases the other, how far to press an issue, and how to love so both are totally contented and happy. Loden and I told each other daily how proud we were of the other and how much we admired our partner's work for the Lord. We each knew our area of work and accomplishments. We cheered one another, gave support, and sat on the sideline to bask in the other's glow. That's living, Dear One.

The work of a married couple is not complete until they are parted by death. As long as both live, there is more loving to be learned, shared, and given to each other and to the world. So freely use the words: "I am so proud of you," "I am so glad I married you," "You mean the world to me," and "I love you so much." Add your own words of love and praise, but give generous doses daily—better still, hourly.

What praise can you give your husband today?

Day 4

Caterpillars and Butterflies

What is your life's pattern from your birth in baptism to your dying breath? Daily you are to offer yourself as a holy, living sacrifice to God as you are one of His priests in His temple, your body. Each day you are also to have a continuous transformation of mind.

> Therefore I urge you, brethren, by the mercies of God, to present your bodies a living and holy sacrifice, acceptable to God, which is your spiritual service of worship. And do not be conformed to this world, but be transformed by the renewing of your mind, so that you may prove what the will of God is, that which is good and acceptable and perfect (Romans 12:1–2).

Transformed is from the Greek word from which we get *metamorphosis*, meaning change. Do you recognize this word as the process which changes a caterpillar into a lovely butterfly? *An Expository Dictionary of New Testament Words* by W. E. Vines defines *transformed*:

> The obligation to undergo a complete change which, under the power of God, will find expression in character and conduct; *morphe* lays stress on the inward change, *schema* lays stress on the outward; the present continuous tenses indicate a process; 2 Corinthians 3:18 describes believers as being "transformed into the same image": (i.e., of Christ in all His moral excellencies), the change being effected by the Holy Spirit.

You were once a caterpillar eating the leaves or fruit of the world. Then you obeyed the law of Christ and were buried in a watery grave of baptism similar to the caterpillar's spinning itself into a cocoon. When nature's law is completed, a beautiful butterfly emerges—very different from the worm! It then enjoys eating the nectar of the Father's sweetest flowers.

You rose from baptism no longer a worldly creature. The Father's law of salvation in the blood of Christ changed you from a worldly creature into a heavenly creature in the likeness of Christ. You now drink His living water and eat His bread of life, looking forward to eating from the Tree of Life in Heaven's fair land.

The Butterfly Effect

As a butterfly and as Christ's priest we have a different way of looking at life, at love, and at ourselves. Each day we have to crucify self and follow Jesus. This leads us to what physiologists call the "butterfly effect." Jesus would call it going the second mile. For the sake of using the butterfly as our emblem, we'll call this second-mile mentality the "butterfly effect." I'll try to paraphrase this truth of physics in "woman talk."

A butterfly is resting on a leaf sipping nectar from a beautiful Amazon lily. After draining the delicate juices, she decides to flit to another lily across the way. When her wings begin to flutter, she sets off a phenomenon: the wave movement begins to stir the air, and by the time that single wing flap gets to Mississippi, it is a category-four hurricane!

Difficulties dissolve into happy endings—not shouting matches.

Would you care to try to explain that in physics? Well, it is so, I am told, and so is the psychological phenomenon of the butterfly effect. This wonderful concept will cause many difficult situations to dissolve into happy endings instead of shouting matches.

When differences of opinion end in a stalemate, one person can make a difference by giving a little. That encourages the other person to change a bit and work at a common solution. You might simply say, "May I tell you why I see it this way? If after you hear me you are still set on your decision, I will follow without complaining." So often, this kind inquiry will have the butterfly effect to calm a storm.

When we lived in Memphis and Loden was commuting to his job in Mississippi, he spent up to fourteen hours a day away from home. We agreed that he was away too much, so we decided to move. But to where? I told him I would go to Batesville, but I could not agree to move to the place he preferred— I gave him my reasons. He chose Batesville to please me, and we both were satisfied. The butterfly effect worked.

When you are in a stalemate, flap your wings before the situation intensifies with a statement like this: "I am sorry I made you unhappy with my attitude. Can we start over and come up with some different solutions to our problem?" You are not at that point changing any of your thoughts, but you are taking a big step by expressing sorrow for causing a rift in your relationship. You removed the big boulder of pride, so a new dialog can begin.

Here are some problem-solving ideas—biblical, polite, and face-saving— that I have gleaned from various marriage counselors.

Define the problem. Set aside a block of time free of interruption to discuss the matter: "Here is what I think we need to decide." Timing is important. Make sure both of you are rested and don't feel rushed into a quick decision.

Discuss the problem. Be calm. Avoid extreme and argumentive phrases such as "You always," "You never," "I will never," and "You can't ever make me change."

Do not use demeaning descriptions of one another. "I can't believe you are that foolish." "You are an idiot to believe that." "No one in their right mind could think such a thing."

Use the phrase "I feel." "I feel this way when you say that or do that." You are not judging. You are using emotion to communicate without regard to his intentions. Your husband now has an open door to come back with his reasoning and his feelings—which may be far from what you thought. He feels free to defend himself with reason instead of anger.

Never judge your husband. "I know you did that because you . . ." or "You are just doing that to make me feel . . ." No one can know what someone else is really thinking, so why make the judgment? Only God knows what is in the heart of another person.

Listen attentively. Look your husband in the eye and concentrate on what he is saying—without interruption. Give rapt attention to understand the true meaning of the ideas your husband is presenting. Take time to digest the words.

Summarize your understanding of his thoughts. Simply say, "Here is what I understand you to be saying. Am I correct or did you intend something different? Wait for his answer: "Yes, you are correct," or "No, you did not understand." Continue this dialogue until you fully grasp your husband's exact position.

Decide on a solution. List potential solutions no matter how ridiculous they may seem. A silly thought may trigger a truly brilliant solution. Be open to a new way of solving the problem.

Sift through the combined solutions. Select the best option and work together to carry out the solution to a satisfactory end.

Postpone the solution if you must. If no solution can be reached after these steps, pray together and ask the Father to provide a solution. Set a meeting time to tackle the problem again to attempt to arrive at a win/win solution. It will happen eventually if you both will practice good problem-solving techniques.

Remember, there is a solution. You just have not found it as yet. Keep praying and asking for wisdom to find the right solution for both of you.

Always practice the butterfly effect.

Write your definition of the butterfly effect. How do you intend to use its beauty with your mate?

Day 5

Metamorphosis

Solomon, the wisest man of his day, made this sage observation: "There is an appointed time for everything. And there is a time for every event under heaven" (Ecclesiastes 3:1). Your baptism marks the beginning of your life as a butterfly. Jesus told of an unclean spirit who went out of a man. The man then swept his house. The spirit returned to find the house empty and clean. He returned with seven other spirits who inhabited the house. (Matthew 12:43–45). The man's mistake was in not filling his house with good things. With all your sins forgiven and left in your watery grave of baptism, you must immediately begin to furnish your house with the jewels of Christ, or your sins will return and multiply.

> For if, after they have escaped the defilements of the world by the knowledge of the Lord and Savior Jesus Christ, they are again entangled in them and are overcome, the last state has become worse for them than the first. For it would be better for them not to have known the way of righteousness, than having known it, to turn away from the holy commandment handed on to them. It has happened to them according to the true proverb, "A dog returns to its own vomit," and, "A sow after washing, returns to wallowing in the mire" (2 Peter 2:20–21).

The dog and the sow did not change their natures, so they naturally went back to doing what their nature dictated. When you are a new creature, you

must learn new ways and change your nature, or you will naturally return to your old worldly habits. Incidentally, the proverb about the dog was written by Solomon (Proverbs 26:11).

Furnish Your House from Romans 12

Do you want to furnish your house with the jewels of Christ? Let's study Romans 12 together.

Verse 3 instructs us to *not _____ more highly of _____ than he ought, but to have sound _____*. We have to die to self and think of others more than self, with special attention on serving our love. Jesus said, "It is more blessed to give than receive" (Acts 20:35),

Verses 4–8 teach *there are many _____ in one body, and each has gifts "according to the _____ given to us."* Don't forget your husband is very different from you and his gifts are not like yours, so cherish him for his gifts, just as you want to be appreciated for your gifts. Think how dull it would be if both of you were exactly alike! Both of you are commanded to increase your talents.

Your goal is to encourage your mate to develop himself to his potential. There is an old axiom that goes something like this: "If you treat a man like he is, he will always remain as he is, but if you treat a man the way you want him to be, he will grow to be that." It is so true. Let your husband know he is capable of being all he can be. Praise him for his growth and encourage him to keep trying new things.

Verse 9: *Let love be without _____*. Always be honest in your words and actions, but always find a way to commend your husband so he will be well fed. He knows when you are not being honest with him. He might say, as Loden did, "I know what you are doing, but I like it; keep doing it." We all like to be built up by the ones we love the most.

Verse 10: *Be _____ to one another in brotherly _____*. Your husband should be the apple of your eye and the focus of your thinking. Remember, you are the one who surrounds him with love and protection. Learn his habits and protect him, even in little things. My Loden never checked the driveway before he backed out of our carport, so when company came, I showed them where to park to be well out of his way. Our daughter says, "Mother, don't set yourself up for failure." Broccoli is healthful food, but if your husband hates it, don't try to force it on him. Find another veggie that will provide him with the vitamins he needs, or just give him a good vitamin.

Verse 10: *Give _____ to one another in honor.* Dear One, this is to us as mothers. Do not let your children come first in your life. Your husband is to be first, only after Jesus. When he knows that, and you show him that he is number one, you will be thrilled with how he treats you and wants to please you. Being a loving wife is truly rather selfish, because your husband will want to treat you just as lovingly as you treat him. You won't have to worry, because taking advantage of his wife is not in the average man's nature. Men are very simple in their desires, and if we meet them, they are only too happy to see that we are contented, because they do not want to give up their good life.

Verse 11: *Not _____ behind in diligence, _____ in spirit, _____ the Lord.* This further emphasizes how we are not to lag in our diligence to serve those we love. In other words, do it more, not less. The older your man gets, the more you have to watch out for him, protect him from falls, and take care of many other little things he can no longer do. Be diligent, not slothful in your service to him. You are serving the Lord when you serve others, especially your husband.

Verse 12: _____ *in hope,* _____ *in tribulation, devoted to* _____. Here is the making of a contented soul, one that is close to Jesus, and one who is centered in life. Hope, patience, and prayer are attributes a Christian is to have in abundance. Work on it, My Dear.

Verse 13: _____ *to the needs of the* _____, *practicing* _____. Turn outward to serve community, friends, and church. We are not to live to ourselves but to show Jesus' way to the world. It is well worth the effort. The home is where people feel connected. If invited into someone's home, you feel welcomed to friendship with your host. Friendships open doors to teach Jesus' love. What a compliment such a thought gives to others! Do you see why God instructs the church not to eat with impenitent Christians? Eating shows approval; the erring will see that he must repent to God to be accepted in the family once again (1 Corinthians 5:11–13).

Verse 14: _____ *those who* _____ *you. Bless and do not* _____. It is by loving that you reach people, not by cursing and hurting. That is the way of the world. When hurt, we are to bless. Although not easy, giving blessings for cursings leads to peace and contentment. Jesus turned many of His persecutors to Him by His words and actions. So can you. When your husband uses hurtful words, reply to him with kindness and gentleness and in a spirit of love. Turn his ire into shame. God will strengthen you to give blessings instead of cursings to those who injure you.

Verse 15: *Rejoice with those who rejoice, and* _____ *with them that* _____. Crying with others is easy, but we have to work on being thankful for others' blessings, especially as it applies to the marriage relationship. Jealously and envy have no place in a couple's life. What one receives, the other must treasure.

Verse 16: *Be of the same _____ toward one another; do not be haughty in _____, but associate with the _____.* If you are not of the same mind, you will have continuous misery. Open your arms to those who truly need a friend, not just to those who are similar to you. Get out of your comfort zone.

Verse 17: *Never pay back _____ for _____ to anyone. _____ what is right in the sight of all men.* You should not try to get even with anyone. Love is our way of life, and we never veer from it. You never act ugly to your husband even if he does so to you. You use the butterfly effect to bring him around. "I am sorry you are angry with me. What can I do to make amends?" Those simple words bring about much more peace than if you strike back. What is right in the sight of all men? The fruit of the Spirit. There is no law against it (Galatians 5:23). But there are many laws against the fruit of the world. When you act in a loving, Christlike way, the other person will usually feel shame for misconduct; if not, attempts to reason are futile.

Verse 18: *If _____, so far as it depends upon _____, be at _____ with all.* Angry words must not come from you. You are a woman of peace, and you will live that way at all cost. Jesus did not retaliate. Even while suffering, He "uttered no threats, but kept entrusting Himself to Him who judges righteously." You are a woman of peace, not war. A child of God does not stoop to the level of the world's way in any situation.

Verse 19: *_____ is Mine, I _____ repay says the Lord.* We humans are incapable of making the right judgment for an offense against us. Only the Father has the wisdom to punish justly, and He says, "I will," so you can depend on it. Who would have thought to have worms eat King Herod as punishment for allowing himself to be viewed as a god? Only God! We must leave such to our Father, for when we plot revenge, it lowers us to the level of the person we want to hurt. Our mission is to love, not to punish. That demeans us as a child of God.

Verse 20: *If your enemy is hungry _____ him and if he is thirsty _____ for in so doing you will heap burning coals of fire on his head.* Kindness in the face of cruelty is often humbling, especially for your loving husband who is taking his bad day out on you. What he needs is some hot food and a glass of orange juice to raise his sugar level. Be sympathetic with his feelings, and he will bless you later. Jesus always made allowances for those in need, and He was full of compassion for those struggling with life, so must we be especially kind to our loves.

Verse 21: *Do not be _____ by evil, but overcome _____ with _____.* Good deeds will never be forgotten, and doing good to those who do evil to you will cause those who know it to think well of you. You never know what influence you will have. Especially in regard to your mate, you need to overcome any hurtful deeds with loving kindness in order to learn a better way and to teach him a better way.

The Rare Jewel of Forgiveness

What subject must you learn to avoid? From Song of Solomon 5:2–8, we learn that Shulamith was asleep when her lover came to her, but she had washed her feet before going to bed. You know the saying: "If an excuse is needed, any will do! She "did not feel like it," or we might say in today's language, "Not tonight; I have a headache." Her lover was hurt, but he left a sweet smelling ointment on the door handle. Shulamith became conscience stricken, arose from bed, and tried in vain to find her husband. The watchmen of the city chastised her.

She said, "Scarcely had I left them when I found him whom my soul loves; I held on to him and would not let him go until I had brought him to my mother's house, and into the room of her who conceived me" (Song of Solomon 3:4). When a problem develops between lovers, both romantic and sexual love come to a halt at the expense of both lovers. Love energizes but anger depletes the body and soul. You must work at learning to forgive one another! Oh, the making up can be wonderful! Forgiveness is the greatest gift given man by the Father through Jesus, and forgiveness is the greatest gift one man can give another, so use it freely.

Learning forgiveness was hard for me. I carried grudges against Loden for days; I wanted him to suffer for what he had done to me. Doesn't that sound very selfish and childish—not Christlike at all? You see how much I needed the lesson on forgiveness! Let me share with you Shulamith's age-old wisdom which is still true today.

The Center of God's Plan

The whole plan of God from before the beginning centered around forgiveness. God knew man would sin, so His plan was in place before time began. Sin separated God from being intimate with His children, and He wanted that intimacy. Jesus was the promised Savior from Genesis in the Old Testament through the Gospels in the New Testament. His sacrifice was to reunite man with God.

If forgiveness was so important through the ages, it should catch our attention in the husband and wife relationship. Forgiveness makes harmony in the union. The intertwining of a man and woman in marriage is God's lesson to the world of the loving union between Christ and His church. We humans are prone to sin, but it separates us from God. Then daily we have to ask for forgiveness to keep our relationship pure and holy through the blood of Christ.

As in our spiritual union with God, so it is in our earthly union of marriage. We are prone to sin against each other, and forgiveness is the only avenue open to heal the wounds and close the gap of hurt. That is why Jesus taught the importance of settling feelings of anger with one's brother (Matthew 5:22–24). Surely your husband comes under that title! Releasing anger was important to Jesus. He taught that the wrong use of anger could send one to hell. The remedy? Go to the brother and be reconciled at once, before trying to worship.

From this teaching we can see the importance of reconciliation. James, the brother of Jesus, was guided by the Holy Spirit to admonish: "Therefore, confess your sins to one another, and pray for one another so that you may be healed. The effective prayer of a righteous man can accomplish much" (James 5:16).

We humans do not view sin in the same way God does because we live with it. We often excuse our actions by saying, "Well, he deserved what he got," or "He asked for it." Do the verses above excuse such statements?

I Have Sinned

The focal point of the parable of the prodigal son is the boy's realization of the severity of his condition and the one possible solution: "I will get up and go to my father, and will say to him, 'Father, I have sinned against heaven, and in your sight; I am no longer worthy to be called your son; make me as one of your hired men' " (Luke 15:18–19). When he went to his father and began to deliver his prepared speech, his father stopped him, forgave him, and honored him with a banquet.

Here is an example of how to make amends with your husband.

Identify the problem. What did you do to hurt him, or how did you sin against him? God does not look upon sin as trivial.

Plan the approach. You must confess your sins (James 5:16), so you must say, "I sinned against you by doing _____. I am very sorry, and I ask your forgiveness."

I wanted him to suffer for what he had done to me.

Ask forgiveness as soon as possible. The best time is when his facial expression convicts you, although in some cases you need time to organize your thoughts. If you must wait, select a time when he is relaxed and the television can be turned off. You certainly need to do it on the day of the offense.

Ask for words of forgiveness. For his sake as well as yours, ask him to say, "I forgive you." If the sin is ever brought up again, ask if he truly forgave you. If so, remind him that love does not keep a record of wrongs done.

You Hurt My Feelings

On the other side of the coin, Jesus says if you have anything against a brother, go to him and settle the matter. If he listens, you have gained a brother (Matthew 18:15). Otherwise, return to him with one or two witnesses. And finally, if necessary, take the matter to the church.

I had to learn to get the chip off my shoulder. I hated to be constantly going to Loden and saying, "You hurt my feelings." I finally began to get rid of those chips and hurt feelings and remembered to say to myself, "I do not have to be hurt unless I want to be." I did not want to be hurt any longer! We began to laugh about what we did to one another. It is far better than the selfish way I was acting. Go to your husband for important things and let love cover a multitude of sins. If you are constantly going to him with hurt feelings, he will start tuning you out. However, if you act as an adult when you do go to him, he knows it is important and will give you his full attention.

A forgiving attitude stokes our feelings of mercy and allows love to flow into the one that has injured us; it allows the wounds to heal. Forgiveness makes for stronger bonds. If you ask forgiveness seventy times seven times, it is time to change your attitude! The more you work at loving, encouraging, and building up your mate, the less you will need to ask for forgiveness because you will not want to hurt him.

 For what do you need to ask your husband's forgiveness? Make your confession statement in your mind and take care of it today.

Your Own Husband

One of the reasons there should be the pearl of peace in your house of love is that you are quite content to be under the leadership of your husband. In Ephesians 5:22 wives are commanded to be subject to their own husbands. You and your husband are a unit, and what the two of you decide under his headship is right for you. That is why you do not air your relationship grievances. Otherwise your friends will hear the side that favors you. That is slander, and you do not want to be guilty of that sin. You work under your husband's care and oversight and no one else's. Once again that is what the marriage law is—both leave their parents and become one flesh. No one has the right to interfere with your marriage.

Don't allow your children to say, "But the Joneses do this," or "The rest of my friends are allowed to do that." Our children knew it did not matter what others did or did not do. We made our decisions based on what we felt God wanted us to do. That approach taught our children that we did not run with the herd; rather, we walked with the Spirit.

How content are you to be under the oversight of your husband?

What blessings have come from your position of submission?

Everyone likes to be thought of as unique, so cherish your husband for the way he is different from you. When you make him feel he is truly one-of-a-kind, and the best of that kind, you give him a feeling of self-worth very necessary to a man's ego.

Do some things drive you up a wall? Yes. What do you do about them? One friend goes into her bedroom, vents her frustration, and then calmly returns quite content as Miss Nice. I'd just say, "That's Loden's way," and get over it. Does it really matter? Is it worth getting upset over? No! Each of us has habits that can be annoying, so just chalk it up to your dear husband's little quirk and love him for all the things he does right. You must allow your husband to be himself, if you want a loving atmosphere in your love house. When I think of what Loden had to endure with me, he was pure apple jade—the finest of all.

Women choose love, and men desire respect.

To what extremes can women go for their own satisfaction? A business person related the following account:

> Trudy went into an antique shop looking for jewelry. She spotted a string of apple jade beads in a bowl mixed in with costume jewelry. "What is the price?" she asked. "Twenty-five dollars," the owner replied.
>
> Trudy's conscience got the better of her, so she asked the owner if she knew how much they were worth. "Yes," the owner replied, "and when they are sold, I will tell my ex-husband, 'The apple green jade beads you gave me were sold for twenty-five dollars, and you will get your half!'"

R-E-S-P-E-C-T

Love or respect? We women choose love every time, and husbands desire respect most of the time. Sampson was judge over Israel (Judges 16:4), and he was in love with Delilah. When he tricked her three times about his source of strength, she wailed to him, "How can you say, 'I love you,' when your heart is not with me? You have deceived me these three times and have not told me where your great strength is" (Judges 16:15).

For many years we women have bound love and actions together, often for the sake of controlling our husbands. We want their love, and we want them to prove it by words and deeds and by giving us our way. Delilah, like many women before and since, wore Sampson down. He went against his best judgment and told her what she wanted to know. One young husband told me, "When my wife starts in on me, I just keep quiet because I know if I say something it will just set her off more."

You know you have power over your husband, so do not abuse it. Women want love; men want respect. When you wear your husband down by harping on him, you are not respecting him!

Men assume women love them because their mothers and grandmothers loved them. A man expects the woman of his life to love him, but respect is something else. Men desire respect in the work place and from their male friends. They especially desire it from their wives. How you speak to your husband, how you treat him, how you react to him—all tell him loudly, "She respects me!" or "She does not respect me!" His perception determines the way he reacts to you. You may think you are the perfect wife, but if he does not think so, then you will not be treated with love.

Trust is vital to respect. The wife in Proverbs 31 did her husband good, so he totally trusted her to act in his best interest. What more could he have wanted? Jesus puts it this way in John 14:15: "If you love Me, you will keep My commandments." It is the same with your husband. He wants you to respect his wishes and treat him with the same devotion you treat Jesus.

You must face this fact: if you do not respect your husband, you do not respect Jesus who requires you to submit to the headship of your husband. Men show their love by protecting and providing for their families. We have to guide them gently in the way we want them to love us.

Say It Again

A young wife came to me distraught because her husband would not give her cards on special occasions like Valentine's Day and her birthday. I advised her that she needed to buy him cards for special occasions and no occasion, letting him know how much she loved him. Then when he bought her a card, she was to show appreciation: leave the card on a table, pick it up when he was looking, and tell him again how much pleasure it gave her to read his card and feel his love all over again. It was not too long until he caught the idea: "My wife really likes for me to give her cards," he told a friend, so cards were forthcoming.

When you want to guide, do it with love and kindness. When your husband does something that pleases you, tell him, tell him, and tell him again how much it meant to you. Praise and positive reinforcement bring us pleasure. Employers, teachers, parents, and wives guide others by this natural process of learning. Guide your husband into ways of pleasing you. Use the words, "It would really help me if you . . ." But request only one thing at a time. Women multitask, but men are geared to one task at a time. Give honest praise and tell your husband how and why his act of kindness aided you.

After our children left home and Loden worked fewer hours, I began asking for his help in the kitchen. He put ice in glasses, chopped food, and helped in preparation and cleanup. We talked and laughed as we worked. I always told him how much I enjoyed his help and companionship. Soon he was volunteering to wash the dishes for me. It became a time of sharing one more phase of life. He was proud of the way he took tasks from me. He told me, "You are so good to me; I want to do good back for you."

Jesus often asked questions in conversation with others. So should you. When you don't understand why your husband acted as he did, ask him. Instead of accusing him of leaving his clothes down to make life harder for you, ask him, "Will you kindly help me by picking up your clothes?" When you don't understand the logic behind his action—and I assure you he did have his logic behind it—ask him to explain his action. "I know your male reasoning was at work, but my female understanding is blank! Will you please explain to me why you acted in that way? Then I will understand." Don't these questions sound better than our often-used harsh words?

Before you speak about a controversial matter, think about the way your words sound and your stance—please, not with your hands on your hips. Always remember Ephesians 4:29: no corrupt words—use words that build up and give grace, and be sure your words always show respect. You can talk to anyone about anything if you respectfully use the right words and the right tone. If a person feels your love, a connection will take place between your minds, and words will flow freely. An attitude of respect is the key to unlocking your feelings, words, and emotions toward him. If we do not respect a person, it shows in everything we do. You can't fake respect.

Practice polishing your jewels; furnish your home with these precious stones. All the money in the world cannot buy such treasures; they are made only with God's guidance from His precious Word.

Memory Verse

"Wives, be subject to your own husbands, as to the Lord."

Ephesians 5:22

Did you catch that phrase "as to the Lord"? You are not pleasing to Jesus if you are not subject to your husband just as you are submissive to Christ.

My Homework

1. Pray for the Father to help you understand and practice the truths He has taught you.

2. Practice, practice, practice because practice makes perfect. The way of Jesus goes against the grain of human nature, so you have to work consciously to incorporate it into your life. We have to learn divine nature and make it our way of life.

3. Keep on doing all the actions of love you were assigned in the previous weeks: praising, kissing, and caressing your dear husband to build him up?

4. Select a night when you can be alone with your husband for at least forty-five minutes. Buy some massage oil or very good lotion. Begin by bathing together. Then begin your massage. Oh, you're not a masseuse? He will think you're wonderful anyway. Begin with his face and head, using the tips of your fingers, and work in a circle. Then go to his neck, right arm, right leg, left leg, left arm, then begin on his neck and work down his body. Have him turn on his back and begin at the back of the legs and work up all the way to the neck. After you begin massaging you will naturally begin to get a rhythm. You will start to knead the muscles and massage them. A massage is one of the nicest gifts you can give him. You can try the bed, but it may be easier to use a pallet on the floor. Give him a pillow for his head and cover him with a blanket. Uncover the part you are massaging so the rest of the body will stay warm. Work to the rhythm of soothing music. Have him rest awhile after you finish. You have just earned at least a hundred Brownie points!

5. Highlight "one another," or similar terms listed below, from the book of Romans. What great admonitions for your marriage!

   ❧ 12:5 "So we, who are many, are one body in Christ, and individually members one of another."

   ❧ 13:8 "Owe nothing to anyone except to love one another; for he who loves his neighbor has fulfilled the law."

   ❧ 14:13 "Therefore let us not judge one another anymore, but rather determine this—not to put an obstacle or a stumbling block in a brother's way."

   ❧ 14:19 "So then we pursue the things which make for peace and the building up of one another."

   ❧ 15:5 "Now may the God who gives perseverance and encouragement grant you to be of the same mind with one another according to Christ Jesus."

   ❧ 15:14 "And concerning you, my brethren, I myself also am convinced that you yourselves are full of goodness, filled with all knowledge and able also to admonish one another."

   ❧ 16:16 "Greet one another with a holy kiss."

A Truth: Patti and Dillon Bayers were first-place winners in a contest by *Good Housekeeping* magazine. Contestants were to define a successful marriage in fifty words or less. Patti and Dillon's entry won first place among tens of thousands of entries. It is good advice; give it serious thought.

We *gave* when we wanted to *receive.*

We *served* when we wanted to *feast.*

We *shared* when we wanted to *keep.*

We *listened* when we wanted to *talk.*

We *submitted* when we wanted to *reign.*

We *forgave* when we wanted to *remember.*

We *stayed* when we wanted to *leave.*

Put me like a seal over your heart, like a seal on your arm. For love is as strong as death, jealousy is as severe as Sheol; its flashes are flashes of fire, the very flame of the Lord. Many waters cannot quench love, nor will rivers overflow it; if a man were to give all the riches of his house for love, it would be utterly despised (Song of Solomon 8:6–7).

"Love never fails" (1 Corinthians 13:8).

Week 9
Special Gifts

From the Father of the Bride: "... O friends, drink and imbibe deeply, O lovers" (Song of Solomon 5:1).

Thought for the Day: "We need love in good measure, and we need to give it. We need to feel that we are wanted and belong. We need to know that the pleasure which our senses and our body can bring us is permissible and good and that our enjoyment does not make us 'bad.' We need to feel accepted and understood. And finally we need to feel worthwhile and essentially worthy in being uniquely the self that we are" (Baruch, *How to Live with Your Teenager.* New York: Charles Scribner's Sons, 1956, 23).

From Sarah, your Mother: "After I have become old, shall I have pleasure, my lord being old also?" (Genesis 18:12).

From Queen Mother: "The heart of her husband trusts in her ... She does him good and not evil all the days of her life" (Proverbs 31:11–12).

From Shulamith: "I am my beloved's and my beloved is mine, he who pastures his flock among the lilies" (Song of Solomon 6:3).

Day 1

Review Your Happy Marriage

Our imaginary journey in our house of love this week sheds light on gifts presented by our Father.

Shulamith stood in the living room robed in her beautiful garments and the splendor of her peaceful and loving countenance. She motioned for us to sit and she began talking.

"You are here today to learn of two gifts that are very special. Each of you will present a gift to the other. Your heavenly Father gave them to you; they are meant to be shared. The special gifts that you give each other are the gifts of intimacy—loving one another physically in the joyous union of your bodies.

"Before we discuss these two gifts, however, let's review what we have learned in the previous weeks. Those principles are necessary before you can truly have the pleasure of using your gifts to the fullest."

Your *"Miracle Grow"* Ingredients

The following characteristics of a happy marriage are necessary ingredients to make a marriage grow toward perfection. Rest assured, husband and wife must be willing to work to develop in Christ's image.

- *Think positive* (Philippians 4:8). Each of you must have positive thoughts about the other and actions that are always loving and positive. All negatives must be handled the day they happen; do not let the sun go down on your anger. Seek a win/win solution for problems. Be willing to compromise and be unselfish in your desires for peace. Be affectionate, truly listen, and be proud of each other's accomplishments. Be playful. Being too serious takes all the fun from life.

- *Feel empathy.* Constantly use the Golden Rule. Put yourself in your husband's shoes and feel what he is feeling. This helps him as he makes decisions, and it helps you as you look to him as your headship and the difficulties both of you have in your respective roles.

- *Honor your covenant.* Put aside selfishness, and work together. Be willing to work at solving even the smallest disagreement, hurt, or trial. Have the same commitment Jesus had when He promised, "I will never desert you, nor will I ever forsake you" (Hebrews 13:5). "Till death do us part"; that is your covenant.

- *Accept each other.* What is the fertile soil needed for love to grow? Love, appreciation, and a feeling of value. Jesus takes us as we are. He cleanses us and gives us loving commands to develop us into His very image. The following quote pretty much sums up this feeling between two lovers:

  It's a situation in which anything is permissible, where two people are so secure with themselves and with each other they don't have to fake anything. They know that everything about them is loved—the good and the bad. It's a love cocoon where we feel warm and protected and safe (Alexandra Penny, *How to Make Love to Each Other.* General Publishing Co. Ltd., 1982, 22).

- *Give mutual love and respect.* When the husband gives the wife proper loving care, the wife is willing to give the husband respect as the head of the home

(Ephesians 5:23). When each gives the other what God commands, then each can deliver to the other his or her heart's desire.

If these five characteristics are alive and well in your marriage, then you will handle conflicts, upsets, and trials in a way that leads to marital peace and growth. As you develop into total oneness, your differences will diminish. You will desire unity more than you desire your selfish ways. You will crucify your selfishness daily. To live outside self is far more satisfying than pleasing only self. As you grow in love, you will resolve differences; you will want your husband to be contented. Forgiveness will become a way of life; love does not remember wrongs suffered (1 Corinthians 13:5).

You will crucify your selfishness daily.

Family traditions add to the solidarity of the marriage and give meaning to special times. Having fun and playing together cements the family and creates lasting memories. Relaxing is necessary for a healthy body, soul, and mind. Add daily family devotions, and you have a recipe for a successful, happy family. Children learn to serve God at an early age by praying, reading scripture, and talking about good deeds done during the day.

Helping Mother cook or make treats for others is also a way to teach the little ones that sharing brings happiness to the giver. Allowing each family member to report a good incident of the day fosters the habit of being positive instead of negative. Have family meals together. Studies of family life have shown the many benefits of eating and sharing time together as a family; all suffer if they do not pray and eat together. There should be joy in the family. Begin to notice the word *joy* as you read through God's Word. The Father is joyous and He desires that His children have a joy that being one with Him brings.

Day 2

Intimacy: The First Gift

An outstanding characteristic of the Song of Solomon is the intimacy of the lovers. Closeness invigorates a marriage, making it alive, special, and fulfilling. You will strive for total intimacy with your husband. You have to work at it, but you know that old saying: "Anything worth doing is worth doing right," so you want to work very hard at developing intimacy. The beautiful love story of Solomon and Shulamith—from courtship to mature love—is God's marriage manual.

How beautiful, how grand and liberating this experience is, when couples learn to help each other. It is impossible to over-emphasize the immense need men [also women] have to be really listened to, to be taken seriously, to be understood . . . No one can develop freely in this world and find full life without feeling understood by at least one person (Paul Tournier, *To Understand Each Other*. Richmond, VA: John Knox Press, 1962, 29).

To be so intimate with your husband that he feels totally at ease with you in every situation is priceless; intimacy is the rarest of jewels. Periodically, review your relationship:

❧ What have we created in our marriage?

❧ Where are we on the road to complete oneness?

❧ What can we do to make our union even more glorious?

These are valid questions, because in our hectic world, we often let slip the most valuable relationship in our lives. These questions are especially important in the first twenty years of marriage when children are being reared and careers are established. Couples often find themselves flying in five different directions.

Remember God's eternal law: we reap what we sow (Galatians 6:7). The promise given two verses down says, "Let us not lose heart in doing good, for in due time we will reap if we do not grow weary."

A satisfying marriage, like any other achievement, must be reached with hard labor, effort, and desire. Do not criticize, harp, or try to change one another, but instead strive to allow one another the freedom to grow and to shed those negative traits.

The central problem in the beginning of marriage is combining the distinct and often antagonistic needs of two individuals into a workable, satisfying union (John Levy and Ruth Monroe, *The Happy Family*. New York: Alfred A. Knopf, 1938, 148).

Isn't this similar to Paul's encouragement: "Do nothing from selfishness or empty conceit, but with humility of mind regard one another as more important than yourselves"? (Philippians 2:3). You both work for mutual maximum satisfaction with minimum frustration. If a couple uses the Golden Rule as their number one guide in behavior, then mutual edification results. Each is free to develop his own strength. Drop the negatives in the name of love and embrace mutual dependence for feeding each other's soul, mind, and body.

The Golden Rule will carry a couple through the dry periods of the relationship—those times when life is not as thrilling or as pleasant as both would wish. Trials, sickness in family, and work-related problems create a negative pull. During these times the couple must stop and look at their marriage with a magnifying glass, determine where the little foxes are digging and expel them. Never forget that Satan is still lurking about just as he was in the Garden of Eden, and each divorce is of great glee to him. Each unhappy marriage gives the world a negative view of God's union with mankind and greatly increases

Satan's pleasure. Don't let him win! Remember the axiom, "This too shall pass," and work problems together and not against one another.

Below is a check list to assess the degree of mutual satisfaction in your marriage. Answer yes or no.

_____ *Do I have warm, positive feelings about our marriage, or is there an area that needs work?* Talk openly with each other. State the law of Ephesians 5:29.

_____ *Have I grown spiritually, mentally, and emotionally since our last self-check?* If not, what is the problem, where do you need to work, and how can your husband help? God says, "Test yourselves to see if you are in the faith; examine yourselves! Or do you not recognize this about yourselves, that Jesus Christ is in you, unless indeed you fail the test" (2 Corinthians 13:5).

Talk over how each of you has grown, where growth is needed, and how each can encourage the other in continuing to develop in every area. Remember to talk in calm, loving words and give each other very rapt attention. These self-tests are needed to keep you on track in your attempt to reach a happy, nourishing, intimate marriage. How have you grown in the last eight weeks?

_____ *Do I depend on our relationship to feed my needs?* Do you turn within yourself or to others for satisfactions that the marriage should give: admiration, acceptance, caressing, empathy.

How can I involve my husband in making these goals a reality?

What new goal do I want to set for myself?

Am I truly trying to meet all the emotional needs of my husband? Is he truly trying to meet all my needs? If not, how can we define those neglected needs and develop a plan for meeting them?

Day 3

Basic Heart Nutrition

A marriage that supplies the following needs is a marriage based on a solid foundation.

❧ The need for security

❧ The need to give or to be needed

❧ The need for self-esteem

❧ The need for pleasure

❧ The need for limits or boundaries

❧ The need for freedom

❧ The need for faith

Security

In order to grow into a healthy individual, a child must feel secure. Many people carry emotional scars because at some time in their childhood, their security was at risk and a feeling of helplessness set in. Feeling loved in a secure marriage is essential to intimacy in marriage. Knowing each will be there for the duration supplies a feeling of security. John was inspired to give us the secret to rid ourselves of fear: "There is no fear in love; but perfect love casts out fear, because fear involves punishment, and the one who fears is not perfected in love" (1 John 4:18).

Each mate approaches perfect love when there is no fear of the other's leaving the marriage or devising punishment for some dissatisfaction within the relationship. Freedom to be yourself, and thus open and intimate with the other, prevails because you feel safe. You can reveal your weakness and know you will still be loved and protected, and that your lover will not use these weaknesses to punish you in times of anger. Anger and punishment do not belong in an intimate, loving union. This is the feeling of the popular song "Stand by Your Man."

Jesus taught, "Do not judge, and you will not be judged; and do not condemn, and you will not be condemned; pardon, and you will be pardoned" (Luke 6:37). You have the security of not being judged by your mate, freeing you to have intimacy of being totally naked in body, mind, and spirit and being cherished on earth as you are in heaven.

✍ How can I learn to accept my husband's weaknesses without judgment?

✍ How does judgment make me feel?

✍ How can I bring myself to make the one I love feel accepted and secure?

Being Needed

If you love, you must give. "It is more blessed to give than to receive" (Acts 20:35). Psychologists have discovered that giving is what makes humans happy, well-rounded, and productive. Selfish people are full of anger, unhappiness, and sadness. Ann Landers and other counselors repeatedly hand out this solution for many problems: give, serve, and make someone happy; then you will be happy. One of the most beloved verses in the Bible states: "God so loved the world, that He *gave*. . ." (John 3:16). To imitate God and Christ, we must be givers, especially to our husbands. When you do something that brings pleasure to your husband, he automatically wants to return the feeling. Try it!

Selfish people are full of anger, unhappiness, and sadness.

The more we give, the more we have to give, and then the more we receive. Scripture reveals that God "richly supplies us with all things to enjoy" (1 Timothy 6:17), and Jesus promises, "Give, and it will be given to you. They will pour into your lap a good measure—pressed down, shaken together, and running over. For by your standard of measure it will be measured to you in return" (Luke 6:38). Lifting your husband up when he is down is one of the great gifts of intimacy. You know your husband well enough to know when a soothing hand is needed, when words of encouragement are like cool water on a hot day. We are the balm that is needed. Isn't that a good feeling? Offer words of encouragement; do not hurl hurtful stones with no concern that he is wounded and needs your balm. No one on earth loves him as much as you do, so show it!

What gift of self can I give my husband this day that I have not given him before?

Self-Esteem

Jesus was successful in His mission. Why? Because He knew who He was, why He was here, and where He was going. To enhance the intimacy of your marriage, you also need to know who you are: the wife of your loving husband; what you are doing here: being his suitable helper; and where you are going: to live with God eternally. Help your husband and yourself to grow in Jesus and obey His commands. Affirm with Paul, "For me to live is Christ and to die is gain" (Philippians 1:21). If this isn't your goal, study God's Word to see if you should change your course.

Who am I? What am I doing here? Where am I going?

You must have self-esteem—a sense of worth—to be productive. Shulamith and Solomon praised one another; they recognized this gift of self-worth. They lifted one another up in word pictures.

Your husband is hungry for your praise, your admiration, your pride in him and what he is doing for the family. That is the male ego—guiding, protecting, and providing. What does it do for his ego when you will not allow him to be head of his house; when you criticize so much of what is important to him; when you do not give praise or thankfulness to him for his efforts; when you tell the children you love them, but never tell him he is loved? How can he love you if you feed him nothing?

What is prayer? Is it not a form of communication to our Father for the purpose of mutual edification? Just as our Father fills our needs, so can you fill your husband's. Read Philippians 4:4–9 and substitute your husband's name in the paraphrase below.

Rejoice in _____ always, and again I say, rejoice! Let your gentle spirit be known to _____, for your dear _____ is near. Be anxious for nothing but in everything ask _____ for what you need, and give _____ thanks for all he has done for you. And the peace I have with _____, which surpasses all comprehension, will guard my heart and mind as we live in Christ together. I will think about _____ in a way that is true, honorable, right, pure, lovely, and of his good repute, and any other trait that is excellent, and if there is anything else about him that is worthy of praise, I will dwell on these things. The things I have learned and received and heard and seen in _____, I will encourage him to continue to practice, and the God of peace will be with us.

Do not neglect your husband's self-esteem, no matter what! Read 1 Corinthians 10:1–12. The Israelites were destroyed because they behaved contrary to the wishes of God, their husband, and they were unfaithful to Him. They were not thankful for what He had done for them, and He finally destroyed them. God recorded these facts to keep us from making the same mistake. Truly the principle applies to your own husband; he is made in the image of God. Never forget that fact.

I really needed Loden's assurances. My mother never complimented her children because she did not want us to get the "big head." I can assure you, her plan worked. I always wanted to hear her say, "Well done," but she died with those words sealed forever from my ears.

Loden's words of approval and assurances were worth more than gold. He pushed me to become and to achieve. I had the desire, but he inspired me, led the way, and gave me kudos when I needed them. He was my super hero for many reasons, but I cherish most his faith in me.

Feed your husband until he is sated with your words of love, encouragement, and pride. He will reward you beyond your wildest dreams. How did twelve unlearned men, under the influence of one very learned man, Jesus, turn the world upside down? He believed in them, told them they would succeed, and depended on them. He gave them the power to succeed in their mission. How many hungry husbands are presently in the world? It hurts me to see pain on husbands' faces when their wives are publicly tearing them down. Don't ever be guilty of uttering a word about your husband that does not build him up. It is a sin (Ephesians 4:29).

Pleasure

Playfulness is a pleasurable gift of an intimate marriage. If you don't play with your husband, who will? No, you don't want to know the answer to that! Of course, sexual pleasure immediately comes to mind, but we will touch on that another day. Playfulness in interaction, teasing in a positive way, doing child-like things, playing games, and attending plays, athletic events, lectures, and symphonies—all add to the adventure of being a twosome. Whatever you do, find time just to be together.

Somehow, even in your hectic schedule, find at least fifteen minutes a day to concentrate on each other. Talk about something other than children, work, and problems. It is okay for you to have a night out with the girls or for him to pal around with the guys sometimes; it renews your spirit and you have happenings to share. Join a club; read poems or books aloud. The important fact is to find what pleases the two of you and then do it.

Often it is the wife who has to come up with activities to enjoy. Plan outings, go out on dates, and go away for a weekend. Notice that the lovers in the Song of Solomon planned new outings to keep their love alive, such as a picnic in the woods. Ward off boredom by planning discussion topics for times when you are alone. On the other hand, the ultimate intimacy is to sit in the same room doing your own thing in total silence. That feeling of unity is love!

Plan three things to discuss with your husband tonight, and do it.

Enjoy your friends. Socializing in the form of eating and playing games is a lost art. Work these activities into your life; they are rewarding and they add to your pleasure. Loden and I were members of a supper club for thirty-six years. We met monthly to talk and play games at a member's house. We shared in the trials, tribulations, and joys of our families. We helped each other through the sorrows of losing children and mates. When death began to invade our group and our children began having grandchildren, our group broke up. So be aware of the ebb and flow of life. Be adjustable. Enjoy each stage and then move on without looking back longingly.

Limits

Each of us needs to know what our husband finds acceptable and live within those boundaries. God created everything with laws—from nature to our covenant with Him. Laws keep us within bounds. You know not to approach certain subjects, so you don't. Family rituals keep the living machinery running smoothly. Each has his task and does it without complaining. Does this make you feel secure?

Early in your marriage, you established rules to live by. For instance, you could no longer run out and buy an expensive item just because you wanted it. It has become "we," not "me." Remember? You developed a whole new code of conduct.

Each partner brings ideas to the table, and they are worked out to the mutual benefit of the marriage. These rules are to be your rules—not your parents' or friends' rules. They are for your own marriage, and you do what works for the two of you. You can change the rules if you want or break one sometimes, just for fun. Be wise in your decisions; they should benefit the whole family and not just one member.

On the other hand, freedom within the marriage is also food for intimacy. Each person should feel free to pursue his development. Our talents from the Father should be explored with the aid of our husbands and not stifled for selfish reasons. "Because I do not want you to" is not a valid reason. I regularly commended Loden for the freedom he gave me to grow, develop, and run our home. It is still precious to me. I wanted him to know I would never misuse my freedom to hurt him or our relationship.

What rules have you and your husband established that are unique to your household?

How do you honor this code of conduct?

Freedom in Faith

The last concept of an intimate marriage is the philosophy by which we live. You must respect your husband's codes of conduct. Placing God first in your marriage will be the most satisfying, because all decisions will be guided by the laws of God—and all His laws are for our good. However, a marriage between a Christian and a non-Christian can be happy if both partners respect the freedom of the other. I think of two couples who worked out a very successful relationship, although the husbands were not religious. They gave their wives freedom to worship without any restrictions.

 Write below the best way of life for a couple to follow, as found in 1 John 5:3.

Let us close this section with a revealing writing, paraphrased from an Internet article that describes the purpose of intimacy in marriage:

> Love is the experience of knowing that another person cares—deeply, warmly, acceptingly, and dependably; this is the most indispensable need of any human being to which all the other heart-hungers are tributaries. To have a steady source of warmth and affection helps to offset the chill of depersonalizing experiences in the outside world. Such love—given and received in a marriage—feeds self-esteem. A husband said, "Knowing that she loves me through all our ups and downs makes me feel ten feet tall." Love helps a person define his identity more sharply as he experiences himself vividly in both passionate and quiet caring. It reinforces feelings of inner security by making the marriage a harbor where one is safe from many of the storms and threats of life. Love is the force which welds a relationship at its points of meeting. The ancient insight of Paul has been confirmed and reconfirmed in the social sciences, counseling relationships, and successful marriages—"the greatest of these is love" (1 Corinthians 13:13). (Howard and Charlotte H. Clinebelle, *The Intimate Marriage*).

Respect your husband's codes of conduct.

Such intimacy is seen in the words spoken by lovers. A massage therapist told of a woman's husband—he had Parkinson's disease—who exclaimed after the therapist had given his wife a massage: "Thank you for taking care of my wife and making her feel better. I love her more than anything else in this world."

John took early retirement to care for his wife who had developed and later died with breast cancer. Life was kind to him after her death. He found a second wife whom he adores. He takes her traveling and even washes the dishes because "she cooks for me. The least I can do is wash the dishes." Another bereaved mate explained: "I looked after her for seven years [she suffered from cancer]. It was a pleasure; and if I had it to do over, I would do it all over again. I enjoyed every minute I gave her."

These couples found intimacy and fed one another rich blessings that nourished their love even further. You can also develop this type of intimacy if you work with your husband; it is a growth process.

 How much am I committed to having an intimate marriage?

Day 4

Sexual Fulfillment: The Second Gift

We are back in our imaginary living room with Shulamith sitting where we left her, still holding her book, "Song of Solomon." She looks at us and begins her remarks.

"How much do you really love your husband, Patsy?" Her question startled me. I thought she knew that I truly loved my Loden and was really trying hard to practice everything I had been taught by Mother Sarah, Queen Mother, and her. I hesitated and quietly replied, "Shulamith, I love my husband more than any other person in this world."

She smiled, opened her book, and began reading,

Put me like a seal over your heart, like a seal on your arm. For love is as strong as death, jealousy is as severe as Sheol; its flashes are flashes of fire, the very flame of the Lord. Many waters cannot quench love, nor will rivers overflow it; if a man were to give all the riches of his house for love, it would be utterly despised.

"This was what I thought of my love for Solomon. The seal was a piece of jewelry with my name on it. Solomon wore it over his heart, according to the custom of our people, as a constant reminder of his love for me. The seal upon his arm was his love for me as he embraced me in our intimate times. If you read the book in its entirety, you will see how very much Solomon and I enjoyed giving one another the gift of our physical union which in turn also gave full expression of our love emotionally, spiritually, and mentally for one another.

"We were as uninhibited as Adam and Eve, for we knew this was a gift from the Father Himself and meant to be enjoyed freely without shame. I am going to teach you about the second gift you will give your husband and he will give back to you. It also is a gift given by the Father Himself for both of you to share with one another. Listen carefully about the gift of making love to one another. No other earthly creature has the privilege of having this gift for pleasure, as well as for procreation, so treasure it and freely give this offering to one another. Never deny this gift of lovemaking to one another.

"Our song describes the union of our bodies for the sheer pleasure of each other. Nothing is said in our story about children, and you know in my time, having children was paramount to a woman's feeling complete. The Father gave you the gift of sexual union for the strength, pleasure, and health it gives to your body, mind, and spirit. I repeat: it is the ultimate gift you give to one another, so give it freely. I cannot stress this enough."

Imbibe Deeply, O Lovers

What do we want to learn about the gift of loving one another in the intimate husband/wife relationship? The Spirit guided Solomon to say: "Eat, friends; drink and imbibe deeply, O lovers" (Song of Solomon 5:1).

Let's go back to the sixth day of creation to appreciate fully the beauty of the union of a man and woman in love: "Let us make man in Our image, according to Our likeness." So the man and woman were created in the image of God, He created him, male and female (Genesis 1:26–28). Note the difference in the creation of man and woman:

> Then the Lord God formed man of dust from the ground, and breathed into his nostrils the breath of life; and man became a living being . . . God said, "It is not good for the man to be alone; I will make him a helper suitable for him." So the Lord God caused a deep sleep to fall upon the man, and he slept; then He took one of his ribs and closed up the flesh at that place. And the Lord God fashioned into a woman the rib which He had taken from the man, and brought her to the man. And the man said, "This is now bone of my bones, and flesh of my flesh; she shall be called Woman, because she was taken out of Man." For this reason a man shall leave his father and his mother, and be joined to his wife; and they shall become one flesh. And the man and his wife were both naked and were not ashamed (Genesis 2:7, 20–25).

We learn from these verses that man was made of the dust of the ground, as was every beast of the field and bird of the sky. But woman was created in a different manner. From his side, next to his heart but under his head, the Lord God fashioned Eve. To understand this wonderful creation fully, consider the two words used for these creations: *formed* and *fashioned*.

Adam was formed as a potter would form a pot from earthen clay, and clay pots were purposely formed as various utility vessels. Does this help explain why men are simple, forthright, and purpose-oriented beings? *Fashioned* was a word used for making palaces, temples, or forms of art. That is the meaning when Peter says the woman is the weaker vessel— one that is of porcelain—a vessel of beauty (1 Peter 3:7). Woman was created not only as a companion for Adam, but also as an aesthetic work. Man was created for purposes, like naming the animals and cultivating the garden. God first gave him lordship over the earth. Then He gave him religious headship when He told him not to eat of the tree of knowledge. That was the covenant Adam had with God, and God does not take covenant-breaking lightly (Hosea 6:7).

Woman was fashioned as an aesthetic work.

God noted that Adam needed someone to meet his personal needs. Eve was fashioned from living flesh, not from the earth. From the beginning woman has been special to her Father. She was made with relationship abilities, beauty, and the feeling side of her Father's nature. Adam was made from the purpose-driven side of his Father. The two were joined into a union that made them as one and then were given the whole spectrum of God's nature—the whole image just as the Godhead is three, but their union and purpose are one. Eve was to be as special to Adam as she was to her heavenly Father. Adam, as head of God's earthly creation, named Eve *woman*. Eve was created to be the "help suitable" for Adam—a helper to meet the needs he could not provide for himself.

Consuming Fire

The following paraphrase by Rabbi Akiba lends an interesting slant regarding man and woman in the bond of marriage:

> If one takes the Hebrew words for *man* and *woman* and removes certain letters, then both become the word for *fire*. There is a consuming fire in each individual, and when man and woman marry, this fire becomes one. It is capable of destroying whole worlds if not properly tended. To quench that fire is impossible; it generates the life of the world. If left untended, the fire would be evil.
>
> However God placed the first letter of His name in Hebrew between the words for man and woman. In so doing, the man and woman retain the fire within them, but they have God's presence in their midst. If God is present in the hearts of the two, then there is warmth and heat, and the couple becomes partners in the act of Divine creation—with God making a godly family unit. However, if the two do not cultivate God's presence, then the fire becomes a consuming fire (article from mikvah.org).

The flame of love that God places in man and woman as husband and wife is of divine creation and should be held in great respect and honor, as is God, the creator of their love. On the other hand, when God is not present in the union, it becomes worldly and evil as evidenced by all the ungodly forms of sex and the consequences suffered as a result.

Think about the times fire represents the presence of God. First, at Mount Sinai in the burning bush and when God brought Moses and the Israelites back to the mount to give them His law and make a covenant with them. The fire terrified the Israelites. The cloud that led the children of Israel by day was a pillar of fire by night. It gave them assurance of God's presence. Isaiah 31:9 declares, ". . . whose fire is in Zion and whose furnace is in Jerusalem."

Again, when the Holy Spirit came upon Jesus at His baptism, He was represented as a dove, but when He came upon the apostles on the day of Pentecost, He was as a flame of fire. The fire of the Lord is holy and good; however, fire without the presence of the Lord is evil. Hell was made to be a fire that would never die—punishment by fire to those whose names are not found in the Book of Life (Revelation 20:14–15). Hell has no light; God's presence will not be there (Matthew 8:12; cf. Revelation 21:23). The fire in the hearts of loving mates is good, but the fires of lust outside marriage are the fires that destroy mankind: AIDS, venereal diseases, HIV, and sexually transmitted viruses that can never be healed. The world has not learned that those who ignore God's laws will suffer the consequences! His eternal law is that we reap what we sow (Galatians 6:7).

One Flesh

When the Father presented Eve to Adam, she was naked, and they were not ashamed. When a husband and wife are in their own habitat, nakedness is not wrong; it is the way the Father planned life in Paradise. Did the Father want Adam to have full appreciation of the beauty of the wife? Yes, God made her especially for Adam's needs, which included sex. Both you and your husband should stand naked before one another in the flesh and spirit and become one as God commanded.

Genesis 1:27–28 gives us the verbal account of the first human family. God blessed the couple and then said to them, "Be fruitful and multiply, and fill the earth, and subdue it, and rule over . . . every living thing that moves on the earth." God's first command was to enjoy their fleshly union as husband and wife. God intended that Adam be "joined to his wife; and they shall become one flesh" (Genesis 2:24). The Father brings this same thought over into the new covenant when the Spirit explains that the fleshly union of the couple is honorable: "Marriage is to be held in honor among all, and the marriage bed is to be undefiled; for fornicators and adulterers God will judge" (Hebrews 13:4).

Read 1 Corinthians 7:5. What is God is teaching you?

Many say 1 Corinthians 7:5 was not a command in light of the verse following, but that is a misinterpretation. Verse 6 tells couples that temporary concessions in sexual relations were for the purpose of prayer — concessions on God's part. Concessions were not mandatory, but Paul's injunction made abstention permissible while couples prayed about something vital in their marriage. However, the breaks in relations were not to be for long because of the possibility that Satan would cause sin to arise from abstention.

What is the only reason given for not having sex with your husband?

God's Wife

In the Old Testament, God used marriage to illustrate Israel's covenant with God (cf. Ezekiel 16). God gives a sorrowful account of His courtship and marriage to Israel. Israel's history from the time He made a covenant with Abraham to their coming to Mt. Sinai was worded as a love story. "You became mine" is the declaration of God. He goes on to describe how He adorned His wife in beautiful clothing, gave her fine food, and made her a queen for the world to admire. As her husband, God had "bestowed His splendor" upon Israel and made her perfect.

God's figurative wife Israel played the harlot and went off into adultery with foreign idols. God alludes to His union with Israel as a husband by accusing her of taking her sons and daughters whom she had born to Him and sacrificing them to the abominable idols. Read verses 30–43 to find what God was determined to do with this wife who had broken the covenant with Him (v. 59). In Jeremiah 3:8 the Lord declares that He was divorcing faithless Israel; He accused Judah of returning to Him with a faithless heart. In Isaiah 50:1 God asks this question, "Where is the certificate of divorce by which I have sent your mother away?"

In the book of Hosea God commands Hosea to take Gomer, a wife of harlotry, and play out Israel's relation to Him. When their second child was born, God said to Gomer, "Name him Loammi [not my people], for you are not My people and I am not your God." In chapter 2 the Lord looks toward the time of the new covenant with the house of Israel when "I will betroth you to Me forever."

The covenant with Israel was typical of a husband and wife's covenant of marriage. The illustration is that of a husband and wife's intimacy which produced children. Israel's whole being—political, social, religious—was to be bound together in the Lord's covenant, the Law of Moses. God promised that "those who wait for the Lord will gain new strength; they will mount up with wings like eagles, they will run and not get tired, they will walk and not become weary" (Isaiah 40:31). *Wait* means to bind together as a rope. Israel was to be bound to the Lord as a wife. Israel's strength lay in keeping her life intertwined with the Lord. Where is a wife's strength? It is in her binding as one with her husband!

What did Shulamith write about Solomon in Song of Solomon 1:4? What do you think she means?

The Church Is Christ's Bride

In the New Testament the bridegroom/bride analogy is used to describe Jesus and His church, the new Israel. Consider the following verses that depict this special union:

Therefore, my brethren, you also were made to die to the Law through the body of Christ, so that you might be joined to another, to Him who was raised from the dead, in order that we might bear fruit for God (Romans 7:4).

Do you not know that your bodies are members of Christ? Shall I then take away the members of Christ and make them members of a prostitute? May it never be! . . . But the one who joins himself to the Lord is one spirit with Him. Flee immorality. Every other sin that a man commits is outside the body, but the immoral man sins against his own body. Or do you not know that your body is

a temple of the Holy Spirit who is in you, whom you have from God, and that you are not your own? For you have been bought with a price: therefore glorify God in your body (1 Corinthians 6:15–20).

That He might present to Himself the church in all her glory, having no spot or wrinkle or any such thing; but that she would be holy and blameless. So husbands ought also to love their own wives as their own bodies. He who loves his own wife loves himself; for no one ever hated his own flesh, but nourishes and cherishes it, just as Christ also does the church, because we are members of His body. For this reason a man shall leave his father and mother and shall be joined to his wife, and the two shall become one flesh (Ephesians 5:27–31).

Once again the union of a man and woman as one flesh is the beautiful picture of the oneness Christ wants with His bride just as God wanted with His wife Israel. The intimacy you have with your husband is a living example to the world of how God wants to be joined to you and to the church as a whole oneness in body and spirit.

 Read 1 John 4:10–11 and describe your feelings about God's instructions to you about your husband.

You Belong to Me

Man and woman were created for God's pleasure. Revelation 4 is the throne scene in heaven. All the heavenly beings are worshiping God on His throne. Lightening flashed (fire again) and thunder rolled. All beings worshiped the Most Holy and elders bowed before Him and said, "Worthy are You, our Lord and our God, to receive glory and honor and power; for You created all things, and because of Your will they existed, and were created" (Revelation 4:11). The King James Version says: "And for thy pleasure they are and were created."

Humans were always meant to belong solely to God, body and soul. Notice how the Holy Spirit reveals the end place of all creation:

It is done, I am the Alpha and the Omega, the beginning and the end. I will give to the one who thirsts from the spring of the water of life without cost. He who overcomes will inherit these things, and I will be his God . . . one of the seven angels . . . came and spoke with me, saying, "Come here, I will show you the bride, the wife of the Lamb" (Revelation 21:6–9).

Revelation 19 describes the Lamb's bride.

"Let us rejoice and be glad and give the glory to Him, for the marriage of the Lamb has come and His bride has made herself ready." It was given to her to clothe herself in fine linen, bright and clean; for the fine linen is the righteous acts of the saints (Revelation 19:7–8).

Insult to Purity

Purity of body and spirit has always been God's will for us. He is holy and He created us to be holy (1 Peter 1:16). You as a wife should be gloriously pure, without spot or blemish for your husband, just as the church is for Christ (Ephesians 5:25–27).

> Professing to be wise, they became fools, and exchanged the glory of the incorruptible God for an image in the form of corruptible man . . . Therefore God gave them over in the lusts of their hearts to impurity, so that their bodies would be dishonored among them . . . For this reason God gave them over to degrading passions [Remember that burning fire within each of us which had become evil within these people?]; for their women exchanged the natural function for that which is unnatural, and in the same way also the men abandoned the natural function of the woman and burned in their desire toward one another, men with men committing indecent acts and receiving in their own persons the due penalty of their error (Romans 1:22–27).

It was Satan who brought the beautiful picture of unity down to the mire of all that is dirty and evil. Pornography, sexual bondage, sadism, and any other aberrant sexual act is an insult to the purity, holiness, and honor of God. Anyone who engages in such activity will reap what they sow.

God intends sexual unity to be for the pleasure of a husband and wife in the sanctity of the marriage bed. It should be held in honor. A senator from Hawaii once stated, "Sex is not a spectator sport." He expressed God's view. Paul wrote, "Immorality or any impurity or greed must not even be named among you, as is proper among saints" (Ephesians 5:3).

God calls for us to be set apart. We are to walk different from the world. If we choose to disobey, He will be our avenger.

> For this is the will of God, your sanctification; that is, that you abstain from sexual immorality; that each of you know how to possess his own vessel in sanctification and honor, not in lustful passion, like the Gentiles who do not know God . . . For God has not called us for the purpose of impurity, but in sanctification. So, he who rejects this is not rejecting man but the God who gives His Holy Spirit to you (1 Thessalonians 4:3–8).

It is time for us as Christian women to realize the seriousness of our calling. If we do not "possess our vessel in sanctification and honor," we are rejecting God.

🌱 What were the two purposes of the sexual act given in Genesis 1–2?

🌱 How will you enjoy the sexual part of your marriage as God intended?

Day 5

No Shame

Song of Solomon was written in Solomon's early years; it speaks of his mother's placing the crown upon his head. It is the love story of Solomon and Shulamith from courtship to mature marital love. *Solomon* means "peace," and *Shulamith* is the feminine of his name, so the two names combined tell us that God intended man and woman to live as one in peace. Solomon's other name was *Jedidiah*, "beloved of Yahweh [Jehovah]." We recognize this song coming from the Beloved of God. It teaches about love and marriage between lovers who lived in a peaceful union by the direction of the Holy Spirit.

Both husband and wife submit to the other's desires.

The New Testament's "Song" teaches us how to walk in love, as the bride of Christ, and commands us to "be subject to one another in the fear of Christ" (Ephesians 5:21). Song of Solomon is God's marriage manual; it instructs us in love's way and in the consequences of failing to obey the love call of the marriage partner (Song of Solomon 5:2–9). Both husband and wife submit to the other's desires and the other's will, but the husband is the recognized God-given head, just as Christ is the head of His bride, the church.

Write below the chain of authority in God's home (1 Corinthians 11:1–3).

Many commentators cannot believe God would give such intimate details of the husband/wife union, so they try to look at Song of Solomon as speaking spiritually of Christ's union with His church, which in itself is a lesson on the purity of the sexual union of you and your husband. However, the book is to be accepted as the literal love life and marriage of Solomon. It is a serious marriage guide; it is for you.

You and your husband become one, but your completeness and fullness and holiness is found only in your union with Christ as His bride. You complement one another in the fullness of Jesus, following in His way. "For in Him all the fullness of Deity dwells in bodily form, and in Him you have been made complete, and He is the head over all rule and authority" (Colossians 2:9–10).

What is your feeling about your sexual union with your husband?

Eyes of Love

Shulamith taught us that there is a difference in the way males and females enjoy the sexual act. The first step in learning to please one another is to understand and appreciate those differences. Notice how each lover describes the other. Males are more visually oriented. The woman's naked body is very stimulating to the male. Remember, Eve was presented without clothes to Adam by the Father, and there was no shame in either Adam or Eve. Learn to allow your husband to enjoy seeing your body. Don't worry about "too much of this or too little of that" which you see in the mirror. He views you through eyes of love, and if you are sensual and meet his needs, he doesn't care, that is, if you have not just totally let yourself go.

Keep yourself in shape for your own health first, then for the pleasure of your husband. An older woman once proudly told me that her husband had never seen her naked. Do you wonder they never had any children! Each of Song's lovers reveled in the other's body and exclaimed about it to the other (Song of Solomon 5:10–16; 7:1–9). They stimulated one another by love talk. Women are more sound-oriented than men, so pretty music and love's words are stimulating to the woman. Men like to see and feel their wives' bodies; we women should respond by allowing him to caress us, and in turn caress him. You may have to teach your husband the pleasure of having his skin gently massaged with fingers, brushes, and other pleasurable things. Let your mind lead you into all kinds of joyous experiments.

For a birthday surprise one year, I paid our children to remove the leaves and branches from their tree house. After they left for school that morning I mounted the ladder and set up a Tarzan and Jane luncheon. Then I donned my Jane outfit and left Loden a note to put on his Tarzan kilt and join me in the tree house. Use your imagination. We still talk about the fun we had!

Talk to Me

Neither of you can read minds, so during your love-making, freely discuss what is pleasurable and what you like. That is hard for some of us, but we must be open about sex. Work on it.

Verbally express yourself while your husband is trying to pleasure you—no talk about needing a new dryer! And do not discuss mundane house needs right after sex! He may think that is what you were thinking about. And what do you do when he turns over and goes to sleep immediately after the sex act? Tell him you would like to snuggle and talk awhile. Each has to understand and respect the other's needs to make sex a joy for both. That is the goal: a win/win for both of you.

Keep your conversation positive and uplifting. For example: "I really like it when you . . ." or "I enjoy it when you touch me and stroke me here" or "How would you feel if we try . . . ?" Don't ever criticize your husband's love-making. Keep your words positive! Notice the adjectives the lovers use in Song of Solomon to describe their love-making. One can follow the progression of their love-making by their words to one another.

Bed Buddy or Lover?

How do you dress for bed? Husbands want to go to bed with a lover, not a buddy, so don't dress in clothes that mimic men's shorts and tee shirts. Wear a sexy gown. When I wanted to buy Loden a present guaranteed to please, I got a sexy new piece of underwear. It was always received with pleasure. Remember God made him that way. Your own dear buffalo!

Husbands want a lover, not a buddy.

Shulamith's banner was love. A banner was used to give information—a battle banner, a banner for the king, a flag, we would say today. The banner that protected Shulamith was her own dear buffalo, Solomon, putting his flag of love over her head. He wanted her and the world to know that his heart belonged to her, and he put a flag over her to let all know she was his and under his protection (Song of Solomon 2:4). A love flag was over their whole relationship. Allow your husband to give you that security, and proudly let his banner of love fly over you.

How does your husband like for you to arouse him? Do you try new ways? Do you ever buy books on love's techniques? Remember, there is no right or wrong.

Use Your Senses

Enhance your love-making with candles, incense, and perfume, as Solomon and Shulamith did (Song of Solomon 1:3, 12–13). Before love time, light incense in your bathroom. Try cinnamon. It is quite a come-on for men. Do not light candles unless you can monitor them. Even then, place them away from the bed. Try bathing by candlelight. Lavender is very complimentary to the female body. Invest in the pure oil of lavender; wear it on your body and put it on your bed sheets. I tried to put dabs on each night to remind Loden of our intimacy. It helped to bring back memories that were precious to us. Purchase oil of lavender at a health-food store and spray your sheets before a night of love.

Take time to bathe or shower together before the love-making begins. Savor the time as you enjoy one another. Touch and kiss on each other. Talk to one another, laugh, and even sing if it enters your mind to do so. This can be a very special ritual that arouses the sexual mood. In today's rush, rush, rush society, couples feel they do not have time for love-making. Take time! Your body, emotions, and spirit need the release and health-giving benefits of the sex act.

When the Father finished His creation, He said it was very good (Genesis 1:31). Everything He created has a purpose in His plan for us.

Select a romantic CD and whisper words of love and admiration as it plays sweet music. Your sighs and moans will assure him that you are being pleasured. Use your eyes to guide, appreciate, and direct your mutual conversation. Flirting with your eyes is always fun for your husband. Remember, he is visually oriented, so keep the bedroom decorated for love.

Solomon and Shulamith's love nest is described as luxuriant with beams of cedar and rafters of cypress (Song of Solomon 1:16–17), types of wood usually reserved for king's houses. Solomon made his wife's bedroom very special.

Color and Flowers

Colors effect moods. Red is stimulating while pink is calming. Blue is peaceful; green brings productivity. Decorate your bedroom in a peaceful, tasteful way with appropriate colors. Your bedroom is your love nest, so make it, along with your bathroom, a special room for lovers.

Try always to have flowers in your bathroom. We use that room often, and fresh flowers lift the spirit so. I used to put flowers in special little vases and attach a love note for Loden. Try this: leave a note in the morning offering him some wonderful pleasure come night. Your husband loves to be seduced.

Romancing is another ploy. Whisper "sweet nothings" in his ear and then promise if he appears at a certain place and time, wonderful happenings will take place. Don't let him down. Think about your gift all day and prepare for time to make him feel super special. If you feed a man physically, sexually, spiritually, and emotionally, he'll fall at your feet and adore you for all your life. And, Dear One, that is not a bad thing! It is quite enjoyable and satisfying to know you are doing him good all the days of his life.

Use Your Charms

Make dates and keep them. Prioritize your activities to include what is important to the intimacy of your marriage and its health. The skin is the largest organ of the body, so pleasure one another by starting your evening bathing together—and leave no inch of skin unloved. There is nothing evil in lovemaking as long as it is pleasurable for both of you, so freely experiment. Remember, the Father created sex for pleasure, so enjoy!

Song of Solomon describes love-making in detail as each part of the body receives kissing and touching. No part is excluded (2:1–6; 4:9–16; 5:1). The mind is the ultimate sexual organ. Notice how the lovers thought about their time together and anticipated their love-making. Seduce your husband before he goes to work so both of you can spend the day anticipating the pleasure of the evening. Shulamith told her lover she had planned their love-making and was going to include some new things along with the old (Song of Solomon 7:10–13).

Plan some new things and do not hesitate to take the lead in love-making. Your taking the lead stimulates your husband.

Follow Shulamith's example and create new and exciting ways to change your love-making methods, anything to make this part of your life fun and playful. No one else can get your husband to relax and enjoy playing roles like you, so use your charms to keep your love-life glowing and growing. Sex is your own special world, so continue to make wonderful, warm memories that will carry you through the dry periods that come in every relationship.

Costume Party

I enjoy the memory of the week our children were away visiting my parents. I prepared a different type of meal each night and served it in a different place in the house. Our costumes, as well as our entertainment, reflected the country we were "visiting" that night. We ate all over the house—on tables, on the floor—anywhere I could think of to make life different and fun.

Don't take for granted that you know what your husband will and won't do. I thought Loden would find this game silly, but afterwards, every so often, he would ask, "When are we going to have another costume party?" So allow your husband to make up his own mind as to whether or not he wants to try something new. If you are enthusiastic, he probably will be too. Dale Carnegie's motto states, "If you act enthusiastic, you'll be enthusiastic." If you begin rekindling your imagination, he will pick up on it and come up with some ideas of his own. Here's an example.

If you don't invent fun, you won't have it!

Once when I returned from my sister's, Loden had planned a scavenger hunt, and oh, was it a fun evening! Another time he had covered our bathroom mirror—all eight feet of it—with pictures of our life together and a welcome home sign, his banner of love over me. Let the fun of discovery and being a child once again develop within you to make life fun and special for the two of you. If you don't invent fun, you won't have it! No one else is going to do it for you.

I Already Washed My Feet

In chapter 5 of Song, Shulamith refused to allow Solomon into her bed chamber, although he was desirous of being with her sexually. She used a very flimsy excuse: "I have already washed my feet and am in bed, and I don't want to get them dirty." Rather like our excuse of "headache" or "too tired," isn't it? Then she became conscience-stricken and got up to let Solomon in, but he was gone; his fragrance remained on the door handles. She tried in vain to find him, and the watchmen of the city beat her. Shulamith was sorry for her refusal; she paid a heavy price for denying her husband.

🌿 Read 1 Corinthians 7:3–5 and list the commands.

Both husbands and wives use 1 Corinthians 7 to berate one another. That is wrong. Often when a husband is not treating the wife in the manner of Christ and she refuses to have sex with him, he quotes this verse. This is the wrong use of God's Word and such is sinful.

However, many wives who do not find sex appealing deprive their husbands. That is also wrong; perhaps the couple needs help to recognize their sins and restore proper love to the marriage. Happily married people do not have a problem working on the frequency of their love-making. One may not feel like it but will use the dear old motto of the class: "Act your way into feeling!" One can also coyly say, "I am not in the mood, but we could both enjoy your getting me into the mood."

Never withhold sex as punishment.

Love finds a way. Remember, agape love steps in when the other four loves lag, so if nothing else works, think of his needs and take care of them in a very loving way. Sex is very calming and invigorating, so even if you start tired, when you set your mind to the body, you will find it is worth the effort and time. It should not have to be said, but it does: "Sex should never be used as a weapon against your husband." You never withhold sex as punishment or to get your way. Dear One, that is a sin not only against your husband but also against God—it is not obeying His Word.

Have you thought about this fact: each wall of your house of love is involved in having a satisfying love life? You need the romance to make it interesting, the erotic to make it satisfying, the friendship to make it enjoyable, the family to make it special.

🌿 How do you feel when you turn your husband away from having sex?

Full of Sweetness

Song of Solomon ends with the lovers once again verbally sharing their love. Read chapter 8 and let the beautiful words sink into your mind. Solomon found peace in his beloved Shulamith, and the book ends with her words ringing to all generations that sex is only for the married, and young women should keep their bodies only for their husbands. She utters the closing words to indicate she was anxious once again to be united in body with her Solomon: "Hurry, my beloved, and be like a gazelle or a young stag on the mountains of spices" (Song of Solomon 8:14).

You too can be like Shulamith and declare to all your love for your husband in this way, "His mouth is full of sweetness, and he is wholly desirable, this is my beloved and this is my friend" (Song of Solomon 5:16).

These lessons are as new as the day and as lasting as the Son. Each came to us through the pages of the Word. Now it is your turn to learn them, live them, and let them pass from your lips to the ears of another. God's Word must be taught by those who have embraced its truths and want others to share in the good promises of the Father. So love that wonderful buffalo of a man and act your way into feeling when you need to—allow the Spirit to make of you a beautiful butterfly that will sip all the sweet nectar God has in store for you.

Don't forget your daily workout; you do not want to go back to the old you. Remember, after three days, you stink! My love and prayers go with you. The next chapter is "Patsy's Potpourri" and will be just what the word implies: a mixture of dried flowers and spices kept in a jar for its fragrance. I hope the various petals will add fragrance to your life and love.

Memory Verse

"Put me like a seal over your heart, like a seal on your arm.
For love is as strong as death, jealousy is as severe as Sheol; its
flashes are flashes of fire, the very flame of the Lord."

Song of Solomon 8:6

My Homework

1. Continue to make prayer a constant source of help and strength for the day.

2. Write down things that you find a little awkward about your sexual union. Then go back and note ways you can overcome feeling this way.

3. Work on feeling as Adam and Eve did about their sexuality. Pray for God's help in giving you freedom of expression in this area of love.

4. Rate your marriage on the intimacy level. On a scale of one to ten (ten being the highest) rate the five areas of intimacy given.

    _____ Positive thinking   _____ Empathy

    _____ Till death do us part   _____ Total acceptance

    _____ Mutual love and respect

5. Which areas do you need to work on? How will you increase the number of the low characteristics? You must have a plan to succeed.

6. This week, come up with a new way to make love with your husband. Make a date with him for that purpose, and carry out your plan. Make it interesting! Include in your plans the reading of the Song, each of you reading the male/female part, respectively. Try to discern what the symbols mean. The fruits discussed are parts of the body. See if you can decide what is meant and learn some new techniques from the two great lovers.

Week 10

Patsy's Potpourri

From the Father of the Bride: "My [daughter], do not forget my teaching, but let your heart keep my commandments; for length of days and years of life and peace, they will add to you. Do not let kindness and truth leave you; bind them around your neck, write them on the tablet of your heart. So you will find favor and good repute in the sight of God and man [especially your husband]. Trust in the Lord with all your heart and do not lean on your own understanding. In all your ways acknowledge Him, and He will make your paths straight. Do not be wise in your own eyes; fear the Lord and turn away from evil. It will be healing to your body and refreshment to your bones" (Proverbs 3:1–8).

From Mother Sarah: I obeyed Abraham and called him Lord of my own free will. He, in return, loved me deeply and mourned and wept for me when I left him for Paradise. When you love your husband as much as I did mine, then you will know the joy I had as a wife (Genesis 23:1–2).

From Queen Mother: "The heart of her husband trusts in her, and he will have no lack of gain" (Proverbs 31:11). You will provide all your husband needs all your life, and you will reap the joys of committed love with him.

From Shulamith: If you fully love your husband, he will exclaim over you as Solomon did when he said to me: "You are a garden spring, a well of fresh water" (Song of Solomon 4:15).

From Patsy: The things I have written to you are truths from God. Follow the footsteps of Jesus to change your life for the better. Since I have been teaching these lessons from God's Word, I have not found one woman who followed these truths to be disappointed in the results. Even if your partner does not follow Christ, you will still reap the promises given. You can have the joy of Jesus in your heart and be at peace. Our expectations of life are seldom realized totally, so we must learn to be adjustable, allow the Father to lead us where He will, and be at peace in knowing we are "standing our ground" where He stationed us. Note the excerpt from Robert Browning's poem, "Rabbi Ben Ezra":

> Grow old along with me!
> The best is yet to be.
> The last of life, for which the first was made:
> Our times are in His hand.
> Who saith, "A whole I planned,
> Youth shows but half; trust God; see all, nor be afraid.

Day 1

From Despair to Contentment

Jane came into the class full of assurance that she was really a good wife who needed to learn techniques to shape her husband into line—her line, that is. I fully understood, because I had those exact thoughts when I first took the course.

Both Jane and I had to learn that no one has the right even to try to change another—that is God's work. But we can allow God to change us into being love and to bring us to His standard of conduct, not ours.

Here is Jane's letter describing her journey from self to selflessness. Notice her success in seeing her husband grow and develop into the man she wanted—not through any forcing of will, but through her loving him in the ways Jesus asked her to love him. She recognized God's power over her husband's life. You will find, too, that He can do a far better job than you ever could.

Dear Miss Patsy,

Thank you for the time that you took to help women like me to be what God wants us to be as wives. When I came to your class of how to be a Christian wife, I thought I had a good marriage. I was so wrong. I listened to you and tried to do what you were teaching us. I was so bad because I was not living God's way, but I was living my own way. My marriage came apart, but I kept working at God's way, the way you showed us in the class. I had peace in my heart.

God's Word was what saved my marriage. Thank you for sharing God's Word. I have to work on doing what you have taken the time to teach us about God's Word: to love my husband the way God wants me to. My husband has come a long way, but the two of us have worked a long time to bring it to this point. I felt at times like I wanted to give up. That is the worldly way out. You showed me the love of God.

Your class has helped me to love my husband. I could not do it without your help. You emphasized that God has a place for us. When we say "I do" in marriage, we are saying "I will" to our God first and then our husbands. That was what saved my marriage.

Miss Patsy, I did not know how to be a wife, but with God's help and your class, you have taken the time to teach and show many women how to love our husbands and how to live as God has taught us. I have to retrain myself every day, and remember how to speak to my husband. Thank you for all your help. I know it won't be easy, but I will keep doing what works and it is God's way, the only way. Miss Patsy, I thank God for you. I know God put you in my life to help me be a better wife and person. I will teach my daughter and grand-daughter the way to be a better person and wife some day. Thank you, Miss Patsy. God bless.

Jane has been working for a few years on improving her serve, and as you can see, she has grown from "I" to "we." You can deduce that changing is not a one-day transformation but the culmination of hundreds of daily efforts.

She told me how tired she was, and I reminded her that learning to live, think, and talk in a different way is very taxing to the body and mind. But like any other exercise routine, the more she practiced, the easier it would become. Those muscles get into a different mode, and before long the new you becomes natural and your energy surfaces. Love is energizing!

Remember the rule about developing a habit? When you begin to reshape yourself in God's mold, life can become painful, but if you keep following the footsteps of Jesus, you will begin to take on His thinking, His actions, and His words. Jane realized she was not allowing her husband to be the head of the marriage, so he was reacting in the opposite direction of her old habits. When she changed her tactics and began living in love's way, she immediately noticed a change in him, his attitude, and his actions. She also noticed that she was begin-ning to love him again and to think of him in a positive way.

Jane had invested years in this "buffalo." If she left him, wouldn't she have to start all over with her same problems? And if she left, would God or Satan be pleased? She began thinking positively and, as a result, their marriage changed for the better. Is her marriage perfect? No. Was my marriage perfect after more than fifty-one years? Not quite!

What progress have you made so far in your efforts to become a lovely butterfly?

What changes have you noticed in your husband?

Day 2

The Mature Years

Life is lived one day at a time, but years pass in a flash! You have only today, so live it well and plan for the tomorrows. Make memories to cherish, not memories to regret. If you continue to live, you will age, and with age comes change, change, and more change. Prepare for the days when you will have reared your children, because then who will be home? Just you two lovers who began the marriage journey years before.

Dear One, you will have to work just as hard on your marriage in the years to come as you did in the honeymoon years. The "empty nest" years are often susceptible to divorce. Two have lived as strangers, occupying the same quarters, but neither knows the person sitting across the table or sleeping on the other side of the bed. Gone is the desire to be together. Do you see the reason you must put your husband first and develop your relationship with him in your busy, hectic younger life? Never put your children before him.

As we near the close of our study, you are still building your house of love. Make sure the four walls of erotic, romantic, friendship, and family love are all strong and sturdy, and that your roof of agape love does not leak. Keep stoking the flame of love God placed within you—repair the walls and roof as needed. Keep Wisdom on retainer for furnishing your home with treasures to be enjoyed, even more now that you have more time to savor them. The fire the Father put within your home is not the burning flame of passion you knew as a young bride but something even better. The flame has settled into bright glowing embers of great warmth and beauty.

Embrace Age with Joy

Love settles from passion to loving stability as your two lives melt into one. The warmth of embers is much more intense than that blazing flame. You begin marriage with the dominate walls of romantic and sexual love, but as the years flow, family and friendship grow brighter. Your agape love grows even stronger. After fifty years, agape love will dominate, and it is the sweetest of all! Therefore, embrace age with joy rather than dread. With all its aches and pains, the beauty of your oneness in the winter years have a majesty and mystic glow that the other seasons do not know. You have more time to appreciate that buffalo. And he will treasure his beautiful, delicate butterfly more than ever.

How can your love abound and overflow for your husband similar to that of Paul's love for the Philippians? (Philippians 1: 8–9).

Your sexual love will intensify in your forties and beyond. Once the children are gone, you can concentrate on pleasing one another without interruption—if you will take the phone off the hook, turn that cell phone off, and drag yourself away from the TV. Marriage counselors suggest that couples have a "toy box" of pleasure-giving goodies: books to learn how to make love to one another, volumes of love poems to read aloud to one another, a large soft brush to use with a delightful smelling dusting powder to give pleasure to one another's body, and paint brushes and washable paint for those Michelangelo nights. (Don't forget to include a plastic sheet to catch the paint drippings.) As your body ages, you will make other adjustments in your lovemaking.

Love settles from passion to loving stability.

Of all the species created, the Father gave only the woman a special body part exclusively for sexual enjoyment, so don't deprive yourself of this health-giving experience. It makes us women easier to live with; it is very good medicine for the woman in many ways. In some cultures, little girls are circumcised in a very cruel and dangerous way. Men in that society do not want their women to enjoy sex—it is only for men! You are blessed to be spared such a gruesome life.

Buffalo for Life

Be thankful for your Bridegroom Jesus. Only where His truth is followed are women treated with the respect of a beautiful porcelain dish rather than a cracked pottery piece! Be thankful for your privilege of being a child of God and a lover to your husband. You belong to each other (1 Corinthians 7:2–5).

Keep in mind that your husband was created a buffalo, and a buffalo he will be all his life. God instilled within him the attributes of that maleness. Even though time takes its toll on both your bodies, your basic attributes do not change. The male body is different from yours; to be healthy and comfortable, he needs sexual relief. A wife's refusal to have sex will often cause great discomfort in his body. The Father designed sex for the purpose of pleasure, procreation, and good health. Medical science is just now discovering how much orgasms in both male and female bodies contribute to healthy bodies and minds. The emotions receive a great boost also. Don't be guilty of depriving your husband of this truly life-giving relief. It is as good for you as for him and helps keep you young. Don't forget to be playful with each other. How long has it been since you had a pillow fight or chased one another around the house? Much fun and many laughs are good for the soul! Don't forget to add special music for your occasions. "Bolero" is famed as the perfect music for lovemaking.

Make Adjustments

Dear One, let me advise you of this truth. The sex act helps to keep your husband's male hormones developing; it keeps him younger in body and spirit, and it is your pleasure to help him stay virile. As we grow older, our bodies slow down. We must make appropriate changes. Hormones are more responsive in the morning than the evening; rearrange your lovemaking times accordingly.

If you are pleasing him, he will not notice the little sags here and there that we women detest. Give him your full attention, and hide the mirrors! If you have had a wonderful love life, you are going to miss it when the time comes that health or age takes the full pleasure from you. When this day comes, don't quit touching, kissing, and talking love's words to one another, and allow each other sexual relief if it is possible. Allow memory to recall special times and places, and enjoy the tender feelings you both felt in younger years. Such recapping of life's adventures helps keep love's flame glowing. Hold hands often and never pass him without touching him and telling him how much you love him.

One part of your sexual life may cease, but not all of it, so use what you have and be thankful and joyous in pleasing one another. Be his lover, tell him of your needs, and let him still be a lover to you. Your assurance gives him a feeling of manhood. We women often think our men should react as we do, but they don't. Never let yourself forget that God made your husband male and He made you female, and the two are not the same, but each blends into the other to make a whole. Treasure that difference and honor that man as your man all your days. Too many women are relieved when their husbands can no longer have sex, and then they deny their husbands the physical love they can enjoy. But he needs to continue to feel that he is a man!

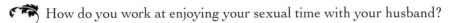 How do you work at enjoying your sexual time with your husband?

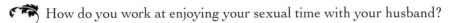 What are you doing to help make these very special memory-making times?

Young at Heart

Your romantic love must also continue. You do not want to develop a brother/sister relationship with your husband. Always treat him as a lover, not a sibling, and certainly not as parent or child. As you grow older, you might have to fight becoming the caregiver and subconsciously falling into the mother role. *But fight you must, with all your might!* Even if he is ill, you must still treat him with honor and dignity, and allow him to be in charge. If you do not, you will have emasculated him!

Keep the love notes, the fresh flowers, and the words of love flowing even in sickness. Laughter and teasing keep the atmosphere fresh and playful. Kiss often especially when he leaves or returns home. Hold him and make him continue to feel like your young buffalo rushing toward you across the plains as Shulamith describes her gazelle rushing to her mountain of spices in Song of Solomon. Your husband will respond to you according to the way you treat him. Continuously feeding him the food of love will also help keep him young in heart and mind.

Once while on the campus at Freed-Hardeman University, a young woman asked, "You are the valentine couple, aren't you?" In the spring of that year, Loden and I had been asked to give the history of the special valentines he presents to me each year on Valentine's Day, complete with exhibits. Our conversation with the young student gave us an opportunity to give her a little free advice about life. You, too, should pass on the knowledge and understanding of love's way to the next generation.

You must not fall into the "mother" role.

As your marriage grows, you will develop your own romantic specialties. Here's a memorable one:

> Susan: "Have you bought Calvin his valentine yet? We only have two more days!"
> Evelyn: "No, I bought him the perfect valentine years ago. It said just what I wanted, so why should I buy another? Each year, I add a line to it and give it to him again. But I don't know what I am going to do in the years to come—I have about filled all the space!"
>
> Evelyn's yearly valentine became intriguing to Calvin's co-workers. They began to ask him every year, "Have you received your valentine? What did Evelyn write this year?"
> One year Evelyn forgot "the valentine," and Calvin came storming into the kitchen demanding, "Where is my valentine? I want it right now!"

Do you think this symbol of their lasting love had any meaning to Calvin? After the community lost both of these unique and wonderful people, I saw their daughter at a Garden Club meeting and asked her, "Did you find the valentine?" She answered me, "Yes, I did, and it is my most treasured possession from them."

Stay romantic all your life.

How have you romanced your husband lately? When have you sent him a love note?

Have you worn a pretty nightgown for him lately? Have you worn sexy underwear for him in the last week?

Your Husband Is Your Friend

Your friendship should have grown oh so close that you almost know what the other is thinking. Loden often remarked that I knew what he was going to say or do before he did it. I'd just sweetly smile, "It's because I love you and study you so much!" Even though I knew pretty much what Loden would decide, I deferred to him. If someone came to me and asked me to speak for him, I'd reply, "You'll have to ask Loden." He landed a surprise in my lap now and then! We did not make decisions for each other.

As friends, feel free to enjoy separate activities with others; however, don't let that be the primary friendship! Your husband is number one always. If you must, change plans to go with him, and do so willingly. You will be well rewarded by his devotion, if you put him first. He will in return give you the same treatment.

Even if you are not a fan of his activities, find a way to join him in his pleasure. I did not often watch football games with Loden, but I made it a point to pass through the den, stop a minute, ask him the score, and discuss a play with him. You can share his interests without participating fully in something that has no real interest for you. I often sat on the couch and read while he watched his games, looking up from my book occasionally to inquire about a play.

At times I even got involved with a game and showed much more enthusiasm in cheering my team than he ever did. I learned to enjoy the football games at our local high school; we attended them together. Loden would say "so she can visit friends," and that was not too far from the truth. But I did go and that pleased him. I bought him a small radio with ear plugs so he could listen to the broadcast as he watched from the bleachers. Find some way to show that you want him to enjoy his pleasure: golfing, hunting, fishing, or whatever. One woman told me she sits and reads while she watches her husband tinker with a car he is rebuilding. She talks to him and gives him the pleasure of her presence.

Kindness in Action

Friends share conversation, so talk with your husband during meals, while riding in the car, and while walking together. Some husbands lament that they ride for hours in the car without their wife ever speaking. Loden was not fond of reading, but he did get hooked on listening to audio books during road trips. When we arrived home with an unfinished, interesting book, he would say, "Now don't you listen to the end without me!"

Friends keep in touch. One loving couple talks to each other throughout the day by cell phone. He needs her input on business decisions, but mostly he just wants to hear her voice. They plan their evening or their week's activities. The phone call always ends with, "I love you." That is what God meant for us—romantic love intertwined with the friendship. You should never have a better friend than your husband. Go to him with your problems. But remember to inform him whether you are going to vent or seek a solution. Men are problem-solvers, you know.

Do him the favor of just listening when he needs a friendly ear. Usually men do not want our advice, so ask him, "Do you just need my ear or my help?" When he walks into the house in the afternoon, you know what kind of day he has had, so kindly ask, "Do you need to vent or cuddle?" That is kindness in action.

My Lips Are Sealed

One of the best counselors I have known gave me this sage advice about giving counsel:

> When someone comes to you with a problem, don't even think about giving them any of your advice, no matter how good it may be. The person knows before they come to you what they are going to do. All they want from you is a sounding board. Also, if you give them advice, they take it and use it, and it backfires on them, then they will be angry with you for bad advice. On the other hand if you give them your advice and time, and they don't take any of your good advice, then you will be angry with them for wasting your time. Therefore, no advice will be forthcoming from your lips.
>
> Your role is to ask questions to get them to think for themselves. Use the key words *how, when, where, why, what,* and *how.* For example, ask, *How do you feel about this situation? What are your options? What do you think the outcome will be if you try the various solutions you have? Why did you decide upon this way of solving the problem? What will be the cost? How do you think the outcome will affect all those who are involved?* These are questions that evoke thought so a person can solve a problem for himself. Then the solution will be a personal one, and the troubled one will put forth the effort to carry out the proposed solution.

I have used this method for years with very good results, and highly recommend it. Your husband needs a sounding board, and you can fulfill that need by simply asking the right questions. It will take a load off your mind and remove nagging doubts from your emotions.

Here is a very real illustration of unkind thinking. You ask your husband to pick up a loaf of bread on his way home from the office. He walks in the door with no sack! Well, it does not take a scientist to know he forgot the bread. How should you handle the matter?

Option 1:
Woman: "Well, I see you are your usual Mr. Forgetfulness. I knew I could not count on you to remember one thing. I don't know why I asked you in the first place to pick up one measly loaf of bread."

Option 2:
Woman: "Did you happen to have time to stop for the bread?"
Man: "Oh, I just let it slip my mind. I will go back and get it."

Woman: "That is okay, Sweetie; going back to the store is far too much trouble for you. I can pick up a loaf tomorrow; I'm going to the store anyway. I will manage without it tonight. I know how tired you must be or you would not have forgotten."

How many Brownie points will each rate you? Which way will add a ruby to your crown and which will put some rust in that halo you think you wear? Choices!

How long has it been since you told him how much his friendship means to you? When did you last plan something fun to do for the day just for the friendship side of your relationship?

Create some unusual, no-cost activities that will be pleasurable for the two of you.

Stretched Two Ways

Your family love will expand on both sides. When you reach the middle years you are stretched on the left with aging parents who have special needs and on the right with children who are beginning their careers and families. Who is in the middle? It's poor you who would like to have your hands stretch forward to embrace your husband, but instead are stretched to each side by the entreaties of parents and children. You must go one way or the other, but never forget your vows: leave father and mother and cleave to your husband. He must always come first.

Make the commitment Loden and I did: "Our home is within one another's arms." Remember it. Learn to say no to parents, children, and friends. And don't feel guilty because your husband is number one in your life.

Keep Changing

One young husband began to complain to his wife about the time, energy, and emotion she invested in her parents' problems. Her dedication to them interfered with her marriage relationship. Everyone has to draw the line at some point. "Your parents can solve some of their problems themselves," he told her. But it was easier to let the daughter take care of them.

Don't feel guilty when you put your husband at the top of your list. Dear Loden insisted that I go and spend time with my parents, my sister Sue, and my teaching in Poland. It tore me emotionally to leave him, but he wanted me to go. And I did need to help my sister with Mother's care in her later years. However, when Loden developed physical issues, my reply to needy calls was, "I can no longer leave him alone; if he cannot come with me, I must decline."

You see what I meant by saying you must be willing to keep changing? As life throws its small and large hailstones on your house of love, it will try to break through that roof of agape love. I had to give up going to Poland and teaching English through the Bible, a work very dear to my heart. But my True Heart needed me more, and the Father opened doors for me to teach where Loden could go with me. We had time together like never before, and it was nice, Dear One.

Our home is within each other's arms.

Always look for the positive and enjoy what you have. Don't lament over what you don't have, because you will never receive all you want anyway. Be willing to compromise with a joyful heart; the glass is half full, not half empty!

 How have I allowed my parents or children to come first in my life?

 Why does my husband know I treasure him above all others? What have I done in the last week to show him how much he means to me?

Storms Blow Over

Agape love shields the other four loves through thick and thin—through all the storms of life. We do have to learn to keep those thin times at bay while we hunker down in love's protection and wait for the bad storms to blow over. We learn proper love because God first loved us (1 John 4:19). By now you have learned that principle, haven't you? Agape love is all in the daily choices we make: Do I look at this as a negative or a positive? Do I treat the person in the way of grace or in my selfish way? How can I wait patiently and allow God to make something good come from this storm?

 What does 2 Corinthians 9:8 mean in terms of agape love and your interaction with your husband? Why will the Father give you grace to develop agape love?

The Father allows bumps in the road; they teach us to slow down, ponder, and learn. The Bible reveals that Jesus learned obedience though the things He suffered. We, too, learn through suffering. When we are happy-go-lucky, we do not usually consider the deeper mysteries the Father wants us to master. Through the agony of the cross, Jesus brought salvation to the world. As a result He was given the title "King of kings, and Lord of lords." Don't look at problems as black holes, but embrace them with joy. They are learning experiences, stretching exercises, faith-builders, and times for prayer. Be thankful for the privilege of asking the Father for the wisdom to deal with life's rocky road.

Difficult situations handled correctly require much faith and trust in the promises of the Father; you will have to grow to recognize this blessing. I went through three really rough trials in my life. In my younger days, I almost lost my dear Loden twice and our daughter once. From these three experiences, I learned that strength from the Father does sustain me! I learned to wait patiently and look for blessings to be gained from walking through the valley of the shadow of death. I learned how very much the Father loves and cares for us. I realized how very precious loved ones are—never take their presence for granted. Enjoy each day of living with them; it is a gift from the Father. Accept it joyfully and with thanksgiving.

Write two truths from James 1:2–8 that apply to you.

Day 3

Review of Love's Way

Love's way is not always noticed, especially by our children, but it is felt. Sometimes they will not fully appreciate your love until they are parents. Then they realize what you sacrificed for them in the name of love.

Likewise, we are building a house of love which may not be noticed by the world, but the Father and Jesus will see. God dwells with us if we are building our house according to His rules. Your husband will adore living in your house of love where the fire of God will keep both of you toasty and warm. You are building the future of our country with confidence that the Father will continue to bless a nation that looks to Him for guidance. The greatest service you can give your country is righteous living.

We provide foundations for the homes our children will build when they marry; they subconsciously construct their house of love according to the plans they learned from Mother and Daddy. Don't ever feel that no one appreciates what you do day after day, love deed after love deed. The Father sees; He is pleased and blesses your efforts. Your children will show their appreciation by bringing their friends to your home. They may really never know why they do this, other than it feels good to be in your house of love. That is the greatest compliment—they want to be inside your love and share it with their friends.

So day after day, toil at shaping yourself into love. Then use the wisdom you learned from the Father to build your house of love with your husband and children. This is the greatest blessing you can give the world, although it never recognizes your labor of love. But your Father and your husband will, and that is what matters most! The effect of your house of love will last eternally.

Without Love

The first three verses of 1 Corinthians 13 provide a commentary on various religious practices of the day.

❧ The Greeks used large bronze jars in the back of theaters to echo and amplify the sounds from the stage. Paul says you are just an echo if you act without love. Faith without love is nothing of note.

❧ The Hindus had a religious practice of a new widow throwing herself onto the funeral pyre so her body, along with that of her husband's, was consumed. Even if she had no love for her husband, she was forced to honor the religious code.

❧ Buddha taught poverty—giving away all possessions—without regard to being desirous of holiness.

These major world religions were nothing compared to the greatest thing—love, the most excellent way. It is selfless—chosen by the heart. And it is always in the present tense. The Father wanted you to know His character so you could emulate it. Love is all you will take with you into eternity.

After beginning by describing what love is not, the chapter ends with the words, "But now abide faith, hope, love, these three; but the greatest of these is love."

Love is greater than faith because the end is greater than the means. Faith connects us to the Father, but love is the goal. Hope leads us to Jesus, but it is love that makes us follow in His footsteps, so love is greater than all. We must develop it in our hearts in order to love our husbands as God intends. Love on earth is merely a reflection. We bask in the love of the heavenly Son and shine forth His warmth as we reflect His glory.

The effect of your house of love will last eternally.

You are striving to have a heart as pure and loving as your parents had in the Garden of Eden. Satan brought sin into the heart of man and destroyed pure love. When you arose from that watery grave of baptism a new creature, you had to learn how to have a new heart, loving and pure like your heavenly Father. You have to work diligently to allow the Spirit to fashion you into holy love. It will be a life-long journey and a never ending struggle to say _____ (insert your name) is love.

Paul began his work for Jesus with the blood of saints on his zealous hands. Jesus taught him a more excellent way, and as you read through his inspired letters, you will see that agape love became central to his thinking as he grew in Christ. It is the most excellent way of life.

What Is Love?

Highlight the following characteristics of love from 1 Corinthians 13:

Love is patient. *Patience* is the natural attitude of love, and love is not in a hurry. The Bible speaks of "the fullness of time" in regards to Jesus' birth. Patience wears an attitude of contentment. The future is in God's hands; God acts in our best interests. Patience is endurance under the weight of everyday life.

How much patience have you developed in your life? List some ways you can become more patient.

Love is kind. *Kindness* is service, goodness, pleasantness, graciousness. It is the opposite of being harmful. Study the life of Jesus and see how much He used kindness to change hearts so He could teach His followers the truth. One can never be nearer God's heart than when being kind.

Jesus' acts of kindness were deeds the other person or persons needed: healing, restoration of life, forgiveness, and food, for instance. He saw the needs of others, and He helped them.

> I shall pass through this world but once.
> Any good thing, therefore, that I can do
> Or any kindness that I can show to any human being,
> Let me do it now. Let me not defer it or neglect it,
> For I shall not pass this way again.

How important is it to offer a sweet good-bye to your husband as he leaves for work each morning and to greet him lovingly when he returns each evening?

How do such greetings set the tone of the day and evening? Is this a part of walking in good works? (Ephesians 2:10). Explain your answer.

Love is not jealous. *Jealous* is the opposite of generous. Love desires the best of everything for others. Does this include your husband? Indeed. On the other hand, jealousy begrudges another the gifts that she wants for herself. It destroys love quickly, replacing it with feelings contrary to love. Jealousy is never content; it possesses the heart and suffocates the spirit. Do not give it even the tiniest place in your life.

Who among you is wise and understanding? Let him show by his good behavior his deeds in the gentleness of wisdom. But if you have bitter jealousy and selfish ambition in your heart, do not be arrogant and so lie against the truth. This wisdom is not that which comes down from above, but is earthly, natural, demonic. For where jealousy and selfish ambition exist, there is disorder and every evil thing. But the wisdom from above is first pure, then peaceable, gentle, reasonable, full of mercy and good fruits, unwavering, without hypocrisy. And the seed whose fruit is righteousness is sown in peace by those who make peace (James 3:13–18).

 List some companions of jealousy from the previous verses.

 Name some ways a husband or wife can be jealous of each other. What effect does jealousy have on the relationship?

Love does not brag and is not arrogant. In others words, love is humble. Do not boast about your kindness, good deeds, or giving. Love's action is not for self-gratification or praise. Jesus surmised, "So you too, when you do all the things which are commanded you, say, 'We are unworthy slaves; we have done only that which we ought to have done' " (Luke 17:10).

Could a husband's bragging be a symptom of his wife's failure to give him the attention and recognition he needs? Does he tout his worth hoping his wife will begin to give him the respect he desires? But bragging can potentially generate resentment, so it might be death to the relationship.

 How do you give your husband the honor, recognition, and respect in deed and actions that he needs in order to feel needed and worthy?

 Why should you feed your husband's ego without his begging for morsels of praise? How do you make him feel like a million-dollar man?

Love does not behave or act unbecomingly. Simply put, love is courteous. Here is a paraphrase of the first page of Emily Post's book on manners: "Manners are simply practicing the Golden Rule." Amen. Being polite to your husband, your family, and others is simply conducting yourself non-offensively and pleasantly. Eating correctly not only looks more gracious, but it is practical. Every move is to make eating as inoffensive as possible. Manners make others feel at ease and important. "Thank you" and "please" should be common words between you and your husband. "I am sorry; please forgive me" should follow any offense.

Ladies and gentleman always conduct themselves in a mannerly fashion. Teach your children proper manners; it a great gift. They will always be at ease in any situation because they know how to act. They will never be afraid to try new ideas and actions because they are in control of themselves.

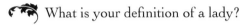 What is your definition of a lady?

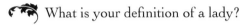 Do you always conduct yourself as a lady? As the wife of your husband and the bride of Christ, how important is it to their reputation and pride for you to be a lady 24/7?

Love does not seek its own. Positively speaking, love is unselfish. Love does not even seek that which is rightfully her own but gives up that right for the other. It is more blessed to give than to receive (Acts 20:35). Give self first to the Lord; then it is easy to give money, time, love, kindness, or a good deed to others (2 Corinthians 8:5). Likewise, in marriage, you must give yourself totally to your husband. Then it is your privilege to give him a lifetime of joyful service. The ruby in Proverbs 31 gave her husband "only good"—*only good*—all her life. Jesus came to serve, not to be served. We are to follow in His steps.

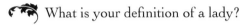 List some ways you excel in doing your husband good.

Love is not provoked. Love does not become angry. Too often one who is good in so many ways spoils her demeanor by being short-tempered. Others are uncomfortable around such a person. Most sins can be classified in two categories: sins of fleshly lust and sins of disposition. Usually, a bad disposition leads to fleshly lust because actions follow the heart. Consider the prodigal son and the older brother. The latter tried to negate the festivities when the father showed love and forgiveness to the younger son. He tried to destroy the joy of the father by his ill temper and jealously.

Henry Drummond had this to say about anger:

> For embittering life, for breaking up communities, for destroying the most sacred relationships, for devastating homes, for withering up men and women, for taking the bloom of childhood, in short, for sheer gratuitous misery-producing power, this influence stands alone.

Drummond is correct. A bad temper will destroy both you and your marriage, so get rid of it. Anger is a sin of the flesh and must be discarded by a child of God. The way of love is always superior to anger in solving life's bumps.

How much progress have you made in eliminating anger? With what have you replaced anger?

Love does not take into account a wrong suffered. It does not remember hurts. What a blessing when we learn to put away the "account of wrongs" of the past. The memory of the deeds cannot be erased, but the deep emotions associated with it can be eliminated. When you pulled your first tooth, you soon forgot the pain and remembered only the action and thrill of the tooth fairy's gift. Usually the loving husband will not purposefully hurt his wife. Hold on to that truth and don't be easily offended.

When you are offended, you must go to your husband and tell him how his action made you feel; resolve the hurt before night falls. Unresolved hurts are like millstones about your neck. They will cause you to drown. Keeping resentment in your heart leads to heart attacks—both physical and spiritual! Nursing a grudge makes life miserable for you and your husband. Get rid of all the negatives. You certainly don't want your husband to remember your bad deeds, do you?

List some ways you can learn to let go of past offenses.

How can letting go of offensives make you better, happier, and more peaceful? How can you turn them into positives?

How can Philippians 4:8 help you overcome the negative memories?

Love does not rejoice in unrighteousness. Love rejoices with the truth. Love does not think evil. It thinks only on truth and the positive things listed in Philippians 4:8. Develop the nature of thinking on the good in life and not the evil. There will always be evil, which will destroy everything in its path if you allow it. Don't give Satan a toehold on any of your thoughts; keep all his evil from your mind. Hold on to positive thoughts of your husband; allow the Father to work on his negatives and pray for one another.

How are you to rejoice? Notice the word *with.* You have the truth of God, not the negatives of Satan. Be joyful that you have access to His truth. The only way to develop the nature of love is to practice, practice, practice every hour of every day the principles laid down by the Father. Satan is there waiting to catch you off guard and cause you to falter.

Jesus asked the Father to help us live above the world. He prayed for you and me:

> But now I come to You; and these things I speak in the world so that they may have My joy made full in themselves. I have given them Your word; and the world has hated them, because they are not of the world, even as I am not of the world. I do not ask You to take them out of the world, but to keep them from the evil one. They are not of the world, even as I am not of the world (John 17:13–16).

What scripture have you learned that helps you to be positive rather than negative? List the positive thinking guideline in that scripture. The more you dwell upon these guidelines, the more they will become your habit of thinking.

How can this verse guide your thinking all the time? How can you use prayer to retrain your thinking?

Love bears all things, believes all things, hopes all things, endures all things. Love never fails. Love's way will continue when all else on the earth is done away. Faith will be lost in reality; hope will be fulfilled. Only love will go into eternity. You develop your nature to be that of Christ's and treat your husband with love; you bear with him in all the trials of life, along with his imperfect ways. You believe in him and tell him this truth over and over. You know from God's promises that you will be victorious in your marriage. You are confident that all the blessings given to God's faithful children will be yours, and you endure because love never fails—neither your love for others nor God's love for you. You live each day to the fullest; you are content with each minute given you. Don't forget to be thankful for the fleas!

Inspired by Nature—Never Give Up!

I have a visible object that inspires me to remember God's love and live in love's way. A very old oak tree, five feet in diameter, towered in our front yard. It was the lone survivor of three giants which stood sentry over our new home years ago. I treasured this remaining aged friend. In 1994 an ice storm took some of the limbs from this majestic tree. A few years later, lightening stuck, but Tree valiantly kept living, even with half its insides destroyed.

Time passed. One morning I went outdoors for the paper, and there was half of my precious oak lying on the ground. The night's storm proved to be stronger than my friend; it was lopped in two. With much sadness Loden and I decided that Tree had to go. Tree was too large for the average chain saw, and since it threatened no power lines, TVA could not cut it. We hired men to cut all of Tree's branches. Soon, a big thirty-foot pole decorated our front yard.

In reality, I did not want to part with my friend; we decided to leave Tree to nature and plant a vine to run up her side for beauty. The next spring, I was amazed! Two limbs began to form and grow from the top of dear Tree. They were straight limbs lifting their leaves to the sky in praise to God for their victory over death, much as a winner of a race raises his arms in victory. From that day, every time I went in and out the drive, I looked at Tree and gained strength to tackle any challenge. I would think, *If Tree can keep trying, so can I.* I thank the Father for this living lesson!

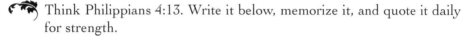

What inspires you to keep trying? God's gifts of nature are especially effective—God's creation and not man's. Jesus often used nature to teach valuable lessons about life and His kingdom, and so can you.

Think Philippians 4:13. Write it below, memorize it, and quote it daily for strength.

What is one problem you are experiencing? How do you think the Father will help you resolve this problem in victory?

Dear One, I implore you. Follow this way of love and you will have the joy of the Lord accompanied by the peace that passes all understanding to guard your heart and mind—God said so (Philippians 4:7). What a marvelous, reassuring thought! No matter what happens to you, be at peace. The Father enables you to stand your ground with your precious husband by your side. This is your hope, your banner of love given by Jesus for His bride to hang over her house of love here on earth.

You have been working for over nine weeks on love. What areas do you need to improve to be fully developed in love's way? Be honest.

How has your husband changed since you began to change your nature?

Day 4

Preparation for Separation

It is a sad thought, but every marriage ends in separation. The only consolation is that we have some control over how the separation takes place. Giving your husband up in love when death separates you is far different from giving him up with the words, "Divorce granted!" These words carry a very different type of pain than the pain of death. The way of love is to prepare for death's separation. Start preparing now, because death comes to every age. Even if you are young and have small children, make plans in the event that you or your husband becomes a victim to accident or illness.

Keep your affairs in order as best you can. Have an accessible place to keep your important papers. Know the laws of your state. Sometimes lock boxes are sealed at death until the court allows them opened, and the mate is unable to withdraw cash from the bank account. Secure your lock box and your bank accounts with both signatures, along with the signature of a trusted friend. Keep your life insurance current.

Make funeral plans. Pre-planning lifts a great burden from the bereaved at a time when many have difficulty thinking clearly. Secure a burial plot. Little things left undone add up to a big problem when the final hour comes. Both of you need to make wills even if you don't own a cent.

You cannot will your children, but you can request the court to honor your desires for the caretakers of them. Incorporate details in your will to make life easier for your mate. That means you need legal aid to help you determine things you would not think about such as not having to make bond to settle the estate. A lawyer will save money in the long run. If you don't have a will, the state will make all the decisions for you, and those decisions will not be to the benefit of your family.

Tackle the Unpleasant

Death is as sure as birth, so don't be queasy about tackling this unpleasant part of life. Loden and I got an above-ground vault for our burial place. When the day came for it to be set up, he told me our new house had arrived. That is how we referred to it—our new house. For a child of God, death holds no fear; it is the doorway to rest for our souls. Perfect love casts out fear, and Jesus has promised us life after death, so why fear?

Part of your planning for life alone will be discussing the options of the mate left. These options include possible relocation. Discussing this ahead of time is invaluable. If you have stocks or any other assets, know where the deeds and stock papers are, know a good CPA, and know a trusted lawyer. All these plans will make the transition from two to one easier.

Too often these matters are not discussed, and the wife is left helpless. My sister Sue was glad that her Tom had taken care of financial matters. He had the house payments and repairs all completed and the records filed so Sue could easily access them. All the official paperwork was made much easier because her loving husband had planned for her. It eliminated a lot of stress.

On the other hand, when Daddy died unexpectedly, Mother knew nothing about writing a check or managing money. My daddy handled all the finances. Fortunately, he had his business affairs in perfect order, and our brother was a business man who could take over. My mother never recovered from Daddy's sudden death and being left alone. She had not prepared herself in any way and was bereft. Protect yourself from this feeling.

Mother knew nothing about writing a check.

🌿 Have you and your husband made preparations for the survivor? Check the list below:

_____ Make wills which include provisions for your children's future.

_____ Have a network of friends to help you in time of need.

_____ Know the location of important papers.

_____ Have access to all finances.

_____ Discuss and plan funeral and burial.

_____ Have contact information on professional help, such as a CPA and attorney.

🌿 How can you prepare yourself mentally for the loss of your husband? What is the difference between being prepared for an event and agonizing over it?

You Are Not Alone

The death of a husband immediately puts the widow into a different world, so we need a network of friends. Join clubs and do volunteer work in the church and community. Not only will you develop friendships, but you also will have the satisfaction of helping others. Create hobbies that give you mental and physical enjoyment. "Loneliness is a second death," my mother kept quoting to us, so make sure you have outside interests to keep loneliness at bay.

Hold on to this truth: when one door in life is closed, the Father will open another. Keep your eye on doors that will open, rather than habitually looking back longingly at the closed door. Look for new adventures, join a grief network, and read books on grieving. Dealing with death is hard work; educate yourself and force yourself to heal.

Sometimes women who are left develop into angry, depressed, needy individuals who continually feed into their pain. Then it is impossible for anyone to help them. Don't allow yourself to become dejected.

A New Beginning

Realize that this is a time for you. You are now free to do things you were never able to do before, so plan to grow in these new areas. View life as an adventure with various stages, and learn to move from one stage to the next. One widow told me, "It is so wonderful to go when I want to go, do what I want to do, and not have anyone to tell me otherwise." Her remarks surprised me because she and her husband were very close—truly one in everything they did. This dear woman now travels, cooks for those in need, keeps her great-grandchildren, and maintains a joyful attitude. Her husband had told her he did not want her to stay home and grieve for him. He wanted her to make a new life for herself. She truly took him at his word!

Keep the knowledge in your heart that God will see you through and make you victorious, for He cares deeply for you. Read Romans 8 often to reinforce the Father's love and His Holy Spirit's aid to you, and feel Jesus' tender mercies enclosing you. Keep these treasures before you and stand your ground with the confidence that the Godhead is with you.

Prayer will draw you closer to God. As a woman, it is your nature to lean upon a stronger one, and Jesus wants to be the one you lean on when you no longer have an earthly mate. You are never alone; constantly talk to the Father. Confess your feelings and receive healing (James 5:16).

Nature says you, a woman, will outlive your dear beloved husband, but your Bridegroom will never leave you. You are the only one who can separate yourself from Jesus. When you are left alone, you are a widow by earthly rules, but you will never be a widow to your Bridegroom. Then you will truly grow closer to Jesus. Widows are very special to the Father and to Jesus.

Read 1 Timothy 5:14. What is God's will for young widows?

What does God want regarding older widows? (1 Timothy 5:5). Why do you think the Father gave this command? How can this work help the church, the nation, and the world?

Day 5

Closing Petals

How many women are grieving over grandchildren's being tossed back and forth because of a wife's deserting her husband? How many grown children grieve because their stepmothers abandon their fathers? More and more women in our society are opting to leave their mates and forsake their children. Women initiate 75 percent of divorce proceedings. That is why you and your husband must begin when your children are babies to teach them God's plan for the home.

As you tenderly carry your precious baby under your heart, ask God to select a special mate for him. Pray that He will help that future mate's parents to bring her up in the Lord. Continue this prayer through the years, until the right one comes into his life. Then pray that both of them will be committed to their marriage vows.

You are the only one who can separate yourself from Jesus.

Your teens will observe how you and their father treat one another. As a result, your children should have a good idea of how to conduct themselves as adults. Don't be afraid to be a parent! From the very beginning into teen years, children learn to respect, honor, and follow adult directions. Refuse permission for them to date someone you know is not good for them.

What is the Father's plan for the home? The parents are to be in charge and bring the children up in the nurture and admonition of the Lord. Be a wise, strong, and firm parent. The child will buck and kick, but after the dust settles, she is usually thankful for your discipline.

I always thanked the heavenly Father and my parents for guiding me in romance. After the tears were dried, I'd pray, "Thank you, Father, for saving me from another bad mistake." Then one day wonderful Mr. Right stuck his head in my car, and we have lived happily ever after, that is, after I learned how to love him. I had prayed many a prayer for my precious Loden; I felt duty-bound to love him because I knew he was that wonderful gift from the Father.

How can you be a strong parent who can say no to your child and stick with that decision?

Why should you tell your child he or she cannot date certain people? Who is in control in your home?

The Potter's Form

Man was made with much deliberation; he was formed in God's image. The words *create* and *form* carry the meaning of a potter using clay to make a vessel for a specific use. The potter knows what use the vessel will have; he has a plan in mind. There was meaning in every step of creation. Man was given the earth to rule and subdue; he was to cultivate it. The religious regulations of the covenant between man and God were the male's responsibility; as the head of the family he dictated the laws for daily living.

The male needed the drive and stamina to fulfill his purpose. The female was to be a help suitable for the man. She was created from the side of man; his own flesh and bones were taken to fashion her. She was destined to perform finer tasks than Adam. She was to give beauty and a feeling of softness to the union.

Awakening from his deep sleep, Adam gazed on his beauty and uttered the first poetry: "This is now bone of my bone and flesh of my flesh; she shall be called Woman, because she was taken out of Man" (Genesis 2:23). The word *woman* has the meaning of being soft. Eve was Adam's soft side. She had come from his own body, and he was delighted with her. He knew he was the hard, tough-as-nails side of the relationship, and Eve was his soft, loving, kind, silky side.

Adam's statement about Eve's being his flesh is used throughout the Old Testament. The two new beings now made one family. God gave them their sexual code for life, and it still stands: "For this reason a man shall leave his father and his mother, and be joined to his wife, and they shall become one flesh" (Genesis 2:24). The two were naked and there was no shame—evil had yet to rear its ugly head. Their love was pure and holy—given to them from the Father.

This is the beautiful beginning of all that is important in the world: God, the union of man and woman, the family, and law to govern. The union of man and woman within marriage was to be the law of sex. Any sex outside marriage was wrong. Also, the sexual relationship was to be between a man and a woman, not by two of the same sex.

Choose to have a part in God's grand plan by being the help suitable to your husband in the way of love. Jesus closed his Sermon on the Mount by telling of a wise man who built his house upon a rock (cf. Matthew 7:24–27). Be wise. Build on God's rock foundation.

Me and My House

The Father is the head of the Trinity, but Jesus and the Holy Spirit are one with Him, and they have an equal standing, but defer to the Father (Philippians 2:6). Likewise, man's role in marriage is to be the acting head. The woman defers to his headship, although she is equal to him in value. Man is the image and glory of God; woman is the glory of man (1 Corinthians 11:7). Man was created to rule, and woman was created to be his helper—not his slave but a helper equal to him, standing side by side with him, under his headship by choice. She helps the man carry out his plans. Without her he is handicapped. Woman is still man's glory, his purpose for conquering the world, his inspiration, and his valued partner.

All of creation, other than man, obeys every command of God by nature. His laws govern animal instinct, the plant world, physics, and chemistry. All are obedient. Man is God's only earthly creature with free will. Man must make moral and spiritual decisions based on knowledge, not feeling. The resounding cry today is the same as on that day when Joshua issued to the undecided Israelites this challenge:

> If it is disagreeable in your sight to serve the Lord, choose for yourselves today whom you will serve: whether the gods which your fathers served which were beyond the River, or the gods of the Amorites in whose land you are living; but as for me and my house, we will serve the Lord (Joshua 24:15).

The King's Crown

Peter commands the husband to love his wife as the weaker vessel and to show the wife honor as a fellow heir of the grace of life, so that prayers will not be hindered (1 Peter 3:7). This is God's grace: a loving husband giving a submissive wife the love she deserves, and the wife giving the husband the honor and respect due him. Together they have the Father, and their prayers rise to His throne for His pleasure.

Your every breath, your every thought should be to have the same union with your husband as the Father, Son, and Holy Spirit are united; to love your husband as Jesus loved His bride; and to give the world an earthly preview of heaven. One can envision the bride, the church, eagerly arising when the trumpet sound is heard throughout the world. The bride knows that Jesus is coming for her. She is washed and dressed in her robes of white, and she eagerly rises to meet her Bridegroom in the air. He joyfully escorts her to the home He prepared for her in that eternal city, and they will live exceedingly joyfully for ever and ever! The Father will have the wedding feast laid for His dear Son and His precious bride, the church.

That, Dear One, is worth fighting for, working for, and living for. May this be your daily challenge: live a life worthy of your calling as the help suitable of an adoring husband. You will be the crown he proudly wears which declares, "There goes a king!" My prayers go with you.

Memory Verse

"Beloved, now we are children of God . . . We know that when He appears, we will be like Him . . . and everyone who has this hope fixed on Him purifies himself, just as He is pure."

1 John 3:2–3

My Take-Home

Grow old along with me, the best is yet to be.
When our time has come we will be as one.
God bless our love; God bless our love.

Grow old along with me; two branches of one tree
Face the setting sun; when the day is done.
God bless our love; God bless our love.

Spending our lives together, man and wife together
World without end; world without end.

Grow old along with me; whatever fate decrees
We'll see it through; for our love is true.
God bless our love; God bless our love.

— John Lennon

My Homework

1. Have you given your love note to your husband? If not give it to him in a very special setting.

2. What is the worst hindrance to your transformation into a beautiful butterfly?

3. How are you and your husband rearing your children in God's way?

4. What are some disciplines that need to be instilled in your children to help them experience a good marriage?

5. How can I be conscious of every action I take as being either loving or being unkind to my dear buffalo?

6. Have I totally eradicated anger? If not, why not?

7. Have I totally eradicated criticism? If not, why not?

8. How have I learned to resolve differences with my husband?

9. Why am I committed to having a loving relationship with my husband?

10. Why speak only words that build up, not tear down?

11. Begin from lesson one and repeat all the assignments given you since then. Do this week after week until they become your nature. Practice makes perfection like a Burmese ruby.

12. Go teach another what you have learned about loving your husband.

13. Pray for marriages everywhere that will please God, so our country will be blessed.

Know that you are always in my prayers. There is nothing more important than for you to realize you have a wonderful husband who loves you and wants to please you in every way. In addition, you have a Bridegroom who will come for you and take you to your new home in heaven. Your earthly husband is to help you prepare for your heavenly Bridegroom. Don't disappoint either one.

Week 11
The Last Days

From the Father of the Bride: "Even though I walk through the valley of the shadow of death, I fear no evil, for You are with me? Your rod and Your staff, they comfort me" (Psalm 23:4).

From Solomon: "A time to give birth and a time to die" (Ecclesiastes 3:2).

From Queen Mother: "She does him good and not evil all the days of her life" (Proverbs 31:12).

From David: "Do you not know that a prince and a great man has fallen this day in Israel?" (2 Samuel 3:38).

From Patsy: "Oh, my darling Loden, how much I loved you" (January 20, 2009, 7:45 A.M.).

From Abraham: "Now he is being comforted here" (Luke 16:25).

I can shed tears that he is gone,
Or I can smile because he has lived.

I can close my eyes and pray that he will come back,
Or I can open my eyes and see all that he has left.

My heart can be empty because I can't see him,
Or I can be full of the love we shared.

I can turn my back on tomorrow and live yesterday,
Or I can be happy for the tomorrows because of yesterday.

I can remember him and only that he is gone,
Or I can cherish his memory and let it live on.

I can cry and close my mind, be empty and turn my back,
O I can do what he would want me to do —
Smile, open my eyes, love and let go.

—Author Unknown

Day 1

The End

To close my love's eyes in death was my last act of tenderness to him. This may sound morbid — unless it is your loved one lying in the bed. Then it is a precious act of closing the last page in the book of your life together. The title reads "The End." Loden was no longer with me, only his well-used "tent" remained. My tenure as a wife had ended.

The beginning of the last normal week of our journey of love reads like a script from a love story's happy ending. We joyfully traveled with our daughter Lisa and her family to Searcy, Arkansas, to witness our granddaughter Madison's college graduation. Loden was especially proud of her 4.0 grade point average and wanted all to know of his thrill — he never reached that level in his academic career! We were pleased to renew friendships with many we had not seen in a long time. They too had grandchildren. We visited with old friends that Loden had known since he was a teenager. They had worked hand-in-hand in developing Christian education.

The extended Loden family later drove to our house in Batesville where the ten of us celebrated a family Christmas dinner ending with Madison's favorite dessert, black bottom pie! What fun we had exchanging gifts and snapping family pictures! Little did we know these would be the last pictures and voice recordings of our dear family patriarch.

We drove to Lisa's for the Castleberry Christmas festivities. Once again we never dreamed our love story was about to come to a crashing end. It was such a loving time of family and friends and sharing good food and presents with those we love so dearly. What a climax to our sequence of family events! I stored them all in my memory bank to bring out and cherish in the days to come.

A few days later, we were on our way to Nashville to visit our "sister-in-love," Mary Jo, and her husband John. "Opryland lights, here we come" was our song. Half way between Jackson, Tennessee, and Nashville, Loden's stomach began hurting. When he asked me to drive, I knew something bad was taking place. Soon after we arrived at Mary Jo's, we were on our way to St. Thomas Hospital's emergency room. I realized later the importance of Loden's walking into the hospital on his own two feet.

Loden had emergency surgery. Three weeks later he made his flight to the next life. Those three weeks were days of love and despair, a time of bonding, a time of reaching out to others, a time of preparing for the end, and a time of no sleep.

I had left Loden and our son Woody to go to Mary Jo's for a night's rest. Both my dear men were having a great time going over business matters and joking with one another. I breathed a sigh of relief in hope that we were on the mountaintop at last, ready to slide down the other side all the way home. I was jolted from that dream when I called Woody the next morning—our dear Loden was in ICU.

He had a ventilator tube in his mouth; he would not be able to talk again. Our only communication was by pen and index cards from Woody's pocket. Loden's message to me was: "Let me die. Turn the machines off." The doctors talked him out of the wish on Saturday, but Sunday morning the message was again written, "Let me go." His last thought was of his family, and he wrote each a note. Lisa told him he had to give me my 2009 valentine, and he penned these words,

Loden to Patsy.
I will love you forever.
Love, Woody

My role drastically changed. I had to become his helper in assisting him to let go of this world and enter the next. I carried out his wishes. As I was singing to him and Lisa was talking to him, he wrote, "Just be quiet." It was then I knew he had left me, because up until that minute, he had not wanted me out of his sight. We had to back out of his line of vision and give him the peace to make his transition. It was a time of quietness and a knowing that our love story was about to end and life would become one of new beginnings. The last hours were spent in hospice as we lovingly let him go to a better place.

The Final Goodbye

Our family stood in the church foyer waiting to enter the auditorium for the service of closing the life our dear loved one. The doors to the auditorium opened to allow us entry, and I focused on the casket that held the tent of my precious Loden.

Suddenly, I was swept backwards to August 23, 1957, to Eden, Texas, where I stood holding onto my father's arm awaiting the opening of the doors for me to walk down the aisle to meet my handsome bridegroom. I eagerly walked those steps with a smile on my face and hope in my heart for a beautiful life with the man who had swept me off my feet. My Prince and I planned a wonderful life together, and we worked to make that dream a reality.

Now I walked down the aisle to tell him, "Good-bye, my love. I will meet you in heaven." This time I walked out of the building behind him, not beside him. I walked with my head held high. My heart was at peace, for my Loden had worked all his life to prepare for this moment. May he rest in sweet peace in Abraham's bosom! It comforted me to know he would be awaiting me at the end of my life's journey.

However, I did not leave the building alone! I left that day with my spiritual Bridegroom, who would help me to find the fulfillment of my new life with only Him as my partner. It will be as rewarding as I allow it to be.

 What is Paul teaching you in 2 Corinthians 11:2?

 What does Ecclesiastes 7:2 mean to you?

Loden and Patsy, 2008, displaying their collection of valentines at Freed-Hardeman University.

Day 2

Preparing for the End

What lessons can I give you to help prepare you for this day in your life? Oh, how we despise that word *widow*, but take heart because widows are precious to our Father and He looks after them. Keep James 1:27 close: write it and practice it. "Pure and undefiled religion in the sight of our God and Father is this: to visit orphans and widows in their distress, and to keep oneself unstained by the world."

When you become a widow, you understand why the Father has a very special feeling for widows. You feel so alone and helpless, but you are not alone, nor are you helpless. Understand that, and don't let yourself be in despair. Remember, life is made of choices, so choose wisely. Take courage from the following promise:

> Make sure that your character is free from the love of money, being content with what you have; for He Himself has said, *"I will never desert you, nor will I ever forsake you,"* so that we confidently say, *"The Lord is my helper, I will not be afraid. What will man do to me?"* (Hebrews 13:5–6, emphasis mine).

During Loden's ups and downs in his struggle for health, the nurses lovingly ministered to him. I walked the hall begging the Lord to grant him life and health. One day it came to me that in my selfishness I was not trusting the Father. I then began praying,

> Oh, dear God, you are my Father who sent the Great Physician. You know what is best for my dearest heart. I am placing him lovingly into the arms of the Great Physician and trusting that You will do what is best for him.

Then mentally, I took my Loden and placed him gently into the arms of Jesus. I was at peace from that hour. The Great Shepherd tenderly embraced my love and carried him to a restful place.

I did not want to bring my husband home a broken man; he did not want that either. That is why it had been so important for him to walk into the hospital under his own power. He finished his life as he would have wanted: working right up to the end, enjoying his family and friends his last good week, and being his own man. We must learn to be careful what we pray for—learn to trust the Lord to do what is best.

Therefore, I can only rejoice with Loden that he is now a whole man living eternally in the promises of his King of kings and Lord of lords. These promises are given to all who listen and obey Jesus: "Not everyone who says to Me, 'Lord, Lord,' will enter the kingdom of heaven, but he who does the will of My Father who is in heaven" (Matthew 7:21).

Write the promises given to the bride of Christ.

Revelation 2:7   Revelation 2:11

Revelation 2:17   Revelation 3:5

Revelation 3:11–12   Revelation 3:21

2 Timothy 4:7–8   1 Peter 5:4

Day 3

The Day of Preparation

Our family, friends, and community were all saddened at the loss of a man who loved his city and worked all his life to make it a better place. Tears and laughter intertwined as family and friends worked to do their part in making preparation for the final honor to be bestowed upon Woody Loden III, Christian, husband, father, friend, community leader, boss, and the many other titles. Loden almost always wore a white shirt and blue pants to work. When he showed up wearing something else, people asked, "Where are you going?" I would tease him and tell him I was going to bury him in his "uniform." However, we decided he should be dressed in his finest—symbolic of preparation for the special place he was going. My last love note was placed next to his heart, but it was not the last of our love.

Lisa decided that we needed a Loden quilt to put on a table to display some of his special things. She worked into the night making a small quilt using various parts cut from his white shirts. She included the paint stains, the tar spots, and the grease that would never wash out. The quilt's border was from his blue work pants, including a hem he had stapled when it came unraveled. (He probably knew if he showed it to me I would discard the pants as being too old—in his mind his clothes never were too old.)

My niece Catherine wanted to help sew the quilt, so we worked side by side, talking companionably. I was teaching her how to sew as I had been taught, and she was a quick study. It was a very special time. We must look for the positives in life and grab them, even amidst pain.

To complete the portrayal of Loden's life, we displayed all the valentines he had given me. Thanks to our local newspaper, the valentines had become a community project. Friends and neighbors were always interested in the current year's valentine. The display satisfied their curiosity. Lisa made a special frame for Loden's last valentine—he gave it to me at the hospital. It was unique as were the others. On Valentine's Day the company that had created previous valentines made a special one for me and had it delivered with a bouquet of flowers. It read:

> Thinking of you this Valentine's Day! We know that you are missing your "Forever Valentine" with whom you had the rarest of loves that so few people ever find. Much love from Nancy and Bill & everyone here who missed Mr. Woody picking up your "Valentine" this year.

So you see, Dear One, you do not just live for yourself. Your marriage can be a testimony of Christ's love to the world.

The Ceremony

Loden's service was so befitting for him. The Freed-Hardeman University chorus sang. Loden's life-long wish came true; he voiced this desire to me often. They sang a special song which truly described his last days: "There's A Stirring." Find the words to this song and be uplifted. I was comforted when one person told me it was the first funeral he had attended that made him a better person. Loden lived his life in service to his God, his fellow man, his family, and his Patsy. It was always my privilege to be his helper!

Practical Lessons for Caregivers

I share the following ideas with you in hope that they will help you on your road of life, especially if you have your loved one in the hospital.

Cut your nails short so you will not harbor bacteria. Staph is a real danger to your loved one. When I was told Loden had staph, I knew the end was near; he did not have a reserve to fight it. The nurse told me that once a person is infected, he is never rid of it. It may go into remission only to surface again when the immune system is low.

Help the nurses all you can. Anything you can do for your patient makes their work easier. They work diligently. We were told that most patients' families sit back and wait to be served.

Tell the nurses daily how much their attention to your dear one is appreciated. Let them know how grateful you are for their work and constant attention to your loved one's needs. These dear people work with pain every day, and it is not easy for them to be cheerful. Our nurses always kept a caring, loving attitude, and it was precious to behold.

Keep records of your patient's progress and inform the doctors and nurses of conditions they may not notice. The nursing staff, the doctors, the nutritionist, and I worked together to supply Loden's needs for healing. You will notice things the medical staff does not have time to notice. Attendants are in the room only at short, irregular intervals. Include the doctors in your "thank you." The more love you give, the more you will receive, and that is what you want for your dear one.

Talk to the nurses about their lives and families. You can minister to their needs and concerns for their loved ones while they are ministering to your loved one. Communicating on a personal level creates a friendship beneficial to both of you and enhances the attention your patient receives. Our family bonded especially with one nurse. She would come kiss Loden goodnight even when he was not her patient.

Talk to families of other patients. Friendly interaction helps you as much as it helps them. One woman in the sitting room looked forlorn; I knew she was hurting. After Woody left, I walked over to her, sat down, and asked her if she would like to talk. She said, "Not really." I then asked her if she would like for me to pray with her, and she did. After that prayer, she opened her heart and told me of her concerns for her twenty-nine year old son who had an inoperable brain tumor. How quickly we learn that we are not the only ones suffering! Sharing pain helps us bear the burden of being a caregiver.

Another young man, walking down the hall with his wife, seemed to have a palsy of some type; walking took special effort. I remarked, "I admire your maneuvering skills." He shared quickly that he was injured and was told he would never walk again, but here he was on his two feet.

In ICU waiting, a man's sister was in emergency heart surgery. Woody led a prayer for his sister, and when the rest of his family arrived, we were all like kin. Reach out to those around you and minister to them—all of you are needing love at that time. The fiery darts of Satan wound each of us. Reach out to each person you meet. Give them tender, loving care, because each of us is a hurting soul in some way.

What is the teaching of 2 Corinthians 1:3–5?

Loden and Patsy swap loving looks over Patsy's 2008 giant valentine.

Day 4

More Lessons to Learn

Don't be afraid to try new treatments. We worked for three weeks as a team trying to find a medication that would allow Loden to sleep at night. One evening I suddenly thought of hypnotism. Loden, desperate for sleep, was very open to this suggestion. A nurse helped me to locate an expert, and we made an appointment for Saturday—too late, as it turned out.

Find ways to relieve your stress and anxiety. Reading carries me through trials, whether my own illness or Loden's. I read a Bible commentary Woody had left to help my spiritual side, and I buried myself in novels to transport my mind to other worlds.

Look out! One morning after another night of no sleep for either of us, I sipped a cup of hot tea the nurses brought me. I looked out the window into a most gorgeous sunrise! How soothing just to sit and watch the wonder in the sky unfold before my very eyes. I prayed such gratitude from my heart to the Father who created this phenomenon.

Visit the prayer room of the hospital. Pray to the Father for strength and peace. Prayer will revive your faith and carry you beyond your fears. You will have a peace to carry on your task of being cheerful for your sick one. If you are fortunate, the hospital will have a garden. Take short breaks and walk there; let nature soothe your brow. Nature always gives love and peace to her admirers.

Remember the power of your touch and gentle words. Loden quickly developed bed sores because he had not eaten in thirteen days; he only had ice chips. He did not like lying on his side—it was uncomfortable to his surgery and back. I put pillows behind him to ease his pain. I touched him and massaged his hands. I told him if he lay on his side, I would do reflexology when it was time for him to sit in the chair. Reflexology helps to heal and relieve pain, and he enjoyed these times of loving touch. The head nurse figured out how to roll and tape pillows to put behind his back. To ease some of his distress, I massaged his head, his hands, and his back when he was sitting up. Don't forget to touch your patient with words of love, comfort, praise for trying, and encouragement to do what the doctor orders. Praise him for walking, because physical activity is necessary for healing. Our bodies are not designed to lie flat. The nutritionist informed me that in that position, it begins to make water. Fluid build-up was one of the monsters we battled. We worked diligently to encourage Loden to walk and sit up. Your words and touch do much to aid the healing process.

Be patient. Your loved one is often in great pain. He is mentally fatigued—as you will be very soon—so great forbearance is necessary. The patient might not want to cooperate, so you must think of ways to convince him. Use laughter and humor to get you through the rough spots. Loden was sometimes too warm and wanted the temperature cooler. I'd ask, "How much?" He would answer,

"One degree." Then he would become cold and ask for one degree warmer. We let this be a joke between us and the children; we finally learned to act as if we were adjusting the degrees.

Keep yourself looking as pretty as you can, under the circumstances. This is important to you and your man. You are his world now; make it as attractive as you can. Your husband draws his strength from you. Give him a wife who looks like she cares about him and herself. Make-up may have to go, but keep your hair looking nice and put on a smiling face so you will look pretty to him. Grooming will also keep your morale high.

Watch your diet. Don't eat and drink junk food. Your system is under attack the same as the patient's, and you need good food to keep your body healthy and functioning at its maximum level. I could not eat the hospital food, so I lived on fruits, yogurt, and salads. When we could, we left Loden in the nurse's care and ate a hot meal in a nearby restaurant. Walk as much as possible to keep your muscles strong.

I did not mind losing weight, but it did have an unusual outcome. Lisa had given me a lovely dress for Christmas. Since it held a precious memory—I wore it our last Christmas together—I decided to wear it for his visitation. I walked into the funeral home, paused briefly, and felt something move about my knees. I looked down and my skirt had slipped off my hips down to my knees! I asked the funeral director, who happened to be passing by, if he had some safety pins. We decided that it was a two-pin emergency. "That's a first for me!" he said. Laughter is always a good thing, even in the most trying of times.

My skirt slipped down to my knees!

Trust the nurses and let them guide you. They will help with your patient's needs and anticipate some pitfalls. Ask them questions. The floor nurses explained Loden's needs with me, and as a result I handled some of his procedures. The nurses had more time to help others and I had more time to love on my man. When we were in hospice, we asked the nurse to wake us through the night; she was most helpful. Our son kept a diary on that final night, which proved to be a source of comfort later. We could understand what was going on when our minds were too weary to register events. A nephew, who is an eye surgeon, told us that often a patient will not die if the loved ones are in the room. I stayed out of the room and allowed the children to keep Loden comforted, but it did not work, so I rejoined them.

Finally, Tuesday morning, Lisa and I went for breakfast while Woody stayed to have a "boy" talk with his dad. He told Loden he had to help me one more time by going, because I was becoming ill and might have to go to the hospital if he did not let them take me home. When he finished his talk, Loden took three more breaths, and was gone. His last act of love for me!

Show love and affection to the nurses. Touch them, hug them, and encourage them. They have a tough job and work long hours on their feet. Nurses have different personalities. Work with them and allow them to work in their own way. Be patient. Help them as they work with your patient. I even helped the cleaning lady change the bed. She gave me some wonderful insights into her philosophy. I called her my ray of sunshine. The more you give, the more you receive. What did Jesus teach in John 13:13–14?

Know when to be quiet. When I had to enroll Loden in the hospice center, I received a booklet which described the dying process. I already knew in my heart that one of the signs was the need for quietness and being alone. Your loved one is preparing the soul to enter into the next realm. You must not invade his space. Your job is to be with him quietly and let him know you are present for him. He probably won't need you, so don't feel neglected if he doesn't. This is your gift — the gift of time for him to take his flight. Read Luke 16:22.

We do not understand this experience, so give the dying one the love and consideration of keeping out of his sphere. I believe Loden was experiencing something we could not see, hear, or understand, so I remained quiet until I thought he was truly on his journey. When the breathing becomes labored, the eyes are open but not focused, it is time to say, "It is okay to leave; you will be in the hands of the Father. I love you." Your loved one needs to know you are in agreement with his desire to go on and that you will be well after he is gone.

 Read the following scriptures and list the comfort from each one:

Philippians 4:13

Revelation 14:13

John 14:1–4

John 15:1–17

Preserve DNA. The information it carries is very important in the medical world. Your family might benefit in the future. Check with your physician or experts in this field to find out how to properly preserve DNA for your future generations. Protect those you love with valuable information in treating your various hereditary diseases. Most physical problems are inherited. Knowledge gives you some power over your life's woes. Read Ecclesiastes 1:9–10. The Father knew we would need such knowledge when He created the earth.

Day 5

Oh, What Will I Do?

After the last guest has gone, and you find yourself alone in the house you have shared so lovingly with your mate, what then? Just remember that you are not alone. Your experience is not unique. Millions of women have gone through what you are experiencing. Jesus told His followers, "Be not afraid." So if you are His child, you are a part of His bride. He is now your only bridegroom, and you are His beloved, so you are not alone or unloved. Turn to others who have walked this path of widowhood and allow them to help you through the coming days.

Keep a journal. It will help you to understand your thoughts and emotions during difficult times. Help is available at any bookstore. Buy books on grief, and study its stages. You might be angry at your loved one for leaving you. Your feelings are normal, but you must not allow yourself to remain at that stage. Walk through the door God has given you and look about with wonder and joy. He will find a new journey, and you can have a full, happy life, if you so choose. No two people are exactly alike, and your cup of sorrow may not have the same recipe as another's. You will experience your own grief in your own way. I never dreamed I would feel as I do, because during Loden's final days I wailed to the Father, "Oh, what will I do when I don't have my Loden?"

However, after I prayed for the Lord to do what was best for my love, I had a peace that I never dreamed possible. I did not have a meltdown, but I did have moments of tears. After each emotional peak, my peace took over once again. I am grateful that Loden went home while he was his own man. He did not have to endure being an invalid, and he left me financially secure. I remain thankful for the years and the fun we had together. Grief never overpowered me. I continue to live one day at a time and work toward the great future Jesus has in store.

Be Not Afraid

When your time comes, you will have to make the same choices every woman is forced to make, so don't be afraid to be yourself. Grieve in the way that is productive for you. Notice, I said *productive*. Never allow yourself to fall into the trap of black grief, allowing Satan to take advantage of your weaknesses and prevent you from moving on joyfully. No one can steal your joy unless you allow it; happiness may be gone for a while, but not joy—unless you allow it. Memorize John 15:11.

My dear Loden had been telling me for a year, "It won't be long before I will take my flight home." We chose to live each day to the fullest, loving one another and taking our pleasure in being together, experiencing life, and dwelling on the positives. Loden prepared for his death. What a great help to know he left our business and his life in order! He had showed Woody and Mark how to locate important papers. Woody helped me get started with the paperwork of closing his life. I truly dislike having to deal with all these matters, but I'm determined to master them; the Father will give me strength for the day. Because Jesus is with me, I am not afraid, and I joyfully look forward to what He has in store for me. I mourned for Loden that last year as I looked at his dear face across the table and knew that the final grains of sand were quickly running through his hourglass.

Patsy proudly displays one of her giant valentines from Loden.

Grab Joy

Life will go on. We are a very small part of the universe, and all we can do is live in our little world and try to make it better. We love those in our world and try to allow the Trainer to fashion us in the image of our Bridegroom. Every phase of life has its joys and sorrows. You decide if you will suck on lemons or enjoy a cool glass of sweet lemonade. The Father will help you to add sweetness to the bitterness of life.

As quickly as possible after the death of your loved one, grab onto occasions that give you pleasure. I belong to a foursome: "Magnificent Magnolias." We are old school chums who enjoy regular outings. What a great source of comfort to have these long-time friends surround me with understanding! After

Loden's death, I lunched with my beloved Magnificent Magnolias (as chocolate lovers, we shorten it to M & M's). When we parted, I asked myself, "What does a woman who is having a down day do?" Immediately the female in me shouted, "Go shopping!" I headed for my favorite group of stores. I did not need anything, but it cheered me just to look. A saleswoman and I chatted easily; and in the course of the conversation, I mentioned that I had just lost my husband. The woman immediately identified with me, telling me of her losses. We women carry each other through the rough times of life, whether we are great friends or new acquaintances. We parted with more love and solace in our hearts. Reach out to others in your grief so they can minister to you. In turn, you give them sympathy for their sorrow.

Bring in the Grands

Our grandchildren came to see me. Treasure these moments, and allow the eyes of youth to help you look to the future with pleasure. Help them make their paths easier to travel because you have shared your wisdom. Praise them, encourage them, and pray with them. Luke and Madison spent Valentine's weekend with me. Since Loden and I had made this such a special day, allowing these two wonderful young adults to bring me cheer was a memorable bonding time for the three of us. Don't allow yourself to have a pity party. Remember the adage: Don't weep because it is over; shout with joy because it happened.

Remember, Jesus endured the pain of the cross for the joy that was set before Him. Because of Him, death has lost its sting, and He will bring you to victory if you allow Him. Death is as much a part of life as is birth, so we must embrace it and use it in a positive way. Otherwise, Satan has won his battle.

Read 1 Corinthians 15:55–58 for your life's marching orders. What is Jesus trying to get you to believe?

Your Time

Consider this time of life as a new adventure. You have lived under someone else's authority: first your parents', then your teachers', then your boss's, then your husband's. But now it is your time. You can do what you want; it is a new day! What have you wanted to do all your life but have not had the time or opportunity? You will be your own worst enemy if you do not find peace, joy, and a work to do with the Lord. It is your fault if you stumble. You will become acquainted with yourself as never before, so be sure you have an interesting person to live with! I know women who have used this time to travel; some go back to school to increase their knowledge in general or to create a new career. Others do mission work, volunteer work, or other worthwhile works to help others. The main thing is to get outside yourself and do for others.

See what Jesus has to say in Matthew 10:38–39. How can these verses influence you?

Also keep in mind that even in experiencing the loss of your husband, you are teaching young women how to love their husbands. You are their example of letting go of one life and taking up another. You still honor your husband; you do want to carry on his good name and the works you had shared, so be a good teacher. Show the world how to endure the worst pain a woman can have. Do so gracefully. People do not know how to handle a weeping widow, but everyone will warm up to a woman who shows courage in the face of sorrow.

 Read James 5:10–11, and express it in your own words.

Parting Thoughts

I leave you with these words:

Therefore, since we have so great a cloud of witnesses surrounding us, let us also lay aside every encumbrance and the sin which so easily entangles us, and let us run with endurance the race that is set before us, fixing our eyes on Jesus, the author and perfecter of faith, who for the joy set before Him endured the cross, despising the shame, and has sat down at the right hand of the throne of God. For consider Him who has endured such hostility by sinners against Himself, so that you will not grow weary and lose heart (Hebrews 12: 1–3).

Consider the enormous teaching in these verses. You will never have to endure what some have experienced. Thank the Father for the blessings you do have! Face each day with courage, knowing you are in loving hands. You don't know the future, but He does, and He promised never to leave or forsake you. What better hope can you have than these promises? Do you realize that you were created to be victorious in life? You are a vital part of inviting the world to become a part of the bride of Christ.

 What does Revelation 22:17 have to say about the bride of Christ.

 How does Hebrews 12:1–3 help you handle life's woes?

 How can you be a gracious hostess for Christ? (Revelation 22:17).

I have enjoyed sharing with you our journey of love. I pray with you these words:

> For this reason I bow my knees before the Father, from whom every family in heaven and on earth derives its name, that He would grant you, according to the riches of His glory, to be strengthened with power through His Spirit in the inner man, so that Christ may dwell in your hearts through faith; and that you, being rooted and grounded in love, may be able to comprehend with all the saints what is the breadth and length and height and depth, and to know the love of Christ which surpasses knowledge, that you may be filled up to all the fullness of God. Now to Him who is able to do far more abundantly beyond all that we ask or think, according to the power that works within us, to Him be the glory in the church and in Christ Jesus to all generations forever and ever. Amen (Ephesians 3:14–21).

You have been practicing the way of love for eleven weeks. I will leave you, but you hold on to your promises from Jesus. Stand in awe and with courage to live life to the fullest. Love that husband of yours each day, each hour, and each minute to the height of God's love. Reap the reward from your earthly husband and your heavenly Bridegroom. God's rich blessings be upon you. Amen. Come quickly, Lord Jesus.

Loden and Patsy, posing for a kiss with their collection of valentines at Freed-Hardeman University.

Epilogue

The Last Valentine

Actions do speak louder than words. I observed the love story of Patsy and Woody Loden firsthand for more than 47 years. During all those years, I never saw them argue—not once. I know they did not agree about everything, but they always presented a united front. They never disagreed in my presence. My brother Woody and I knew we could not get a foothold when trying to wedge between them! Patsy and Woody Loden were one—in public and at home.

They lived love. I fondly remember the many pet names that they had for one another and the homecomings celebrated each day when Dad got home from work. Mom never met Dad at the door expecting him to serve as referee for our daily discipline problems. Mom protected Dad from our trivial sibling strife; our home environment was warm and loving—not perfect, but filled with forgiveness. Angry moments never lasted long; punishment for wrongs was swift. Bruised hearts heal quickly in a secure cocoon of loving embraces coupled with discipline. Our home was blessed to have both.

This discipline, love, and united front that my parents provided encouraged me to try any and everything! It gave me knowledge and fortitude to charge full throttle into life. I was secure. I knew who I was; their parental support bolstered me to pursue life's challenges.

Most of all, I am grateful for my rich Christian heritage. My parents taught me the Biblical principle that above all I am God's child, loved by Him. They taught me that with His help I could navigate life first and foremost as a Christian. How many times they prayed that Woody and I would find Christian spouses! I knew that this was their prayer; I believed God would provide us a Christian mate. He did! I met Mark Castleberry in 1982, and we married in 1987. I felt that Mark was to be my husband as a result of much prayer.

As a new bride, I felt well equipped. (Of course, I only thought I knew everything!) My mom was always there to encourage, buffet, and coach me when I made mistakes. I still have much to learn and many improvements to make, but in reflection, I feel my mom and dad's love and guidance supported me in my love and commitment towards Mark; it nurtured our marriage. My parents' example provided foundation for my own commitment to Mark. I knew it was for life; we could face any hardship and still love.

I loved watching them in the later years. It was like watching Jell-O roll down a hill—absorbing the bumps, reshaping, and continuing the journey. Mom and Dad had trials. They handled them and moved on. I learned, as I watched, that as time passed, when trials came they made adjustments and their love grew. They constantly came up with new ways to express their love based on life's daily updates.

Epilogue

Woody loved his Patsy. As Mom mentioned, Valentine's Day was greatly anticipated. Over the last decade and a half, Dad always prepared a very special valentine for his love. Though a very simple man in dress and material needs, he spared nothing to produce a one-of-a-kind valentine. Our whole family enjoyed watching the collection grow! We learned so much from the love and tenderness shown each year as the Valentine was plotted, executed, and delivered. During Dad's final hours he had some unfinished business for each of us, his family, but he could not give this verbally, because his vocal cords were bruised from tubes and dry from lack of moisture. He asked for pen and paper and wrote his final thoughts to each of us, but to his Patsy, he wrote his last valentine:

Loden to Patsy
Patsy, I will always love you.
Woody

This last Valentine of a long love story is very precious to me and my family. Their loving example will serve to better generations in the years to come.

Thank you, Mom and Dad.

Resources

Bloom, Linda and Charlie. *101 Things I Wish I Knew When I Got Married*. Novato, California: New World Library, 2004.

Cloud, Henry and Townsend, John, *Rescue Your Love Life Workbook*. Brentwood, TN: Integrity Publishers, 2005.

Drummond, Henry. *The Greatest Things in the World*. New Kensington, PA: Whitaker House, 1981.

Eggerichs, Emerson, *Love & Respect*. Brentwood, TN: Integrity Publishers, 2004.

Eggerichs, Emerson and Sarah. *Motivating Your Man God's Way*. USA: Love and Respect Ministries, Inc. 2002.

Eichman, Nancy. *The Road to Forgiveness*. Nashville, TN. Gospel Advocate Co., 2006.

Feldhahn, Shaunti. *For Women Only*. Atlanta, GA. Multnomah Publishers, 2004.

Getz, Gene A. *Encouraging One Another*. Wheaton, IL. Victor Books, 1981. Other books by Getz: *Building Up One Another, Loving One Another, Praying for One Another, Serving One Another*.

Glickman, Craig, *Solomon's Song of Love*. West Monroe, LA. Howard Publishing Co., 2004.

Gray, John, *Men Are from Mars, Women Are from Venus*. New York: HarperCollins Publisher, 1992.

Hay, Louise L. *Love Yourself: Heal Your Life*. Carlsbad, CA: Hay House, Inc., 1990.

Lawrence, Brother. *The Practice of the Presence of God*. Amberson, PA. Scroll Publishing Company, 2007.

Markman, Howard; Stanley, Scott; Blumberg, Susan L. *Fighting for Your Marriage*. San Francisco, CA. Jossey-Bass Inc., Publishers, 1994.

Montagu, Ashley. *Touching*. New York: Harper & Row, 1978.

Nelson, Tommy. *The Book of Romance*. Nashville, TN: Thomas H. Nelson, 1998.

O'Connor, Dagmar. *How to Make Love to the Same Person for the Rest of Your Life*. Garden City, New York: Doubleday & Company, Inc., 1985.

Ornish, Dean, M.D. *Love & Survival*. New York: HarperCollins Publishers, 1998.

Pearl, Debi. *Created to Be His Help Meet*. Pleasantville, TN: No Greater Joy Ministries, Inc., 2004.

Pearl, Michael. *Holy Sex*. Pleasantville, TN. No Greater Joy Ministries, Inc., 2002.

Penny, Alexandra. *How to Make Love to Each Other*. New York: G. P. Putnam's Sons, 1982.

Richards, Larry. *Forgiveness*. Nashville, TN: Thomas Nelson Publishers, 1996.

Schlessinger, Laura. *The Proper Care & Feeding of Husbands*. New York: HarperCollins, 2004. Any other book by Dr. Laura is good.

Sell, Charles M. *Achieving the Impossible: Intimate Marriage*. Portland, OR: Multnomah Press, 1982.

Smalley, Gary and Trent, John. *The Blessing*. Nashville, TN: Thomas Nelson, 1986.

Smalley, Gary. *For Better or for Best*. Grand Rapids, MI: Zondervan Publishing House, 1979.

Smalley, Gary. *The Joy of Committed Love*. Grand Rapids, MI: Zondervan Publishing House, 1988.

Smalley, Gary and Trent, John. *The Language of Love*. Pomona, CA: Focus on the Family Publishing, 1988.

Smalley, Gary and Trent, John. *Love Is a Decision*. Dallas, TX: Word Publishing, 1989.

Smalley, Gary. *Secrets to Lasting Love*. New York: Simon & Schuster, 2000.

Thomas, Gary. *Sacred Marriage*. Grand Rapids, MI: Zondervan Publishing House, 2000.

Printed in the USA
CPSIA information can be obtained
at www.ICGtesting.com
CBHW062349271023
1462CB00012B/5